iPhone 15
for Seniors

Complete Beginners and Seniors Guide
For Non-Techy Savvy to Seamlessly
Navigate iPhone 15 Smartphone

Fritsche King

Disclaimer and Terms of Use

The author and publisher of this book and the accompanying materials have used their best efforts in preparing this book. The author and publisher make no representation or warranties with respect to the accuracy, applicability, fitness, or completeness of the contents of this book. The information contained in this book is strictly for informational purposes. Therefore, if you wish to apply the ideas contained in this book, you are taking full responsibility for your actions.

Printed in the United States of America

TABLE OF CONTENTS

TABLE OF CONTENTS..III

INTRODUCTION 1

CHAPTER ONE 3

GETTING STARTED 3

OVERVIEW 3
SPECIFICATIONS AND FEATURES...3
FEATURES 5
THE IPHONE 15 MODELS...5

    iPhone 15 Series Release Date 6
    iPhone 15 Series Price 6
    The iPhone 15 Series Cameras 7
    iPhone 15 Series Displays 7
    iPhone 15 Series Design 8
    iPhone 15 Series Colors 9
    iPhone 15 Series Performance 10
    iPhone 15 Series Action Button 11
    iPhone 15 Series USB-C port...11
    iPhone 15 Series Dynamic Island...12
    iPhone 15 Series Roadside Assistance via Satellite 12

WHAT'S NEW IN IOS 17? 13

    StandBy Mode...13

OPEN CAMERA APP MODES WITH NEW SHORTCUT ACTIONS...14

    72-hour passcode grace period..14
    Autocorrect gets an improvement 15
    New Journal app 15

NEW MESSAGES IMPROVEMENTS AND FEATURES 16
NEW CONTACT POSTERS 16
DELETE PASSWORD VERIFICATION MESSAGES AUTOMATICALLY 17
CREATE A GROCERY LIST IN REMINDERS...17
CONVERSATIONAL AWARENESS WITH AIRPODS 18
NO MORE 'HEY, SIRI' 19
CONSECUTIVE SIRI REQUESTS 19
AIRTAGS CAN BE SHARED WITH MORE PEOPLE..20
THE MAPS APP GETS A BOOST 20
SHARING IS EASIER WITH AIRDROP AND NAMEDROP..21
SENSITIVE CONTENT WARNINGS 22
HOW TO DOWNLOAD AND INSTALL IOS 17..22
FREQUENTLY ASKED QUESTIONS 24

CHAPTER TWO 25

CONFIGURING THE NEW IPHONE 15 SERIES **25**

OVERVIEW 25

HOW TO SET UP YOUR NEW IPHONE 15 SERIES 25

FIRST, BACK UP YOUR OLD PHONE 25

SETTING UP YOUR NEW IPHONE 26

QUICK START 26

   Set Up Manually 27

ADDING OTHER ACCOUNTS AND SETTING PREFERENCES 28

HOW TO SET UP PHYSICAL AND ESIM 28

   A Quick Word on eSIM 28

   Setting up the Physical SIM Card 29

   Turning on the eSIM 29

   Handling Dual SIM Configurations 30

HOW TO TRANSFER DATA FROM OLD DEVICE TO THE IPHONE 15 SERIES 31

   iCloud Backup 31

   iTunes or Finder Backup: 32

   iCloud Backup 32

   iTunes or Finder Backup: 32

HOW TO WAKE AND UNLOCK YOUR DEVICE 33

   Waking up 33

   Unlocking your iPhone 15 Series 33

   Home Screen 34

HOW TO POWER ON AND OFF YOUR DEVICE 34

   Turning on 34

   Powering off 34

SOME BASIC GESTURES TO USE WITH YOUR NEW IPHONE 15 SERIES 35

   Pinch to zoom on videos 35

   Tap and hold to open closed tabs in Safari 36

   Quicker zooming in on Apple Maps 36

   Swipe down to hide the keyboard in iMessage 36

   Tap and hold to change keyboards 36

   Shake to undo 36

   Swipe down to save email drafts 37

   Tap and drag to select images 37

   Tap and hold to archive messages 37

   Tap and drag to switch scrubbing speed 37

   Swipe down to listen to the text 38

   Swipe right to go back 38

   Swipe left to view details in the Message 38

   Swipe left or right to remove digits in the calculator 38

HOW TO SET UP APPLE ID 38

HOW TO ACCESS AND USE ICLOUD 41

FREQUENTLY ASKED QUESTIONS 42

CHAPTER THREE **44**

FOCUS AND SECURITY **44**

OVERVIEW 44

HOW TO SET UP A FOCUS 44

HOW TO CREATE A PERSONAL FOCUS 46

HOW TO SET A FOCUS TO ACTIVATE AUTOMATICALLY 48

HOW TO ALLOW CALLS FROM EMERGENCY CONTACTS WHEN YOU SILENCE NOTIFICATIONS 49

HOW TO DEACTIVATE A FOCUS 50

HOW TO DELETE A FOCUS 50

FACE ID AND PASSCODE 53

How to set up Face ID 53

HOW TO ADD ANOTHER APPEARANCE TO FACE ID 55

HOW TO DEACTIVATE FACE ID 57

HOW TO SET UP A PASSCODE 57

HOW TO CHANGE WHEN YOUR PHONE LOCKS AUTOMATICALLY 58

How to erase data after ten failed passcode entries 59

How to turn off the passcode 60

FREQUENTLY ASKED QUESTIONS 62

CHAPTER FOUR **63**

FACETIME **63**

OVERVIEW 63

HOW TO ENABLE FACETIME ON IPHONE 15 SERIES 63

Check for Updates 63

SIGN IN TO YOUR APPLE ID 63

CHANGE THE FACETIME SETTINGS 65

MANAGE CALLER ID 66

ENABLE OR DISABLE FACETIME FOR SPECIFIC CONTACTS 66

GROUP FACETIME 66

APPLY THE FACETIME EFFECTS 67

TROUBLESHOOTING FACETIME ISSUES 68

HOW TO MAKE AND RECEIVE FACETIME CALLS 68

Making a FaceTime Call 68

Receiving a FaceTime Call 69

How to create a link to a FaceTime call 69

Creating a FaceTime link 69

How to make a Group FaceTime Call 71

How to Create a Live Image on a FaceTime Call 72

How to start a Group FaceTime call from Messages 73

How to exit a Group FaceTime call 73

How to add someone to a call 74

How to edit FaceTime audio 75

Recording a FaceTime Call 75

Editing the FaceTime Audio 76

How to block unwanted callers on FaceTime 76

FREQUENTLY ASKED QUESTIONS 77

CHAPTER FIVE 78

SIRI ON YOUR IPHONE 15 SERIES 78

OVERVIEW 78

HOW TO USE ENABLE SIRI 78

How to use Siri 80

How to edit Siri's response 81

How to change Siri's voice 83

How to change the way Siri responds 84

How to change the name Siri calls you 85

What Siri can do for you? 86

How to make corrections in case Siri doesn't get what you say 87

FREQUENTLY ASKED QUESTIONS 89

CHAPTER SIX 90

USING THE PHONE APP 90

OVERVIEW 90

HOW TO MAKE CALLS VIA THE CONTACTS LIST, KEYPAD, AND FAVORITES 90

Making Calls from Contacts 90

Making Calls from the Keypad 91

Making Calls from Favorites 92

How to make an emergency call 92

HOW TO ANSWER OR DECLINE CALLS 94

Answering a Call 94

Declining a Call 94

How to avoid unwanted phone calls 95

HOW TO USE EMERGENCY SOS 97

HOW TO BLOCK PEOPLE FROM REACHING YOU ON DIFFERENT CALL APPS 98

HOW TO MANAGE BLOCKED CONTACTS 99

HOW TO USE THE VOICEMAIL FUNCTION 100

HOW TO VIEW ALL MISSED CALLS 102

HOW TO ADD CONTACTS TO FAVORITES 102

FREQUENTLY ASKED QUESTIONS 103

CHAPTER SEVEN 104

USING THE SAFARI APP 104

OVERVIEW 104

HOW TO VIEW WEBSITES IN SAFARI 104

HOW TO TRANSLATE A WEBPAGE OR IMAGE...106
   Translating a Web Page...106
   Translating an Image...107
HOW TO PREVIEW WEBSITE LINKS...107
HOW TO USE A READING LIST...108
HOW TO CHANGE BETWEEN DARK AND LIGHT THEME...109
HOW TO CARRY OUT A SAFE AND ADVANCED SEARCH...110
HOW TO CHANGE LANGUAGE IN SAFARI...112
HOW TO VIEW SAVED TABS..113
HOW TO BRING BACK SAFARI TO THE HOME SCREEN...113
HOW TO USE TAB GROUPS..114
   How to change the name of tab groups...115
   How to change how tab groups are arranged..116
   How to delete a tab group...116
   How to view all the tabs in a tab group..117
HOW TO BOOKMARK A PAGE..117
   How to add a bookmark...118
   How to open a bookmark..119
   How to edit a bookmark..120
   How to delete a bookmark..120
HOW TO VIEW SEARCH HISTORY...121
HOW TO CLEAR BROWSER SEARCH HISTORY..122
FREQUENTLY ASKED QUESTIONS...123

CHAPTER EIGHT...**124**

USING THE CAMERA APP...**124**

OVERVIEW...124
HOW TO LAUNCH THE CAMERA APP...124
HOW TO LAUNCH THE CAMERA APP USING SIRI..126
HOW TO CHANGE THE CAMERA ASPECT RATIO...126
HOW TO SET THE FLASHLIGHT TO BE ON ALWAYS...127
HOW TO ENTER INTO LIVE MODE...127
HOW TO TAKE STEADY SHOTS WITH YOUR CAMERA TIMER..128
HOW TO TAKE PICTURES AND VIDEOS USING THE CAMERA APP...129
HOW TO CHANGE BETWEEN THE REAR AND FRONT CAMERA..132
HOW TO DISABLE IMAGE MIRRORING FOR THE FRONT CAMERA..133
HOW TO ADJUST COLOR AND LIGHT IN THE CAMERA APP...134
HOW TO EDIT PHOTOS AND VIDEOS...135
   Editing Photos..135
   Editing Videos..136
HOW TO ROTATE, FLIP, AND CROP IMAGES...136
HOW TO UNDO AND REDO EDITS..138
HOW TO ADJUST AND STRAIGHTEN THE PERSPECTIVE...139

How to apply filters 141

How to take portrait images.. 142

How to take panorama images 143

How to record a time-lapse video 144

How to revert an edited video or image 145

How to copy and paste edits to images 146

How to edit time, location, and date in the Camera app 147

How to record a slo-mo video 147

How to share photos and videos 148

Basic Camera settings 151

Frequently Asked Questions 152

CHAPTER NINE 153

USING THE CALENDAR APP 153

Overview... 153

Downloading the iPhone Calendar App... 153

iPhone Calendar App Views and Icons 154

How to Create an Event... 158

How to Edit an Event... 160

How to Delete an Event... 160

How to Search for an Event... 160

View and Manage Calendars... 161

Viewing the Calendar.. 161

Managing Events 161

How to Use Siri to Create Events 162

Frequently Asked Questions 163

CHAPTER TEN.. 164

NOTES APP 164

Overview... 164

How to Access the Notes app 164

Using the Home Screen... 164

Using Siri 165

Using Spotlight Search 165

Using Control Center 165

How to create a new note... 165

How to type and format your note 168

How to add media to your note 169

How to sort notes.. 171

How to view attachments in notes 172

How to organize and search notes.. 172

How to view notes in folders 174

How to create a smart folder.. 175

How to share and collaborate on your note... 176

How to delete or archive notes 177

Frequently Asked Questions 178

CHAPTER ELEVEN **179**

MAPS APP **179**

Overview 179

How to access the Maps app 179

How to get your current location... 180

How to search for a location 181

How to view search results 182

How to get directions.. 183

How to choose a transportation mode 185

How to begin navigation 187

How to zoom in and out on the map.. 188

How to rotate the map 189

How to end navigation 190

How to bookmark a map 191

How to see the overview of your route 191

How to customize map settings.. 192

How to report an issue 193

How to mark my location 195

How to create a new guide 196

How to explore nearby areas 197

Frequently Asked Questions 198

CHAPTER TWELVE **199**

NEWS APP **199**

Overview 199

How to access the News app.. 199

How to set up Apple News 201

How to navigate the news app 202

How to read articles on the news app 203

How to share and save on the news app.. 205

Sharing an article 205

Save an article... 206

How to follow channels and publications on the news app 207

How to customize your newsfeed 208

How to view notifications on the news app 209

How to use the search bar on the news app 210

How to use the news audio feature to listen to news 212

Frequently Asked Questions 213

CHAPTER THIRTEEN 214

REMINDERS APP 214

OVERVIEW 214

USING THE REMINDERS APP 214

HOW TO MAKE A LIST 214

HOW TO CREATE A SMART LIST 217

ORGANIZE YOUR REMINDERS WITH TAGS IN THE IPHONE REMINDER APP 218

HOW TO USE SUBTASKS 218

HOW TO USE SIRI COMMANDS 219

HOW TO SET LOCATION-BASED REMINDERS 220

HOW TO SET REMINDERS THAT USE THE MESSAGES APP 220

HOW TO VIEW YOUR "COMPLETED" REMINDERS 221

WHAT CAN WE EXPECT FROM IOS 17? 221

10 KEY TIPS TO GET MORE FROM THE APPLE REMINDERS APP 222

FREQUENTLY ASKED QUESTIONS 225

CHAPTER FOURTEEN 226

ITUNES STORE 226

OVERVIEW 226

HOW TO LAUNCH AND SIGN IN TO ITUNES STORE 226

HOW TO BROWSE AND SEARCH FOR CONTENT 227

HOW TO VIEW CONTENT IN THE ITUNES STORE 229

HOW TO PURCHASE AND DOWNLOAD CONTENT 230

HOW TO ACCESS PURCHASED CONTENT 231

HOW TO DOWNLOAD AND STREAM CONTENT 232

HOW TO ACCESS YOUR ACCOUNT SETTINGS 233

HOW TO REDEEM GIFT CARDS OR CODES 234

FREQUENTLY ASKED QUESTIONS 234

CHAPTER FIFTEEN 236

APPLE APP STORE 236

OVERVIEW 236

HOW TO ACCESS THE APP STORE 236

HOW TO EXPLORE THE APP STORE 237

HOW TO SEARCH FOR AN APP IN THE APPLE APP STORE 241

HOW TO INSTALL AN APP 243

HOW TO MANAGE YOUR DOWNLOADS 245

HOW TO UPDATE APPS 246

HOW TO MANAGE APP SUBSCRIPTIONS 247

HOW TO LEAVE REVIEWS AND RATINGS 248

HOW TO USE PRIVACY AND PERMISSIONS 250

HOW TO ACCESS THE APP LIBRARY IN THE APPLE APP STORE 251

FREQUENTLY ASKED QUESTIONS 252

CHAPTER SIXTEEN **253**

FILES APP **253**

OVERVIEW 253
HOW TO ACCESS AND NAVIGATE THE FILES APP 253
    Browse Locations 254
VIEWING FILES AND FOLDERS 254
    Creating Folders 254
    Organizing Files 254
    Favorites 254
    Search 254
HOW TO BROWSE YOUR FILES 255
HOW TO MANAGE FILES AND FOLDERS 257
HOW TO ACCESS ICLOUD DRIVE 259
HOW TO CONNECT OTHER CLOUD SERVICES IN THE FILES APP 260
HOW TO SEARCH FOR FILES 261
HOW TO VIEW AND SHARE FILES IN THE FILES APP 262
    Using the Files App to Share Files 262
HOW TO TAG AND SORT FILES 263
FREQUENTLY ASKED QUESTIONS 264

CHAPTER SEVENTEEN **265**

APPLE MUSIC **265**

OVERVIEW 265
HOW TO SIGN IN TO APPLE MUSIC 265
HOW TO SUBSCRIBE TO APPLE MUSIC ON YOUR IPHONE 15 SERIES 267
HOW TO BROWSE AND PLAY MUSIC 268
HOW TO CREATE A PLAYLIST 270
HOW TO SHARE APPLE MUSIC WITH FAMILY MEMBERS 271
HOW TO LISTEN TO MUSIC SHARED WITH YOU 272
HOW TO DOWNLOAD MUSIC FOR OFFLINE LISTENING 273
HOW TO CHANGE OR CANCEL YOUR APPLE 275
MUSIC SUBSCRIPTION 275
    Changing Your Apple Music Membership 275
    Canceling Your Apple Music Membership 275
HOW TO CONNECT APPLE MUSIC TO OTHER DEVICES 276
HOW TO MANAGE YOUR SUBSCRIPTION 277
HOW TO CUSTOMIZE APPLE MUSIC SETTINGS 278
HOW TO LISTEN TO AUDIOBOOKS IN APPLE BOOKS ON IPHONE 15 PRO 279
HOW TO PLAY AN AUDIOBOOK 281
FREQUENTLY ASKED QUESTIONS 282

CHAPTER EIGHTEEN **283**

APPLE PAY AND FAMILY SHARING **283**

OVERVIEW 283

APPLE PAY 283

SETTING UP APPLE PAY 284

HOW TO USE APPLE PAY ON IPHONE 15 SERIES VIA FACE ID? 287

HOW TO CHOOSE DEFAULT CARD FOR APPLE PAY ON IPHONE 15 SERIES? 288

HOW TO ENABLE & USE APPLE PAY EXPRESS TRANSIT ON IPHONE 15 SERIES? 288

   Setting up Express Transit 289

HOW TO USE EXPRESS TRANSIT FOR MAKING PAYMENTS? 289

HOW TO ADD A DEBIT OR CREDIT CARD 289

HOW TO FIND LOCATIONS THAT SUPPORT APPLE PAY 291

HOW TO CHANGE YOUR SHIPPING AND CONTACT DETAILS 292

HOW TO PAY IN AN APPLICATION OR ON THE INTERNET 293

HOW TO SET UP AND MANAGE FAMILY SHARING 294

   Setting up Family Sharing 294

   Managing Family Sharing 296

HOW TO START A FAMILY GROUP 297

HOW TO CHECK IF A MEMBER HAS ACCEPTED YOUR INVITATION 298

HOW TO JOIN A FAMILY GROUP 299

HOW TO ENABLE FIND MY 300

   Enabling Find My 300

   Using Find My 301

FREQUENTLY ASKED QUESTIONS 302

CHAPTER NINETEEN **303**

APPLE HEALTH AND CONNECTIVITY **303**

OVERVIEW 303

HOW TO SET UP APPLE HEALTH 303

HOW TO USE APPLE HEALTH TO TRACK HEALTH ISSUES 305

HOW TO MANAGE WORKOUTS IN APPLE HEALTH 306

HOW TO CONNECT TO A BLUETOOTH DEVICE 308

HOW TO PAIR AND UNPAIR A BLUETOOTH ACCESSORY 309

   Pairing a Bluetooth Accessory 309

   Unpairing a Bluetooth Accessory 310

HOW TO CONNECT TO A WI-FI NETWORK 310

HOW TO SET UP A PERSONAL HOTSPOT 312

HOW TO CONNECT TO A VISIBLE AND HIDDEN NETWORK 313

   Connecting to a visible Wi-Fi Network 313

   Connecting to a Hidden (Non-Broadcast) Wireless Network 313

FREQUENTLY ASKED QUESTIONS 313

CHAPTER TWENTY **315**

BASIC FUNCTIONALITIES **315**

OVERVIEW 315

TIPS AND TRICKS 315

USING DO NOT DISTURB 320

HOW TO USE FOCUS MODE 321

HOW TO MULTITASK 322

    Using the App Switcher 322

    Switching Between Applications 322

    Using Slide Over 322

    Use Split View 322

    Close Apps in the App Switcher 322

    Use Picture-in-Picture (PiP) mode 323

HOW TO PIN APPS TO THE SCREEN 323

HOW TO TURN ON DARK MODE 323

HOW TO REDUCE AND INCREASE FONT SIZE 324

    Reduce Font Size 324

HOW TO USE CRASH DETECTION 325

HOW TO USE THE WATER-RESISTANT FEATURE 326

TROUBLESHOOTING ISSUES 327

    How to fix iPhone 15 Black Screen Issue 327

    How to fix iPhone 15 Series Battery Life Problems 327

    Restart your device 328

    Update your Device 328

    Lower the screen's brightness 328

    Disable the Always-On Display 329

    Turn off 5G 329

    Examine Your Apps 329

    Deactivate Keyboard Haptics 330

    Reset All Settings 330

    Opt for Low Power Mode 331

    How to fix lost 5G on iPhone 15 Series 331

    How to fix iPhone 15 Bluetooth Problems 332

    How to fix iPhone 15 Wi-Fi Problems 333

    How to fix iPhone 15 Charging Problems 334

    How to fix iPhone 15 Cellular Data Problems 334

    How to fix iPhone 15 Sound Problems 335

    How to fix iPhone 15 Activation Problems 335

HOW TO SOLVE FACE ID ISSUES ON THE IPHONE 15 336

HOW TO SOLVE OVERHEATING ISSUES WITH THE IPHONE 15 336

FREQUENTLY ASKED QUESTIONS 337

CONCLUSION 337

INDEX **338**

INTRODUCTION

Apple has unveiled the new iPhone 15 series which includes the iPhone 15, iPhone 15 Plus, iPhone 15 Pro, and iPhone 15 Pro Max. Similar to the iPhone 14 family, there are four versions in the series. However, the iPhone 15 series includes several firsts, like the Dynamic Island on non-pro versions and a USB Type-C charging connector. The new Dynamic Island and a 48 MP primary camera, which were formerly exclusive to the iPhone Pro, have been added by Apple to the iPhone 15 and iPhone 15 Plus. Its display, in-camera functions, battery life, and computer efficiency have all improved. Removing the Lightning connector in favor of the more widely used USB-C is one of Apple's largest updates to the iPhone.

The camera is the main upgrade. Beyond just improving the CCD, the 48MP camera's capability is enhanced by very clever software that optimizes the picture. This eliminates the need for massive file sizes to take up all of your storage space while doubling the resolution and balancing light and detail. Additionally, the camera can determine if you want to snap a portrait or not and allows you to change that choice afterward. Once the photo is taken, you may even move the focus between the subjects in it. The Main camera offers customers a new 24MP super-high-resolution setting that uses computational photography to produce images with amazing quality and manageable file sizes that are perfect for sharing and saving. An extra 2x Telephoto option allows customers to experience three optical-quality zoom levels (0.5x, 1x, and 2x) on an iPhone dual-camera system for the first time, thanks to clever hardware and software integration."

Despite this, the business launched 6TB ($29.99/month) and 12TB ($59.99/month) iCloud storage tiers to demonstrate that it understands that more pixels in cameras produce larger photographs. The new flagship iPhone 15 Pro and iPhone 15 Pro Max are costlier and feature Apple's first 3nm mobile processor, the A17 Pro. They are also lighter and stronger than previous models, with an Action button, a new design, and even better cameras than those in the range. You can even use these devices to record immersive mixed-reality scenes for Vision Pro.

The majority of users will notice significant visual enhancements, including as 20% quicker peak performance, improved energy economy, and hardware-accelerated ray tracing for a more engaging gaming experience. (With an extra connection, USB 3 rates are achievable for 20x quicker transfers.) The iPhone Pro's Action Button is a customizable button that can do a lot more than its predecessor. You can use it to change the mode from ring to silence. It may also be used to adjust volume, execute shortcuts, and other things. With every contact, you get immediate visual feedback.

It's a significant gain for photographers. Users benefit from a 5x optical zoom at 120mm focal length telephoto in addition to a 3x telephoto camera. Instead of developing a periscopic camera to do this, the business designed an inside housing that produces a comparable outcome. With an eye toward developing future environments, you can also record 4K video in Pro Res mode with the iPhone and, if desired, use USB-C to transfer all of that data to your Mac for real-time on-location editing. This essentially implies that you will be able to record incredible visuals and experiences with Vision Pro, including the ability to produce 3D spatial video.

CHAPTER ONE
GETTING STARTED

Overview

Chapter one talks about the new iPhone 15 Series which includes the likes of iPhone 15, iPhone 15 Plus, iPhone 15 Pro, and iPhone 15 Pro Max including its specifications and different features. Additionally, you will also get to know the new additions found in iOS 17 and how you can update your software.

Specifications and Features

Here are the specifications for the different iPhone 15 Series:

IPhone 15:

- **Display Size**: 6.1 inches
- **Operating System**: iOS 17
- **Price:** $799
- **CPU:** A16 Bionic
- **Base storage**: 128GB
- **Refresh rate**: 60Hz
- **Charging port**: USB-C
- **Battery life:** All day

- **Colors**: Pink, black, yellow, green, blue
- **Front camera**: 12MP
- **Rear cameras**: 48MP main, 12MP ultrawide

IPhone 15 Plus:

- **Display Size**: 6.7 inches
- **Operating System**: iOS 17
- **Price**: $899
- **CPU:** A16 Bionic
- **Base storage**: 128GB
- **Refresh rate**: 60Hz
- **Charging port:** USB-C
- **Battery life:** All day
- **Colors**: Pink, black, yellow, green, blue
- **Front camera**: 12MP
- **Rear cameras**: 48MP main, 12MP ultrawide

IPhone 15 Pro:

- **Display Size**: 6.1 inches
- **Operating System**: iOS 17
- **Resolution**: 1179 x 2556 pixels
- **Protection**: Ceramic Shield glass
- **CPU:** A17 Bionic
- **Base storage**: 128GB, 256GB, 512GB, 1TB
- **Refresh rate**: 60Hz
- **Charging port:** USB-C
- **Battery life:** All day
- **Colors**: Black Titanium, White Titanium, Natural Titanium, Blue Titanium
- **Front camera**: 12MP
- **Rear cameras**: 48MP main, 12MP Ultrawide

IPhone 15 Pro Max:

- **Display Size**: 6.7 inches
- **Operating System**: iOS 17
- **Resolution**: 1290 x 2796 pixels
- **Protection**: Ceramic Shield glass
- **CPU:** A17 Bionic
- **Base storage**: 128GB, 256GB, 512GB, 1TB
- **Refresh rate**: 60Hz
- **Charging port:** USB-C
- **Battery life:** All day
- **Colors**: Black Titanium, White Titanium, Natural Titanium, Blue Titanium
- **Front camera**: 12MP
- **Rear cameras**: 48MP main, 12MP Ultrawide

Features

The iPhone 15 series represents a significant shift in line with Apple's established three-year redesign cycle. This version showcases a revamped design that exhibits distinct differences when compared to its predecessors, namely the iPhone 12, iPhone 13, and iPhone 14 series. The iPhone 15 series has introduced a range of significant upgrades, particularly in the iPhone 15 Pro models, which have received the majority of these enhancements. Below is a comprehensive overview of the iPhone 15 and iPhone 15 Pro series, providing you with all the essential information you need.

The iPhone 15 Models

There are four models in the iPhone 15 generation — the iPhone 15, iPhone 15 Plus, iPhone 15 Pro, and iPhone 15 Pro Max. The iPhone 15 Mini is not available, unlike its predecessor, the iPhone 13 generation, where Apple introduced the iPhone Mini model. However, Apple decided to discontinue the iPhone Mini model in the iPhone 14 generation. Furthermore, it is important to note that Apple did not introduce an iPhone 15 "**Ultra**" model with enhanced features beyond those of the iPhone 15 Pro Max, despite previous speculations.

iPhone 15 Series Release Date

Apple unveiled the latest version of its flagship smartphone, the iPhone 15, on September 12th. The preorders can be made directly through Apple's official website or authorized carriers such as AT&T and Verizon. The release date for the phones is set for September 22, and they will be available for purchase at Apple stores as well as other authorized retailers.

iPhone 15 Series Price

Except for the iPhone 15 Pro Max, the pricing for the iPhone 15 generation remains consistent with that of the iPhone 14 generation during its initial release. The iPhone 15 Pro Max introduces a storage capacity of 256GB, as opposed to the 128GB offering of its predecessor, the iPhone 14 Pro Max. Consequently, the base model price has been raised by $100, resulting in a new starting price of $1,199, in contrast to the previous price of $1,099.

- **The pricing for the iPhone 15 is as follows:** $799 for the 128GB model, $899 for the 256GB model, and $1,099 for the 512GB model.
- **The pricing for the iPhone 15 Plus is as follows:** $899 for the 128GB model, $999 for the 256GB model, and $1,199 for the 512GB model.
- **The pricing details for the iPhone 15 Pro are as follows:** $999 for the 128GB variant, $1,099 for the 256GB variant, $1,299 for the 512GB variant, and $1,499 for the one terabyte variant.
- **The pricing for the iPhone 15 Pro Max is as follows:** $1,199 for the 256GB model, $1,399 for the 512GB model, and $1,599 for the one terabyte model.

The iPhone 15 Series Cameras

Apple has recently unveiled significant enhancements to the camera capabilities across its entire lineup of iPhone 15 models. The primary cameras of the iPhone 15 and iPhone 15 Plus have been enhanced, with an increase in resolution from 12 megapixels (MP) to 48MP. The new camera provides optical quality zoom, which is superior to digital zoom. It achieves a 2x zoom by utilizing a cropping technique that focuses on the middle 12MP of its 48MP sensor. The inclusion of this significant new feature in Apple's iPhone 15 and iPhone 15 Plus presents users with a valuable choice. By default, the iPhone 15 and iPhone 15 Plus employ a binning process that reduces the resolution of captured photos from 48MP to 24MP. This technique is intended to enhance the level of detail and clarity in the resulting images. According to Apple, despite the increased number of megapixels, 24MP photos are still stored at a size that is considered practical. However, it is currently unknown how much storage a 24MP photo uses in comparison to a 12MP photo, although it is anticipated that the former would require a larger amount of storage.

The iPhone 15 Pro and iPhone 15 Pro Max is equipped with a 48MP main camera that captures high-quality 24MP photographs. Additionally, Apple has incorporated widely favored preset options for focal lengths, including 24mm, 28mm, and 35mm. The iPhone 15 Pro is equipped with a standard 3x zoom lens, while the iPhone 15 Pro Max features Apple's latest 5x zoom lens boasting a focal length of 120mm. The recently introduced 5x zoom lens bears resemblance to the periscope-style 10x zoom lens found on the Samsung Galaxy S23 Ultra. However, Apple has coined it as a **"tetraprism"** design. Apple has further announced its plans to introduce spatial video recording functionality to the iPhone 15 Pro models. This innovative feature will enable users to capture videos in a three-dimensional format, specifically designed to complement the capabilities of the Apple Vision Pro AR headset. The headset itself is scheduled for release in the early months of the following year.

iPhone 15 Series Displays

The iPhone 15 generation maintains its customary display size without any alterations. The iPhone 15 and iPhone 15 Plus have been equipped with enhanced displays, featuring a higher brightness level of 2000 nits, in contrast to the 1200-nit display found in the iPhone 14.

- The iPhone 15 boasts a 6.1-inch Super Retina XDR OLED display with a refresh rate of 60Hz.
- The iPhone 15 Plus boasts a remarkable 6.7-inch Super Retina XDR OLED display, offering users a visually stunning experience with its vibrant colors and sharp resolution. The display operates at a refresh rate of 60Hz, ensuring smooth and fluid visuals for an enhanced user experience.
- The iPhone 15 Pro boasts a 6.1-inch Super Retina XDR OLED display, featuring the cutting-edge technology of 120Hz ProMotion. Additionally, this model offers an always-on display feature.
- The iPhone 15 Pro Max boasts a sizable 6.7-inch Super Retina XDR OLED display, which offers stunning visuals. Additionally, it features a 120Hz ProMotion technology that ensures smooth and fluid scrolling. Moreover, the device includes an always-on display feature, allowing users to conveniently view important information at a glance.

It is disheartening to observe that the iPhone 15 and iPhone 15 Plus manufactured by Apple continue to possess a relatively modest 60Hz refresh rate. This particular characteristic can be considered a significant drawback for a smartphone that commences at a price point of $800 in the year 2023. It is worth noting that even the Google Pixel 7a, priced at $500, and offers a more seamless display experience with its 90Hz refresh rate. There have been reports indicating that Apple and its partners faced challenges in incorporating a high refresh-rate display into the iPhone 15 and iPhone 15 plus, primarily due to constraints in production capacity.

iPhone 15 Series Design

The design of the iPhone 15 is a topic of great interest and anticipation among technology enthusiasts. The iPhone 15 models have been equipped with Apple's most recent design, featuring gently curved edges in contrast to the more angular edges seen on the iPhone 14 series. The incorporation of contoured edges in the iPhone 15 generation is expected to enhance the overall ergonomic experience, resulting in a more comfortable grip for users. The iPhone 15 Pro and iPhone 15 Pro Max feature a Titanium frame that exhibits a brushed metal appearance, offering a sleek alternative to the traditional polished steel. This design choice not only enhances the aesthetic appeal but also contributes to a reduction in overall weight, resulting in a lighter device. Indeed, the iPhone 15 Pro is 6.6 ounces compared to the 7.27-ounce iPhone 14 Pro, and the iPhone 15 Pro Max is 7.81 ounces compared to the heavy 8.47-ounce iPhone 14 Pro Max.

The iPhone 15 Pro and iPhone 15 Pro Max also feature thinner display bezels that make for a more premium look. In addition, the current iPhone Pro models offer the advantage of being more convenient and potentially more cost-effective to repair compared to their predecessors. This is primarily due to the glass back design, which allows for easier removal during repair procedures.

iPhone 15 Series Colors

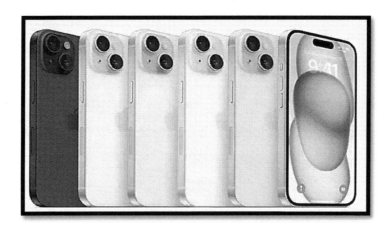

The iPhone 15 and iPhone 15 Plus showcase Apple's latest innovation in design, incorporating a back glass that is infused with vibrant colors and adorned with a frosted matte texture. This exquisite feature is offered in a selection of five captivating color choices, namely blue, pink, yellow, green, and black.

The iPhone 15 Pro and iPhone 15 Pro Max offer a selection of titanium frames in various colors, including natural titanium, blue titanium, white titanium, and black titanium.

iPhone 15 Series Performance

The iPhone 15 and iPhone 15 Plus are equipped with the A16 Bionic processor, which is also featured in the iPhone 14 Pro series. As a result, we can anticipate comparable performance to the previous generation's premium smartphones. The iPhone 15 Pro and iPhone 15 Pro Max are powered by Apple's newest A17 Pro processor. Apple asserts that the A17 Pro exhibits a CPU that is 10 percent faster and a GPU that is 20 percent more rapid in terms of graphics processing. However, the specific benchmarks or devices against which these comparisons are being made remain undisclosed by the company. Apple has prioritized enhanced graphics and gaming capabilities by incorporating hardware-accelerated ray tracing, a technique that produces stunning lighting effects, into the iPhone 15 Pro models. This advancement is made possible by the powerful A17 Pro processor. The company has emphasized that the iPhone 15 Pro models can run full console titles such as **"Resident Evil Village," "Resident Evil 4," "Death Stranding,"** and **"Assassin's Creed Mirage."**

iPhone 15 Series Action Button

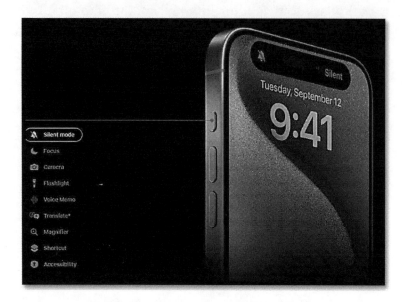

In the latest versions of the iPhone, namely the iPhone 15 Pro and iPhone 15 Pro Max, Apple has made a notable change by replacing the well-known iPhone ring/silent switch with a novel feature known as the customizable Action button. Users can personalize the function of the Action button according to their preferences. This includes options such as enabling or disabling the flashlight, swiftly accessing applications like Camera, Voice Memos, and Translate, activating a Focus mode, or executing a Shortcut. Additionally, it is possible to configure the device to utilize the conventional ring/silent switch. The ring/silent switch has remained unchanged since its inception on the first iPhone, and it continues to be present on the iPhone 15 and iPhone 15 plus models.

iPhone 15 Series USB-C port

The Lightning port has been replaced by Apple with a USB-C port across the entire range of iPhone 15 models. The charging speed remains consistent at 18-20W, which is equivalent to the previous Lightning charging technology. Currently, it is feasible to utilize a USB-C cable to charge a secondary device, such as the recently released AirPods Pro 2 with USB-C, directly from an iPhone 15.

There are notable distinctions in the USB-C ports found on the iPhone 15 models and the iPhone 15 Pro models. The iPhone 15 and iPhone 15 Plus exclusively offer USB 2 transfer speeds, typically reaching 480Mbps. Conversely, the iPhone 15 Pro and iPhone 15 Pro Max feature a USB-C port that supports USB 3 speeds. The iPhone 15 Pro models are capable of achieving speeds of up to 10 GB/s, indicating their usage of the USB 3.1 Gen 2 standard.

iPhone 15 Series Dynamic Island

The Dynamic Island feature, initially introduced in the iPhone 15 Pro and iPhone 14 Pro models, has now been incorporated into the iPhone 15 and iPhone 15 Plus devices. This innovative addition replaces the notch, which was originally introduced with the iPhone X back in 2017.

iPhone 15 Series Roadside Assistance via Satellite

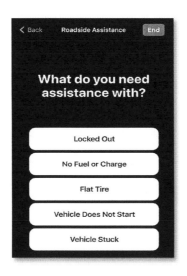

Apple has recently introduced a cutting-edge safety feature known as Roadside Assistance via satellite. This innovative feature enables users who find themselves stranded with car issues in regions lacking Wi-Fi or cellular signal to establish a connection with AAA, a renowned provider of automotive assistance services, for prompt help and support. The complimentary service is provided for two years following the activation of a compatible iPhone, and it is compatible with AAA memberships. For individuals who do not possess an AAA membership, the service operates on a cost-per-use model. The inclusion of satellite-based Roadside Assistance was first introduced with the iPhone 15 series, although it is also compatible with the iPhone 14 series. The feature enhances the current safety capabilities, which include satellite-based Crash Detection and Emergency SOS functionality.

What's new in iOS 17?

There are tons of additions to the new iOS 17 and they will all be discussed below:

StandBy Mode

The StandBy mode is a feature that allows a device to conserve power while remaining operational. As earlier stated, the latest version of iOS, iOS 17, introduces a new feature known as StandBy mode. By activating this mode on your iPhone while it is connected to a power source and positioned in landscape orientation, your device can function as an intelligent display. This mode offers the ability to showcase various features such as displaying the current time, widgets, Live Activities, and more. This particular feature proves to be quite useful, particularly in scenarios where individuals tend to charge their iPhones in the kitchen while engaging in cooking activities or on their bedside tables during nighttime. However, it is important to note that this feature may not be compatible with all models of iPhones. Currently, the effective usage of this feature is limited to the iPhone 14 Pro and Pro Max models due to their inclusion of an always-on display. iPhones that are compatible with iOS 17 can use StandBy mode, although it is important to note that the screen will automatically turn off after a specific period.

Open Camera app modes with new shortcut actions

iOS 17 offers the capability to use the Shortcuts app for creating customized actions. These actions enable users to swiftly access various modes within the Camera app, such as Video and Portrait, instead of the default Photo mode. This implies that there will be no need to navigate through the Camera application to capture a video of an interesting event occurring right before your eyes, only to ultimately fail in doing so. Here, we will discuss the process of creating Shortcut actions for the Camera app in the second public beta of iOS 17.

Additionally, we will explore the steps required to add these Shortcuts to your home screen.

1. To begin, access the **Shortcuts application**.
2. Locate the plus (+) symbol situated in the upper-right corner of your screen.
3. To proceed, select the "**Add Action**" option.
4. Search for Camera.
5. To create a shortcut for a specific Camera mode, simply tap on the desired mode from the carousel located under the Camera Mode section.
6. To access the camera function, tap on the "**Open Camera**" option located at the top of your screen. This action will prompt a dropdown menu to appear.

By accessing the dropdown menu, users can rename this Shortcut to reflect the specific Camera mode it opens. This can be done by simply tapping on the "**Rename**" function. To include this shortcut on your home screen, simply tap "**Add to Home Screen**" from the menu.

72-hour passcode grace period

Have you ever changed your passcode, only to later encounter difficulty recalling it while attempting to access your device? In iOS 17, users have the option to use their previous passcode within a 72-hour timeframe to reset their current passcode in the event of forgetting the newly set passcode. This innovative addition will undoubtedly alleviate the burden for individuals and prevent significant inconvenience.

Autocorrect gets an improvement

The keyboard on iOS 17 for iPhone devices will receive an upgrade. The keyboard will use a transformer model, similar to the one used by OpenAI in its language models. This will enhance its ability to accurately anticipate the user's next input, be it a proper noun or an expletive. Autocorrect can assist with grammar, much like word processing software such as Microsoft Word. Although the provided information is interesting and useful, the main conclusion is that most people will no longer need to repeatedly type profanities to ensure their inclusion in a message.

New Journal app

Journaling is a beneficial practice that aids in stress management, goal attainment, and various other aspects of personal development. Shortly, iPhone users can anticipate the introduction of a new journaling application, aptly named Journal, which is set to be released alongside the highly anticipated iOS 17 update. While there are existing journaling applications available, Apple's journaling app distinguishes itself by using on-device machine learning technology to generate tailored prompts that assist users in their journaling endeavors. Additionally, users will have the capability to schedule notifications as a means of reminding themselves to engage in writing activities. The application ensures the privacy of all entries through on-device processing, end-to-end encryption, and the option to secure the app with a lock feature.

If you prefer typing over using traditional writing tools like pencils or pens and notebooks, this application can assist you in establishing and maintaining a consistent journaling habit. Even individuals who already engage in regular journaling can derive various advantages from utilizing the application.

New Messages improvements and features

iOS 17 also brings several enhancements to the Messages application. The newly introduced Check-In feature allows users to promptly and effortlessly notify their family members or friends about their safe arrival at the intended destination. As a parent, you can use this innovative feature to ensure the safe arrival of your child at their friend's residence. Users will also have the added convenience of being able to navigate directly to the earliest unread message within a conversation in the Messages app. This can be particularly advantageous if you are engaged in a dynamic group conversation. Picture yourself attending a one-hour-long meeting, only to discover upon exiting that the group chat you are a part of with your friends has accumulated 50 notifications. iOS 17 offers the capability to navigate back to the initial unread message, enabling users to review the complete context of the most recent conflict or controversy. Ultimately, the consensus is that nobody has a preference for tea that has gone bad.

In the Messages app, there is a feature that allows users to reply to a specific message by swiping on it. This enables a direct response to the selected message. In the previous version, it was necessary to perform a long press on the message and subsequently choose the Reply option. Users also have the option to generate stickers for their messages using their photographs. Apple refers to these interactive graphics as Live Stickers, which can be enhanced with various effects and conveniently stored on your iPhone for future use. You now have the opportunity to transform your pet's side-eye expression into an enjoyable sticker, although it is likely that your pet will remain displeased.

New Contact Posters

One of the exciting new additions that iOS 17 introduces to your iPhone is the Contact Posters feature. Consider these posters as customizable contact cards with extensive personalization options. In earlier iterations of iOS, it was possible to assign unique ringtones and thumbnail photos to individual contacts stored on your device. Contact Posters offer an enhanced level of customization, allowing users to personalize their contacts by incorporating emoji pictures, modifying the color and font of contacts, and providing additional customization options. Apple has also announced that Contact Posters will be accessible for third-party calling applications, extending beyond the confines of your iPhone's contact list. The incorporation of customizable lock screens with Contacts in this feature resembles Apple's approach, leading to speculation that Apple may eventually extend customization options to other apps and features on the iPhone. It is hoped that Apple will persist in providing individuals with increased customization possibilities in the forthcoming period. For instance, granting users the ability to modify the display, color, and font for distinct conversations within the Messages application.

Delete password verification messages automatically

Within the iOS 17 operating system, users can access a specific feature by navigating to the Settings menu, followed by the Passwords section, and subsequently selecting Password Options. Notably, a novel functionality named Clean up automatically can be found under the Verification Codes category. If enabled, this option will automatically delete messages in Messages and Mail that contain verification codes after you've inserted the code using AutoFill.

Create a grocery list in Reminders

To use this functionality, it is necessary to upgrade the Reminders application after upgrading to iOS 17. Upon launching the application for the first time following the installation of iOS 17, users will be prompted to upgrade. Subsequently, there are several sequential actions involved in creating a grocery list.

Here are the steps:

1. Launch a new reminder.
2. To access additional options, locate and tap the three dots (...) located in the upper-right corner of your screen.
3. To access the list information, tap on the "**List Info**" option.

4. To select the "**Groceries**" list type, tap on "**Standard**" next to the "**List Type**" option.

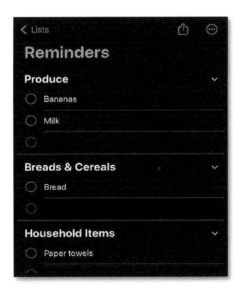

Once activated, the Reminders feature will automatically categorize various grocery items into sections such as Produce, Breads, and cereals.

Conversational Awareness with AirPods

In recent years, the use of wireless Earbuds, such as AirPods, has become increasingly popular. These sleek and convenient devices allow users to enjoy their favorite songs. The release of iOS 17 will bring several enhancements to the second-generation AirPods Pro. These improvements include Adaptive Audio and Personalized Volume, which aim to enhance the overall listening experience. However, the feature that has garnered the most excitement is Conversation Awareness.

The second-generation AirPods Pro features Conversation Awareness, which enables them to detect the initiation of speech and subsequently adjust the music volume, minimize ambient noise, and enhance the clarity of voices coming from the direction in front of the user. Say goodbye to the hassle of adjusting the volume on your AirPods or iPhone just to greet someone.

Apple is expected to develop and enhance this feature in the future. In the future, an enhanced version of this software could potentially enable your AirPods to detect and respond to nearby individuals engaging in conversation with you, thereby automatically adjusting the volume level accordingly.

No more 'Hey, Siri'

With the introduction of iOS 17, Siri can now be activated without the need for a greeting. With the latest update, users can simply utter the word "**Siri**" to activate the digital assistant, which will then be ready to receive any inquiries or directives. This functionality bears resemblance to the way Amazon's digital assistant, Alexa, can be summoned. It is advisable to maintain a polite and respectful demeanor when interacting with your digital assistant. By doing so, you will potentially establish a positive rapport that could prove beneficial in the event of a hypothetical robotic uprising. Demonstrating kindness towards your digital assistant, such as Siri, may potentially influence future generations of robots to spare you from any adverse consequences.

Consecutive Siri Requests

In iOS 17, users will have the added capability to make consecutive requests to Siri. After activating Siri, users can instruct their digital assistant to send a text message to their partner. Additionally, they can seamlessly proceed to ask Siri to set an alarm for a later time without the need to repeat the phrases "**Hey Siri**" or "**Siri**". This feature enhances the conversational experience with Siri, allowing for a smoother interaction.

Personally, it aids in maintaining a coherent train of thought while seeking assistance from Siri.

AirTags can be shared with more people

AirTags provide a convenient solution for effectively monitoring personal belongings such as wallets or luggage. The latest iOS 17 update enables the registration of AirTags with multiple individuals, facilitating seamless item tracking for friends and family members. The latest update also enables multiple individuals to use a shared item, such as a piece of luggage, without necessitating any modifications to the tracking system.

The addition of this new feature has the potential to alleviate certain minor inconveniences associated with AirTags. If you are in the company of an individual who possesses an AirTag device, you will be promptly notified of the presence of an unidentified AirTag in your vicinity. Although these notifications can assist individuals in protecting themselves against undesired surveillance, the process of receiving these alerts can become burdensome when the AirTag in question is owned by one's partner or a friend.

The Maps app gets a boost

The Maps application of Apple is set to receive an upgrade with the release of iOS 17. The latest update offers users the ability to conveniently download maps for designated areas, enabling them to access turn-by-turn navigation, estimated arrival times, and additional features even without an internet connection.

In addition, Apple has announced that it will enhance the visibility of park trails in the United States, making them more easily accessible through their application. Furthermore, the company will integrate a feature that allows electric vehicle drivers to conveniently check the availability of charging stations directly within the app.

The ability to use offline Maps can prove highly advantageous for individuals engaging in hiking activities on unfamiliar trails or for those traveling or driving through remote areas. Apple's latest addition, along with the Emergency SOS via Satellite feature on the iPhone 14 and the Apple Watch Ultra, suggests that the company is actively expanding its product range to cater to various digital requirements in home, office, and outdoor settings.

Sharing is easier with AirDrop and NameDrop

iOS 17 introduces enhanced sharing capabilities through Airdrop and a novel feature called NameDrop, enabling seamless content sharing with others. In the iOS 17 version, users will no longer be required to remain within proximity to complete the sharing of content via AirDrop. If you initiate the AirDrop process within the designated range, it is not necessary to remain within range for the completion of the file transfer, even if it takes a considerable amount of time. With SharePlay, users will have the ability to enjoy music or videos collectively by simply bringing their iPhones in close proximity. NameDrop is an innovative feature that enables users to conveniently exchange contact information with another individual by simply bringing their iPhone or Apple Watch in proximity to the recipient's device.

Sensitive content warnings

The newly introduced feature in iOS 17 aims to provide users with enhanced protection against encountering unsolicited explicit images or videos. Apple has announced that users will have the ability to blur images or videos before viewing them. This feature will be accessible on various platforms such as Messages, AirDrop, and Contact Posters in the Phone app, FaceTime messages, and third-party applications. It appears that certain individuals utilizing dating applications will need to comprehend the appropriate usage of language and refrain from sending unsolicited explicit photographs to others.

How to download and install iOS 17

The usual procedures to download and set up the latest iOS 17 version on your iPhone are as follows:

1. First of all, make sure your iPhone model is compatible with the update before trying to install a new version of iOS. It's common for Apple to offer upgrades that are limited to certain iPhone models. iOS 17 is the latest version of Apple's operating system.
2. Before carrying out any significant software changes, you must make a backup of the data on your iPhone. This can be accomplished using iCloud or by using iTunes or Finder to connect your iPhone to a computer.
3. Verify that your iPhone is connected to a Wi-Fi network. Updates for software might be big files that need a lot of bandwidth to download over a cellular network.

4. To prevent your iPhone 15 Series from shutting down while updating, make sure it has enough battery life or connect it to a charger.

5. Go to: to download and install the most recent version of iOS. To do this select **Settings > General > Software Update**.

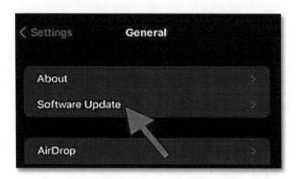

6. You will then see a list of available updates as they become available. Next, choose **"Download and Install**." You may need to enter the passcode on your device.

7. A screen with the terms and conditions will appear. Give them your permission to carry out the installation.
8. Your device will begin to download the update. The amount of the update and the speed of your internet connection might affect how long this takes.
9. Select "**Install**" when the download is finished. After restarting, the update will be installed on your iPhone. This might be a lengthy procedure.
10. After the update is installed, follow any on-screen instructions to finish off the setup process. This includes setting up any settings and logging in with your Apple ID.
11. At this point, you can now restore your applications and data from your backup if you backed up your data before the upgrade.

Frequently Asked Questions

1. What are the new features of iOS 17?
2. How do you download and install the new iOS 17?
3. What are the new features of the new iPhone 15 Series?
4. What are the different specifications of the new iPhone 15 Series?

CHAPTER TWO
CONFIGURING THE NEW IPHONE 15 SERIES

Overview

Congratulations if you have purchased any of the new iPhone 15 Series. The next things include the likes of setting up your new device, setting up either physical or eSIM, transferring data from an old device to the new device, waking up and unlocking and so much more.

How to set up your new iPhone 15 Series

Being organized usually makes things go more easily, so for the simplest setup possible, make sure you have the following ready:

- Your old phone (not necessary, but it's a good idea to have it on hand)
- Your SIM card (eSIM activation does not need it)
- Your Wi-Fi information
- Apple account information (using an iPhone requires having an Apple account).

First, Back Up Your Old Phone

Create a backup of your previous phone first. This will facilitate the process of moving your info if it's an iPhone. The easiest way is to back up to iCloud by selecting Back up Now from the menu after selecting Settings, iCloud, and iCloud Backup. Moreover, you can use Apple's Quick Start function to swap between iPhones by only turning on Bluetooth on your previous model and keeping it close by when you power on the new one. Be sure to download the Move to iOS Android app from Google Play if you're switching from Android. During the setup of your new iPhone, choose Move Data from Android from the Apps & Data page. Return to your Android phone, launch the app, choose **Continue**, and then adhere to the on-screen directions. While certain items cannot be transferred, you can carry over your calendars, email accounts, contacts, messages, pictures, and videos. Even some applications will make the transition.

Setting up Your New iPhone

To switch on your new iPhone 15 Series, insert your **SIM card** (if you are using an eSIM, skip this step) and press and hold the power button. The Apple logo and the greeting **"Hello"** in many languages will welcome you. Next, you have the option to **set up manually** (the difficult approach) or Quick Start (the simple way). Whether or whether this is your first iPhone will determine which route you choose.

Quick Start

Try Quick Start for the quickest route to setting up your new iPhone if you're an experienced Apple user and have your old iPhone close at hand. As soon as you get your new iPhone near your old one, make sure it's fully charged and that Bluetooth is on, and make sure you want to use the same Apple ID on both devices. Your old device should display an animation; move it over with your new one until the picture displays in the viewfinder. On your old iPhone, wait until you see Finish on New [Device]. You can pick precisely what you want to back up and which settings—including those for your Apple Watch if you have one—you want to carry over after entering your password at the prompt to begin the Face ID setup process.

As an alternative, choose **Other Options** and choose to **restore from a Mac or PC backup or an iCloud backup**. After that, input your Apple ID and password, and while your iPhone restarts with all of your settings, preferences, applications, and more in place, go get peppermint mocha. That is to say, it will be identical to your previous device, only updated.

Set Up Manually

Choose **Set Up Manually** if you're new to Apple products or if you simply want to start again and like tinkering with menus. Just follow the directions on the screen to have your iPad or iPhone activated. To restore or transfer your data and apps, you will need to first connect to your Wi-Fi network, activate your eSIM or insert your physical SIM card into the new device, set up a six-digit passcode, enable Face ID, and select whether to **Restore from iCloud Backup, Restore from Mac or PC, Transfer Directly from iPhone, or Move Data from Android**. Those switching from Android should keep in mind that the Move to iOS app is available.

After that, you will set up services like your iCloud account, FaceTime, iMessage, and Location Services, as well as choose whether to enable automatic updates. Sign in with your Apple ID. Additionally, you'll be prompted to set up Siri (which you should!), which entails speaking a few words to the assistant to help it recognize your voice. Finally, you can customize icon and text size with Display Zoom and True Tone (where available) display settings. Screen Time keeps track of how much time you spend on your device and allows you to set limits. Even though there are a lot of options and inputs, the entire process only takes a few minutes. Better still, you can access all of these options again later in the Settings app; none of these selections are enforceable.

Adding Other Accounts and Setting Preferences

The rest is just a matter of customizing your choices. Desire to set up an email account? Select Add Account after selecting Settings, Mail, and Accounts. Do you want to control which apps update in the background and use up more battery life? Open **Settings**, select **General**, **Background App Refresh**, and play around with the toggles. On web forms, do you want to save time? Open **Safari**, go to **Settings**, **Autofill**, and preload your contact information. By selecting Settings, Battery, and then Battery Percentage, you can also enable the battery percentage view.

How to set up physical and eSIM

A Quick Word on eSIM

Since the iPhone XS, Apple has enabled eSIM technology. Essentially, it functions as an electronic SIM card in place of the little, actual chip that you place into your phone to enable cellular access. The first smartphone to do away with the actual SIM card slot entirely is the new iPhone 15 series (in the US). This implies that an eSIM is the only device you can use to establish a cellular connection. Don't worry if you're not acquainted with the procedure; it's extremely simple. You will be prompted to move your number from your previous iPhone during setup. After you provide your consent, your new iPhone's cellular data will be activated, and you'll be ready to go in a minute or two. Remember that when you do this, your previous physical SIM card will no longer function.

If you are switching from an Android phone—whether or not it supports eSIM—you will have to scan a QR code that your carrier provides. This may even be the case with an iPhone if you're experiencing trouble—just call your carrier and they should be able to work things out swiftly.

Setting up the Physical SIM Card

The steps:

1. Find the SIM card tray on your iPhone. This is normally on the right-hand side of the device (when looking at the screen).
2. Use the SIM card ejection tool or a paperclip to gently press into the little hole on the SIM card tray. This will pop out of the tray.
3. Place your physical SIM card into the slot. Make sure it fits firmly and corresponds with the SIM card slot.
4. Carefully press the tray back into the device until it snaps into place.
5. To confirm the SIM card is detected, restart your iPhone.

Turning on the eSIM

The steps:

1. To get eSIM activation, get in touch with your cell carrier. Make sure they can provide you with a QR code or the activation data, and that they support eSIM.

2. To see the eSIM settings, go to **"Settings"** on your iPhone.

3. Choose "**Cellular**" by swiping down and selecting it.
4. Select "**Add Cellular Plan**" from the "**Cellular**" menu.

5. Use the camera on your iPhone to scan the QR code, if one was given by your carrier. If your carrier supplied the activation data, you can also manually input them.
6. Your iPhone 15 Series will walk you through the configuration procedure. It may be necessary for you to input extra data that your carrier has given.
7. Once the configuration is finished, use your eSIM in addition to your regular SIM card. This is known as activating the eSIM.

Handling Dual SIM Configurations

1. Access the Dual SIM by going to "**Settings**" > "**Cellular.**"
2. You have the option to designate a data, voice, and messaging default line. By default, this establishes the line that is used for calls and messages.

3. Tap on the line you want to use to change lines when making calls or sending texts.

How to transfer data from old device to the iPhone 15 Series

To guarantee a seamless data transfer, whether you're moving from an Android smartphone or an older iPhone, ensure you take the following steps:

1. **Backup your Old Device**

Make a backup of your previous device before moving any data. You can do this in many ways:

iCloud Backup

- Connect your outdated iPhone to a network.
- Navigate to **[your name] > "Settings" > "iCloud."**
- After swiping down, choose **"iCloud Backup."**

- Tap "**Back up Now**" and watch as the backup is finished.

iTunes or Finder Backup:

- Use a USB cord to connect your outdated iPhone to your PC.
- Launch Finder or iTunes.
- When your iPhone appears, choose it.
- Tap "**Back up Now**" and bide your time till the backup is complete.

2. **Set Up Your iPhone 15 Series**

It's time to set up your iPhone 15 once you've backed up your old device:

- Hold down the power button on your iPhone 15 to turn it on.
- To choose your language, region, and Wi-Fi network, adhere to the on-screen directions.
- Select to restore your data from an earlier backup when requested.
- Choose the iCloud Finder backup of your choice.

3. **Restore the Data**

Once the backup provider has been chosen, follow the steps below:

iCloud Backup

- Enter your Apple ID and password to log in.
- Select the relevant backup item from the list.
- Await the iCloud data restoration on your iPhone. The quantity of data may determine how long this takes.

iTunes or Finder Backup:

- Use a USB connection to link your iPhone 15 to your PC.
- Launch the iTunes Finder.
- When your iPhone appears, choose it.
- Click "**Restore Backup**" and choose the previously made backup.
- Select "**Restore**" and give the procedure some time to complete.

4. To finish configuring your iPhone 15, follow the on-screen directions. This includes activating or modifying various settings, setting up Face ID, and setting up a passcode.

5. You can choose to update your apps to the most recent versions after the first setup. Click on your profile image in the App Store, then choose "**Update All**" to update all of your applications at once.

How to wake and unlock your device

The typical procedures for waking up and unlocking an iPhone are as follows:

Waking up

1. If the **"Raise to Wake"** option is activated, you can use it to wake your iPhone instead of pressing the power button, which is often found on the right side of the device. Just elevate your iPhone to activate **"Raise to Wake,"** and the screen should come on by itself.

Unlocking your iPhone 15 Series

- If Face ID can identify your face on your iPhone, you should be able to access your home screen by swiping up from the bottom of the screen, which will open the lock icon at the top of the screen.

- You'll need to input your passcode if Face ID doesn't work or if your iPhone isn't equipped with these capabilities. To unlock the smartphone, touch the **"v"** button after selecting your passcode's characters or digits on the lock screen.

Home Screen

- The home screen is where you can access your applications and functions after unlocking your iPhone.

How to power on and off your device

Use these instructions to turn your iPhone 15 Series on and off:

Turning on

1. Find the iPhone 15 Series' side button. Usually, it is located on the device's right side.
2. Once the Apple logo appears on the screen, press and holds the side button for a short while. This shows that the iPhone is turning on.
3. When you see the Apple logo, release the side button to resume the booting process of your iPhone. It may need a minute to boot up completely.
4. After the device has powered up, you'll need to enter your password or use Face ID, if enabled, to open it.

Powering off

1. Once again, find the side button on the right side of your iPhone 15 Series to turn it off.
2. Push and hold the left side of the device's volume up or down button and the side button at the same time. Depress the two buttons simultaneously.
3. Hold down both buttons until the screen displays the "**slide to power off**" slider.

4. Start the shutdown procedure by swiping the slider from left to right.
5. Your iPhone 15 Series will turn off and show a spinning wheel. The screen will become entirely dark once it has been turned off.

You have successfully turned off the 15th-generation iPhone. As stated in the **"Powering On"** instructions, all you have to do is press and hold the side button until the Apple logo appears once again.

Some basic gestures to use with your new iPhone 15 Series

Learning the swipes and touches required to navigate your iPhone doesn't take long. Its ease of usage is one of its main selling points, but several lesser-known motions have hidden uses.

Pinch to zoom on videos

Although you may not be using this gesture wherever it is accessible, you are undoubtedly acquainted with it. You can use the pinch gesture to enlarge images and maps, and you can even use this gesture to magnify films that are playing from local storage. That's not an issue if your iPhone's camera has them, and it's a terrific way to view additional personal information in your recordings.

Tap and hold to open closed tabs in Safari

Do you want to return to the page you clicked off of too soon? Have you already forgotten what you just read? To access your recently closed tabs, press and hold the new tab icon (a plus) in the Safari app. You can also launch the tab view by using the icon in the bottom right corner of the app. In the tab view, you can also drag and drop individual tabs to rearrange them.

Quicker zooming in on Apple Maps

Although it's not always possible to place your fingers correctly for a pinch-to-zoom function in Apple Maps, there are workarounds. You can zoom in or out with a double touch and a two-finger tap, respectively. By the way, to zoom in or out of the current map on Google Maps for iOS, double-tap, holds, and then slides your finger up or down the screen.

Swipe down to hide the keyboard in iMessage

Slide down on the message right above the keyboard to hide it if you're in an iMessage thread and want to be able to browse through the chat history without being distracted by it. You can choose to resume typing as soon as you press within the text input area again since the keyboard will return to the screen.

Tap and hold to change keyboards

You can choose a character and return to the original keyboard without having to touch again if you hold down on the number symbol on the keyboard instead of just pressing. It works both with the special character keyboard and in reverse. Although it doesn't matter, it should make your typing a bit faster.

Shake to undo

Even though it has been available for a long time, most iPhone users are still surprised to hear about it. Shake to reverse your most recent activity in a variety of applications, including Apple products like Messages and Mail. For example, it will restore previously saved messages or erase the last word you typed. You can disable the function in Settings by going to **Accessibility > General**.

Swipe down to save email drafts

This one was introduced to the Mail app by Apple more recently. While writing an email, you can swipe down to return to your inbox and see other emails without losing the one you're now writing. This allows you to save several drafts, which you can then retrieve at a later time by touching and holding the compose button that shows up in the lower-right corner.

Tap and drag to select images

With the release of iOS 17, choosing numerous photos for any given reason is much easier than it was in the past. In the Photos app, tap choose. You can drag and touch to choose many images at once in addition to selecting individual photos. It is comparable to using your desktop computer's Shift key while holding it down.

Tap and hold to archive messages

This is an additional useful one for iOS Mail. A message is erased (with a confirmation notice) when you press the trash button below it. Instead, you can choose to archive or delete it by tapping and holding the trash button. Of course, Mail's primary settings allow you to configure the swipe actions to archive or remove messages from the main folder list.

Tap and drag to switch scrubbing speed

The pace at which you can drag and touch the playback bar to move between music and podcasts is known as the scrubbing speed. Toggle the progress bar to drag up instead of left or right. You can then move left or right while keeping your finger held down since this alters the scrubbing speed and gives you more precise control over the leaps.

Swipe down to listen to the text

This one takes a little more planning, but having it ready is beneficial. Select **Speech and Speak Screen** under **Accessibility** in General in Settings. When this function is enabled, you can read aloud any text on any screen by dragging it down with two fingers. You can change the reading speed by adjusting the control panel that appears as a floating panel.

Swipe right to go back

iOS 17 has a return button that sometimes appears in the upper-left corner. However, you can also use a motion to **"go back"** in several apps, such as Mail and Safari, by swiping right from the left side of the screen. It functions in the majority of big applications and native Apple apps, and third-party developers are free to use it or not.

Swipe left to view details in the Message

It just takes a single swipe to the left to get more information about the vibrant bubbles in Messages. When messages arrive on the recipient's smartphone can be seen. This one is for Messages as well. You can search through all of your messages by dragging them down from the top of the main page, just as you do with many other applications.

Swipe left or right to remove digits in the calculator

There is also another one for those who like the built-in Calculator app that comes with iOS 17. Rather than tapping C to delete all the digits at once, you can remove one digit at a time by swiping left or right on the primary number display area. Tap and hold to bring up the little Copy option above if you want to copy your final response to another app.

How to set up Apple ID

You can access several Apple services, like the App Store, iCloud, and iMessage, by setting up an Apple ID on your iPhone 15 Series.

Here's how to set up Apple ID:

1. On your iPhone, press and hold the power button until the Apple logo shows up on the screen. This shows that the device is turning on.
2. Follow the prompts on the screen to get to the "**Hello**" screen. Here's where you'll begin configuring your iPhone.
3. Choose the language and location that you want to use. This will enable you to customize your device to suit your preferred language and region.

4. If you haven't previously, put your SIM card into a Wi-Fi network or connect to the internet to set up your Apple ID.

5. The iPhone 15 Series usually comes with sophisticated biometric authentication options like Face ID. You can choose not to use the authentication method by skipping this step and following the on-screen instructions to set up your chosen method.

6. To safeguard your smartphone, create a secure passcode. A password is necessary for both privacy and security. Make sure it is difficult to predict but that you can recall.

7. At this point, you have the option to restore from a backup stored in iTunes or iCloud if you're upgrading from an earlier iPhone. Your data, settings, and applications will be transferred to your new iPhone as a result. This step should be skipped if you're starting up as a new device.

8. Click the "**Sign in with Apple ID**" option to sign in using your current Apple ID or to establish a new one. By choosing "**Don't have an Apple ID or forgot it**?" and following the on-screen directions, you can create one if you don't already have one.

9. You will be asked to input your password and Apple ID. Your name, email address, and a strong password must be entered when creating a new Apple ID.

10. Depending on how you have it up, you may need to send a verification number to your email address or another reliable device to confirm your identity. Proceed with the instructions to finish this stage.

11. Select the iCloud services you want to use, including Contacts, Drive, Images, and more. This configuration will dictate the information kept in your iCloud account.

12. If you would rather not utilize Apple's virtual assistant, you may skip this step and instead opt to activate Siri.

13. Choose to activate True Tone display technology and share app statistics with Apple. These options are not required.

14. Finish the Setup After reviewing your options and making sure everything is to your satisfaction, click "**Get Started**" or "**Continue**" to finish the setup.

How to access and use iCloud

The procedures below can be used to access and use iCloud on the iPhone 15 Series:

1. First of all, ensure you're logged in with your Apple ID before using iCloud on your iPhone 15. You can do this by entering your Apple ID details in **"Settings"** > **"Sign in to your iPhone"** or by doing this during the first setup.

2. After logging in with your Apple ID, choose "**Settings**."

3. Swipe down and choose "**iCloud**."
4. You can turn on and off different services in the iCloud settings according to your preferences. **Among the important options are:**

- **Photos**: Your images and movies will be automatically backed up to iCloud.
- **Contacts**: Contacts are synchronized across all of your Apple devices.
- **Notes**: Make sure your notes are current and available across all of your devices.
- **Calendar**: Sync the appointments and activities in your calendar.
- **Mail**: You can sync your email if you use an iCloud email account.
- **Files**: Access the files on your iCloud Drive.
- **Find my iPhone**: This feature helps you find your missing iPhone.

5. To view how much capacity you have on iCloud and what's using it, go to the iCloud settings and touch on "**Manage Storage**." If necessary, you can upgrade your storage plan.
6. Open the "**Files**" app on your iPhone to see files saved in iCloud Drive. You can access all of your iCloud-stored documents and files using this app.
7. If you have activated this option, your images and videos will be automatically backed up to iCloud. Open the "**Photos**" app on your iPhone to see them.
8. You can use the "**Find My**" app to find your iPhone if it's stolen or lost. For further protection, you can use this software to remotely lock or wipe your smartphone.
9. Data on your iPhone can be automatically backed up to iCloud. Make sure the toggle switch next to "**iCloud Backup**" is switched on to allow this. Go to "**Settings**" > "**iCloud**" > "**Backup**."
10. You can safely save and sync payment details and passwords across all of your Apple devices using iCloud Keychain. To activate it, go to the iCloud settings.
11. To get your iCloud data through a web browser, visit iCloud.com and log in using your Apple ID. From there, you can see files, emails, images, and more.

Frequently Asked Questions

1. How do you set up your new iPhone 15 Series?
2. How do you set up physical and eSIM?

3. How do you wake up and unlock your new device?
4. How to power on and off your device?
5. How do you set up Apple ID?

CHAPTER THREE
FOCUS AND SECURITY

Overview

Chapter three discusses the process of creating a focus mode and using it effectively on any of your new iPhone 15 Series. Additionally, this chapter also talks about how to create and use Face ID and passcode on your device.

How to set up a Focus

The basic instructions for configuring an iPhone's Focus function are as follows:

1. Turn on your iPhone 15 series and finish the basic setup, which involves selecting your area and language and establishing a Wi-Fi network.
2. To log in, use your current Apple ID or create a new one if you don't have one.
3. To reach the Control Center after configuring your iPhone, swipe down from the upper-right corner of the screen.
4. Locate the **"Focus"** symbol in the Control Center. It usually resembles a crescent moon. Proceed to tap on it.

5. You will be requested to configure a Focus mode if you haven't already. Select **"Set Up**."

6. A variety of Focus modes, including **"Personal," "Work," "Sleep,"** and custom modes, will be shown to you. To create a custom mode, choose "Custom." Alternatively, select the mode that best fits your present activity.

7. Proceed to adjust the parameters for the Focus mode you have selected. This might include deciding which notifications to let through and who can see them, establishing an auto-reply message, and deciding which applications to allow or prohibit while in this mode.

8. The Focus mode may be set to activate automatically or on a schedule, according to your preferences. Customize these options to suit your tastes.

9. To finish setting up your Focus mode, hit **"Done"** or **"Save"** after making the necessary customizations.
10. You can now program your preferred Focus mode to start automatically or just press on its icon in the Control Center to start it. This will assist you in reducing outside distractions and maintaining work concentration.

How to create a Personal Focus

On your iPhone 15 Series, setting up a personal focus is a terrific method to control your notifications and make sure your phone isn't always taking up your time.

To configure a personal focus on your iPhone, follow these steps:

1. First things first, unlock your iPhone and go to the home screen.
2. Locate and touch the **"Settings"** app to open the settings. Usually, it bears a symbol of a gearwheel.
3. Navigate to the **"Focus"** option by scrolling down the Settings menu. You might find it under **"Do Not Disturb."**
4. To establish a new focus, tap **"Focus"** to access the focus configuration. Here, you can tap the **"+"** button to create a new Focus mode or see any that you have already established.

5. Select a name for your new Focus mode that accurately describes its function. Think about terms like **"Work," "Study," "Driving,"** or **"Sleep."**

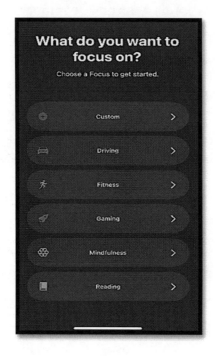

6. At this point, you will be asked to choose a custom focus that works for the task at hand. Options such as **"Personal," "Work," "Fitness,"** and others are available for selection. To further customize your focus, hit "**Custom**."

7. You can choose which certain applications and users are permitted to give you alerts during this period to customize your Focus mode. If necessary, you can also decide to accept alerts that have a time limit.

8. Plan Focus modes for certain times, places, or based on calendar events by selecting "**Turn on automatically**." This will enable you to automate when this Focus mode activates. You might program it to turn on when you're at the gym or during your working hours, for example.

9. Toggle Focus more on or off by tapping "**Done**" or "**Turn On**" once you've adjusted it to your liking. For each Focus mode, you can also create a unique home screen page that will aid in maintaining your attention on certain activities.

10. You can easily reach the Control Center by swiping down from the top-right corner of your screen to turn on or off Focus mode. Use this button to activate or disengage the Focus mode that is presently in use.

11. Make sure your Focus settings are still meeting your requirements by periodically reviewing them. Returning to the Focus settings in the iPhone Settings app allows you to make changes whenever you'd like.

12. To end a Focus mode, just click the Control Center or Settings app's "**End Focus Mode**" button.

How to set a Focus to activate automatically

The main procedures for configuring an iPhone's automatic focus modes are as follows:

1. To access the Control Center, swipe down from the top-right corner of the screen.

2. To enable Focus Mode, go to the Control Center and look for the "**Focus**" symbol or option. It could resemble a symbol of the moon or a bell. To activate Focus mode, tap on it.

3. A variety of Focus settings, including "**Do Not Disturb**," "**Personal**," "**Work**," and others, will be shown to you. Choose the one that works best for you or design your focus mode.

4. You can add your touch to a custom focus mode by deciding which contacts and alerts are permitted in this mode. Additionally, configure time- or location-based automated activation triggers.

5. Open the **Settings** app on your device to configure your Focus mode to turn on automatically.

6. Go to "**Focus**" by navigating to the Settings app. You can find it by going to "**Notifications & Focus.**"

7. To configure the Focus mode to activate automatically, choose it by tapping on it.

8. Locate and enable the option labeled "**Automatic Activation**" or "**Turn on automatically.**"

9. You will have a variety of triggers to pick from, contingent on the features that are accessible on the iPhone 15 series. Time-based, location-based, and app-based triggers are examples of common triggers. Decide which one best meets your requirements.

10. Adjust the particular parameters for the trigger you've selected. For instance, when configuring a time-based trigger, be sure to provide the beginning and ending times of the Focus mode.

11. Don't forget to save your configurations once you've adjusted the automatic activation settings.

How to allow calls from emergency contacts when you silence notifications

Here's a basic rundown on how to do this:

1. First of all, you will need to access settings on your device. To access the settings, use the iPhone's "**Settings**" app. usually, this is located on your home screen.

2. Locate the "**Do Not Disturb**" or "**Notifications**" option in the Settings menu.

3. Tap "**Do Not Disturb**" to view its options and turn it on. To activate "**Do Not Disturb**" mode, flip the switch. Most of your iPhone's alerts will disappear as a result.

4. In the "**Do Not Disturb**" settings, you should usually see an option labeled "**Allow Calls From**." Click on it.

5. If you tap on the "**Emergency Contacts**" or "**Favorite Contacts**" option, you should be able to pick which contacts may call you even if "**Do Not Disturb**" is turned on.

6. In "**Do Not Disturb**" mode, you can now choose which contacts to accept calls from. You won't be cut off from these contacts even if your phone is silent.

7. You may have other customization options, such as permitting calls from non-contacts repeatedly or accepting calls if someone phones you repeatedly in a short amount of time. To suit your tastes, change these settings.

8. After configuring these options, be sure to close the "**Notifications**" or "**Do Not Disturb**" settings. You can now take calls from the designated emergency contacts on your iPhone even when you have your notifications turned off.

How to deactivate a Focus

The steps:

1. To access the Control Center, swipe down from the upper right corner.

2. Locate the Focus icon in the Control Center. Usually, it has the appearance of a crescent moon or an image of the moon.

3. To access the Focus settings, tap the **Focus icon**.

4. There should be an option to deactivate or turn off the active focus mode under the Focus settings. Press this menu item.

5. There's a chance you'll be asked to verify the deactivation. If so, press "**Deactivate**" or "**Turn Off**" to be sure.

6. If your iPhone has gesture controls, you can swipe up from the bottom to quit the settings after turning off the Focus mode.

How to delete a Focus

Here's how to remove a Focus from an iPhone:

1. You need to unlock your device. Use Face ID or your password to unlock your iPhone if it is locked.

2. On your iPhone's home screen, find the **"Settings"** app (it looks like a gear symbol). Tap to launch it.

3. Locate and hit **"Focus"** after swiping through the Settings menu.

4. Press and hold the desired Focus mode to erase. To remove the **"Work"** Focus mode, for instance, just touch on **"Work."**

5. Tap the "**Edit**" option that appears on the next screen.

6. There should be a "**Delete Focus**" option at the bottom of the Edit Focus screen. Press this menu item.

7. You'll get a pop-up confirmation window asking you whether you want to remove the Focus. To confirm your selection, press "**Delete**."

8. The Focus mode will now be removed. Press "**Done**" to close the Edit Focus window.

Face ID and Passcode

How to set up Face ID

The iPhone 15 Series' Face ID setup is a simple procedure that improves the security and usability of unlocking your smartphone and granting access to different functions.

Here's how to configure it:

1. If you have previously set up your iPhone 15 Series without Face ID, you can enable it later by heading to "**Settings**." Initially, you will have the opportunity to set up a Face ID.
2. Launch the iPhone's "**Settings**" application.
3. After swiping down, choose "**Face ID & Passcode**."

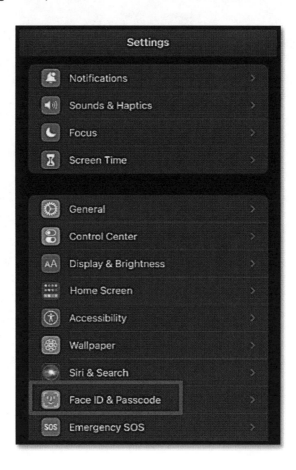

4. If you have configured a passcode for your device, you will be requested to enter it. Input it to continue.

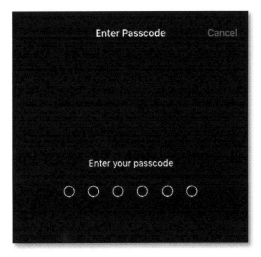

5. Go to the "**Face ID & Passcode**" settings and choose "**Set up Face ID**."
6. Make sure your face is well-lit by holding your iPhone in front of your face at a comfortable distance. You'll be guided by Face ID as you place your face within the on-screen frame.
7. Turn your head slowly in a circle to let Face ID take pictures of your face from various perspectives. During this procedure, make sure you are staring at your iPhone directly.
8. After the first scan is finished, you'll be prompted to do it again. This helps Face ID recognize your face from different perspectives.
9. After the second scan is finished, you'll get a notification that says, "**Face ID Is Set Up**."
10. You have the option to activate or disable Face ID for certain tasks, such as opening applications from the App Store, paying with Apple Pay, and unlocking your iPhone. These options are customizable under "**Use Face ID For**."
11. The Face ID setup on your iPhone 15 Series is complete. Now, all you have to do to unlock your phone and approve different tasks is to just raise it and glance at it.

How to add another appearance to Face ID

The basic procedures to add look to Face ID are as follows:

1. To begin, use your current password or Face ID to unlock your iPhone.
2. Select the **"Settings"** app from your home screen to open the settings. It resembles a symbol for gears.
3. To access these options, scroll down in the options menu and choose "**Face ID & Passcode**." You'll need to enter your passcode right now.
4. **"Set Up an Alternative Appearance"** or a similar option should be shown under the **"Use Face ID For"** section. Press this menu item.

5. As you add a new appearance, your iPhone will walk you through the process if you follow the on-screen instructions. Capturing distinct face characteristics usually entails staring at your iPhone from multiple orientations and perspectives. Make sure you pay close attention to the directions.

6. Your iPhone will notify you when it's ready to use once the other look has been successfully applied. You can now use your main or alternate look to unlock your smartphone.
7. To make sure Face ID works consistently, it's a good idea to test Face ID using both looks. To activate Face ID, lock your smartphone, wake it up, or touch the screen, then position your face following the on-screen instructions.

How to deactivate Face ID

Here's how to turn off Face ID on an iPhone are as follows:

1. To access the settings, you'll need to enter your passcode.
2. To access the Settings app, find it on your iPhone's home screen and press on it.
3. From the Settings menu, scroll down to the **"Face ID & Passcode"** option.
4. For security reasons, you'll be asked to enter it once again.
5. You should notice an option to deactivate Face ID under the **"Face ID & Passcode" settings**. The actual language may change, but the idea behind it should be the same.
6. When asked, verify that you want to turn off Face ID.
7. Your iPhone's Face ID will be disabled after verification.

How to set up a Passcode

The steps include the following:

1. If it hasn't been unlocked previously, you should endeavor to unlock your device before you proceed. To set up a passcode, you'll need to go into the settings of your smartphone.
2. Open the Settings app, which resembles a gear symbol, and can be found on your iPhone's home screen. To see the Settings menu, tap on it.
3. In the Settings menu, go down until you see the **"Face ID & Passcode"** option.
4. You will be asked to verify your identity using Face ID. You will need to first set up a Face ID if you haven't already.
5. The next step is where you'll enter your current passcode if you've already set one up and want to change it.
6. Select **"Turn Passcode On"** from the **"Passcode Options"** menu. If this is your first time establishing a passcode, this option can be called **"Set Passcode."**
7. You'll be asked to do this. Although you may use any combination of letters, numbers, and special characters for your password, it is best to select a strong,

one-of-a-kind passcode for optimal protection. Make sure it is difficult to predict but that you can recall.

8. To ensure its correct, you'll need to enter your new passcode once again. This step verifies that the passcode you entered was correct.

9. You may be able to enable Face ID for faster access. If you would like to finish this setup, just follow the on-screen directions.

10. Your iPhone 15 Series will be configured when your passcode has been properly entered and verified. Your smartphone is now more secure since it is passcode-protected.

11. Lock your iPhone by tapping the power button or letting it lock automatically to make sure your passcode is operating properly. Next, attempt to unlock it using the passcode you just created.

How to change when your phone locks automatically

Here's how to change an iPhone's auto-lock settings:

1. You must first unlock your phone if it has already locked itself. Using Face ID, you can do this by simply inputting your passcode.

2. Tap the "**Settings**" app to open it from your home screen. It is often symbolized by an icon of a gearwheel.

3. Find the option about your phone's display settings in the Settings menu by scrolling down and selecting "**Display & Brightness**" (or a comparable option). It can be found under a different category, such as "**Display & Sound.**"

4. Navigate to the Display & Brightness (or related) settings and find the "**Auto-Lock**" option. This is where you can change how long it takes for your iPhone to lock its screen automatically.

5. Select the time interval that best fits your needs from the list of available options for the auto-lock time. You'll be given the option to set the timer for **"30 Seconds," "1 Minute," "2 Minutes," "3 Minutes," "4 Minutes," or "5 Minutes."** You can choose "**Never**" if you want your iPhone to never automatically lock, although it's not advised for security and battery-saving reasons.

6. Your iPhone will immediately implement the updated option when you pick the preferred auto-lock time. Exiting the Settings app is possible.

Keep in mind that adjusting the auto-lock time may shorten the battery life of your smartphone. While a longer auto-lock period may need more energy, a shorter auto-lock time will save battery life. It's a good idea to strike a balance between the need for power conservation and your choice for ease.

How to erase data after ten failed passcode entries

Here are the steps:

1. Launch the "**Settings**" app.
2. After swiping down, choose "**Face ID & Passcode**."
3. To access the settings, enter your passcode.
4. Move the cursor down to "**Erase Data**."
5. Press and hold the option labeled "**Erase Data**."

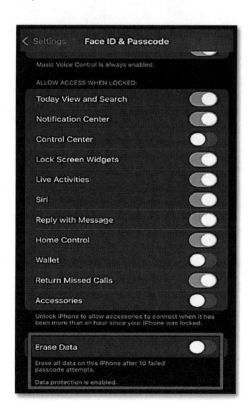

If you activate this function, your iPhone will immediately remove all data after 10 unsuccessful tries at entering the password. This is a security precaution to safeguard your information if someone attempts to use your device without permission.

How to turn off the passcode

To deactivate the passcode on an iPhone, follow these basic instructions:

1. To access your device, if you have activated a passcode, you will need to enter it.
2. On your home screen, the "**Settings**" app is shown by a gear symbol. Tap on it.
3. After swiping down, choose "**Face ID & Passcode.**"

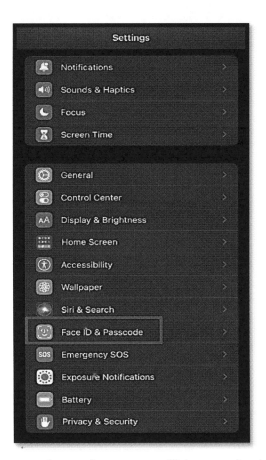

4. To access the passcode settings, you will be required to enter your existing passcode.

5. After accessing the Face ID & Passcode settings, tap the **"Turn Passcode Off"** or **"Disable Passcode"** option after scrolling down.

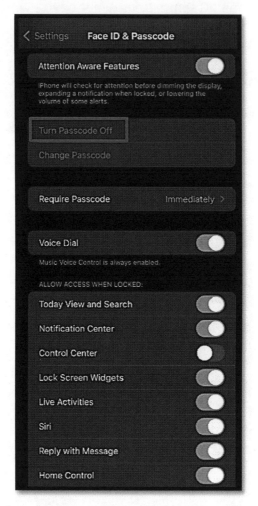

6. You'll get a confirmation notice alerting you to the security risks associated with disabling the passcode. Verify that you want to go forward.
7. You may need to input your existing passcode one more time to complete the procedure.
8. The passcode on your iPhone has been deactivated; you should no longer need to input it to unlock your device.

Be advised that disabling the passcode may make your iPhone less secure as it will now be accessible without verification to anybody who has physical access to it. Use this function sparingly and only in situations when you have a clear purpose for turning off the passcode.

Frequently Asked Questions

1. How do you set up a Focus?
2. How do you create a personal focus?
3. How do you disable and delete a focus?
4. How do you set up a Face ID?
5. How do you set up a Face ID or another appearance?
6. How do you set up a passcode?

CHAPTER FOUR
FACETIME

Apple's video and voice calling app, FaceTime, enables users to communicate with friends and family worldwide.

Overview

Chapter four discusses everything there is to know about FaceTime on your new iPhone 15, iPhone 15 Plus, iPhone 15 Pro, and iPhone 15 Pro Max. Get to learn how you can use FaceTime to communicate with your friends and family members either via video or audio call.

How to enable FaceTime on iPhone 15 Series
Check for Updates

Make sure the operating system on your iPhone 15 Series is up to date before we proceed with setting up FaceTime. Apple updates iOS often, bringing new features and bug fixes. The new Apple OS is iOS 17.

The steps:

1. Launch your iPhone's **"Settings"** app.
2. After swiping down, choose **"General."**
3. Click on **"Software Update."**

To make sure your iPhone is running the most recent iOS version—which could contain FaceTime improvements and bug fixes—tap **"Download and Install"** if an update is available.

Sign In to Your Apple ID

Your Apple ID, which serves as your exclusive identity inside the Apple ecosystem, is personally linked to FaceTime.

Make sure you are logged in with your Apple ID to activate FaceTime:

1. Launch **Settings**.
2. After swiping down, choose "**FaceTime**."

3. Tap "**Sign In**" and provide your Apple ID information if you haven't previously.

You can use FaceTime's whole feature set after logging in, including group calls, audio and video conversations, and more.

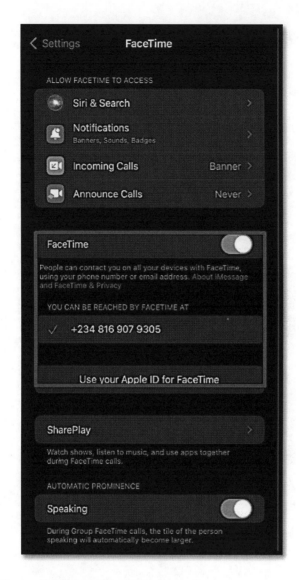

Change the FaceTime Settings

FaceTime has several options that you can tweak to personalize and optimize for your needs. That's how:

1. First of all, launch **Settings**.
2. After swiping down, choose **"FaceTime."**
3. FaceTime can be turned on or off by using the button located at the top of the screen.

Choose whether you want FaceTime to use your mobile data for calls if Wi-Fi is not available under the "**Calls**" section. Those who want to have FaceTime conversations while they're out and about but have restricted data plans may find this useful.

Manage Caller ID

With FaceTime, you have the option to choose which email address or phone number appears during a conversation.

To adjust your Caller ID preferences:

1. Launch the "**Settings**" app.
2. When you scroll down, choose "**FaceTime**."
3. Choose the phone number or email address you want to use as your caller ID while making FaceTime calls under "**Caller ID**."

If your Apple ID is connected to many different contact methods, this functionality will come in rather handy.

Enable or Disable FaceTime for Specific Contacts

You can choose which contacts to allow or prohibit FaceTime for. It may be done as follows:

1. Firstly, launch the **Contacts** app.
2. Locate the person for whom you want to activate or disable FaceTime.
3. Press the name of the contact.
4. After swiping down, choose "**FaceTime**."
5. Turn on or off FaceTime for that particular contact.

This protects your privacy and convenience by letting you decide who may contact you over FaceTime.

Group FaceTime

Group FaceTime is a feature of FaceTime that is particularly noteworthy since it allows you to hold simultaneous voice and video chats with numerous individuals.

To initiate a FaceTime group chat:

1. Launch the **FaceTime** app.
2. In the upper-right corner, tap the **"+"** symbol.

3. Proceed to add the contacts you want to speak with on the call.
4. Press "**Audio**" or "**Video**" to start the call.

Additionally, via a group discussion in the Messages app, you can initiate a Group FaceTime call:

1. Go into Messages and open the group conversation.
2. At the top of the screen, tap the name of the group.
3. Choose "**FaceTime**."

FaceTime Group is an excellent means to maintain contact with friends, family, and coworkers, regardless of where you are in the world or the same location.

Apply the FaceTime Effects

FaceTime has several entertaining effects that can be used during conversations, such as Memoji and Animoji.

To use these effects:

1. Tap the star symbol located at the bottom of the screen while you're on a FaceTime call.
2. Select an effect, such as Text, Memoji, Animoji, or Filters.

These effects give your FaceTime talks a lighthearted and intimate feel.

Troubleshooting FaceTime Issues

Try the following troubleshooting actions if you have poor call quality or connectivity difficulties while using FaceTime:

1. Verify that you have a dependable cellular or Wi-Fi connection.
2. Restart FaceTime by logging out and back into the app.
3. Occasionally, a simple restart might fix a connection problem.
4. Verify that the most recent version of iOS is installed on your iPhone.
5. **Reset network settings**: This will reset all of your network-related settings, so use it as a last option. To reset your network settings, navigate to **"Settings" > "General" > "Reset" > "Reset Network Settings."**

How to make and receive FaceTime Calls

The steps below can be used to place and receive FaceTime calls on the iPhone 15 Series:

Making a FaceTime Call

1. To start, use your password or Face ID to unlock your iPhone 15 Series (iPhone 15, iPhone 15 Plus, iPhone 15 Pro, and iPhone 15 Pro Max).
2. The FaceTime app is usually shown by a green symbol with a white video camera on your home screen.
3. You will need to sign in with your Apple ID if you haven't previously. You may skip this step if you are already logged into your Apple ID.
4. To add contacts, touch the **"+"** or **"Search"** button while you're in the FaceTime app. A contact's name, phone number, or email address may be used to find them.
5. Tap on the name of the person you want to call after locating them.
6. You have the option to place either an audio or a video call. Tap the video camera icon to start a video call. Tapping the phone icon will initiate an audio call.
7. Hold off till the person on the other end answers. Your FaceTime call will begin if they accept.

8. Tap the red **"End"** button located on the screen to put a stop to the call.

Receiving a FaceTime Call

The steps:

1. If you're using FaceTime and someone calls you, the call will show up as a pop-up notice or as an incoming call notification on your iPhone's lock screen.
2. To accept the call, either hit the green **"Accept"** button or swipe right on the notice. You can hit the red **"Decline"** button or swipe left on the notice to end the call.
3. After accepting the call, use the on-screen controls to manage different call settings, such as muting your microphone, turning off your camera, or going to speaker mode.
4. Tap the red **"End"** button located on the screen to put an end to the FaceTime call.

Be aware that for FaceTime to function, you and the person you are calling must have FaceTime enabled on your devices and have an active internet connection (cellular data or Wi-Fi).

How to create a link to a FaceTime call

Most FaceTime conversations begin with a direct phone call between two iPhone users. However, there is another method of making calls using the FaceTime applications on Mac, iPad, and iPhone: by linking them.

Creating a FaceTime link

Anyone can join a call using a FaceTime connection, even if you don't know their phone number. This makes it ideal for chatting on the phone with someone whose number you don't know or for making a call that is available to a large number of people. You can FaceTime users with Windows or Android smartphones in the same way.

1. Open the FaceTime app on your iPhone to make a connection. Then, in the upper-left corner, choose **Create Link**.
2. You can instantly share the link with contacts or via an app by selecting it from the option that appears. If all you want to do is save the URL to your clipboard, choose **Copy** instead of any of these alternatives. If you do this, the link will need to be pasted somewhere to be saved and shared.

3. You can also take a screenshot of a link while on a call by pressing the options toolbar and choosing **Share Link**. *Note:* Open FaceTime, press the i symbol next to your impending meeting, then click **Delete Link** to stop a connected meeting before anybody joins.
4. The Join button will appear at the top or bottom of the screen once someone clicks the link. For the app to use its microphone and camera, it may also need to provide authorization.
5. The individual who shared the link will get a message to allow them to join the call when they hit Join. You can allow them to join the call by tapping the options toolbar inside the call or by clicking the checkbox button on the notice.

6. The meeting will end when everyone gets off the phone and the connection expires. If you want to repeat the process, you will have to create a new link.

How to make a Group FaceTime Call

On the iPhone 15 Series, do these actions to initiate a Group FaceTime call:

1. Let's start by getting your iPhone 15 Series unlocked. You can enter your passcode or use Face ID to do this.
2. Navigate to the FaceTime app on your home screen to access it. The symbol is green and has a speech bubble enclosing a white video camera icon.
3. To open FaceTime, just tap on the app.
4. You have to enter your password and Apple ID if you haven't previously. To make a FaceTime call, you must complete this step.
5. **Launch a New FaceTime Call:**
- Press the '**+**' (plus) button located in the upper-right corner of the FaceTime app to initiate a new FaceTime call.
- As an alternative, you can choose which contacts you want to add to your group call by tapping the "**Contacts**" option.

6. **Add Contacts to the Call:**
- Type the contacts' names or phone numbers into the search field to add them to the group FaceTime call.

- You'll see ideas as you write. To include the recommended contacts in your call, just tap on them.
- To form a group, you can add more than one contact.

7. Begin the Group Call:

- To begin the group FaceTime call, touch the "**Video**" or "**Audio**" option after adding all the appropriate contacts.
- In case you choose a video, your camera will go on and the video call will start. It will be an audio-only call if you choose audio.

8. Managing the Group Call:

- Access several settings throughout the conversation by tapping the screen, such as adding new participants, turning off your camera, or muting your microphone.
- Additional controls, such as navigating between grid and tile views, are also shown by swiping up.

9. End the Call:

- Just hit the red "**End**" button to decline the call.

How to Create a Live Image on a FaceTime Call

The typical procedures to take a Live Image while on a FaceTime call are as follows:

1. Begin a FaceTime call with the individual whose live image you want to take. Make sure the FaceTime call is established.
2. To activate Live Photos, press the **Live Photos symbol** (a collection of concentric circles) in the camera app before snapping a picture. Locate and activate Live Photos during a FaceTime conversation if you have an iPhone 15 series or earlier model. The camera settings or the FaceTime interface may provide this option.
3. To take a Live Photo during a FaceTime chat, push the shutter button (the white circle), provided that Live Photos are enabled. This will record a little video clip in addition to the picture.
4. The photo will appear in your Photos app once it is taken. To get to it, use the Photos app, and then choose the "**Live Photos**" album.

How to start a Group FaceTime call from Messages

With Messages on the iPhone 15 Series, you can initiate a Group FaceTime call to conveniently communicate with numerous friends or family members at once.

The steps to start a Group FaceTime call are as follows:

1. Start by unlocking your iPhone using Face ID or your password.
2. To open the "**Messages**" app, tap its icon on your home screen.
3. Tap the compose icon (pencil) in the top right corner of the Messages app, and then choose the contacts you want to include in your group chat. You can then choose an already-existing group conversation or create a new one. Tapping on the names of contacts allows you to pick many of them.
4. The group members will be displayed at the top of the discussion window. To access the group information menu, tap the group name or any member's avatar.
5. There are several options available under the group details menu. Click "**FaceTime**" to start a group FaceTime conversation with the chosen individuals.
6. By touching the corresponding symbols (microphone for audio, camera for video), you can choose whether to make the call audio or video before it starts. Moreover, you can pick more contacts by choosing "**Add Person**" and adding other participants to the call.
7. Tap "**Start**" to start the Group FaceTime call after choosing your options. You will then be able to connect with the chosen participants using your iPhone.
8. Use many controls to muffle your microphone, turn off your camera, change the volume, and more while on the call. To see more options, including screen sharing, effects, and filters, swipe up.
9. Click the red "**End**" button located at the bottom of the screen to stop the Group FaceTime call.

How to exit a Group FaceTime call

On any of your iPhone 15 Series, ending a group FaceTime conversation is a simple procedure.

Take these actions:

1. First of all, use Face ID or your password to unlock your iPhone if it is locked.

2. To launch FaceTime, find the FaceTime application on your iPhone's home screen and press on it.

3. If you haven't already, you can join the group FaceTime call by tapping the notification of an active call, opening the **FaceTime app**, choosing the call from your list of recent calls, or entering the contact names or numbers and choosing the group call.

4. The call controls will appear on your screen as soon as you enter the Group FaceTime session. Depending on your iOS version, these controls could seem a little different, but you should see buttons for muting, switching the camera, and other features.

5. **End the Call:**

- The most popular way to use the red phone symbol, which is often seen at the bottom of the screen, is to touch it. Pressing this **"End"** or **"Leave Call"** button will end the call right away.

- An alternative method to access the control center is to swipe up from the bottom of the screen. Proceed to see the ongoing FaceTime conversation, and then choose **"End"** or **"Leave Call"** to end it.

- To end a FaceTime call while it's locked, swipe left on the call notice and choose **"End"** or **"Leave Call**."

6. To prevent unintentional exits, iOS may sometimes prompt you to confirm that you want to end the conversation. Just press **"End"** or **"Leave"** to be sure. Upon confirmation, you will end the group FaceTime session and remove your voice and video from the discussion.

How to add someone to a call

On your device, follow these steps to invite someone to a FaceTime call:

1. To begin a FaceTime call, launch the FaceTime application on your iPhone and connect with the person you want to speak with. This can be accomplished by either calling their phone number or email address if it isn't stored in your

contacts or by looking for them in the FaceTime program and pressing their name.

2. The call interface with options will be shown at the bottom of the screen while you are on a FaceTime call.
3. Tap the screen to display the call controls, then locate the **"+"** or **"Add Person"** button to include someone in the call. Tap on this. It could show up as an icon with a plus sign or just the phrase **"Add**."
4. After selecting a contact, your contacts list will be shown to you. To add someone to the call, scroll or search for them, then press their name.
5. A FaceTime invitation will be sent to the person you want to invite; wait for it to arrive. They are asked to join the call, and you will see a message on your screen.
6. When someone accepts your invitation, a notice is sent to their smartphone. Under the iOS version they are running, they may accept your invitation by pressing **"Join"** or a comparable option.
7. After they accept the invitation, you can all have a group FaceTime session. They will be joined to the call.

The person you are asking for the call must also be using an Apple device that is compatible with FaceTime and has an active internet connection for this to function.

How to edit FaceTime audio

To capture and edit FaceTime audio on an iPhone, follow these basic steps:

Recording a FaceTime Call

1. To activate screen recording, swipe down from the upper right corner of the screen to access the Control Center. To begin recording your screen, tap the **Screen Recording icon**, which resembles a circle within another circle.
2. Launch the FaceTime app and start the call as you would typically do to begin a FaceTime call.
3. Both the audio and video will be recorded via the screen recording feature during the FaceTime call. By pressing the red status bar at the top of the screen

or going back to the Control Center and tapping the **Screen Recording icon** once again, you may stop the recording.

Editing the FaceTime Audio

With a third-party app, you can edit the audio from the FaceTime call after it has been captured. You may find several apps on the App Store that can assist you with audio editing.

Here's a broad overview:

1. Go to the App Store and type in "**voice recording**" or "**audio editing**." A few well-liked choices include Ferrite Recording Studio, Voice Record Pro, and GarageBand.
2. To import the recorded audio, use the audio editing application and choose the FaceTime audio file that was captured. The app you choose may have an impact on this procedure.
3. You can make any desired adjustments to the audio, such as trimming, cutting, or adjusting the level, by using the editing tools in the program.
4. Transfer the audio file to your iPhone as soon as you're happy with the changes.
5. You can now use cloud storage services or messaging applications to share the altered audio file.

How to block unwanted callers on FaceTime

On the iPhone 15 Series, blocking unsolicited calls during FaceTime is a helpful technique to protect your privacy and stop unsolicited messages. **Here's a step-by-step instruction on how to accomplish it:**

1. Open **Settings**:
- Unlock your iPhone and go to the home screen.
- Press and hold the "**Settings**" app, which has a gear-shaped symbol.
2. **After swiping down, choose FaceTime:**
- Scroll down to "**FaceTime**" in the Settings menu, and then touch on it.
3. Click on "**Blocked Contacts**":

- There are other options available to you inside the FaceTime settings. Find **"Blocked Contacts"** and give it a touch.

4. **Add a contact in the block:**
- Tap **"Add New"** or the addition (+) symbol, which is usually found in the top right corner of the screen, to block an undesired caller.

5. **Select the person to block:**
- A list of your contacts will appear. Locate the contact you want to block by scrolling through or using the search box. To add someone to your blocked list, tap on their name.

6. **Confirm the block:**
- It will ask you to confirm that you want to block the contact when a confirmation popup appears. Press **"Block"** to continue.

7. **(Optional) Unblock a contact:**
- To unblock a contact at any time, return to the FaceTime settings' **"Blocked Contacts"** section, swipe left on the person you want to unblock and choose **"Unblock."**

8. **Check whether the contact has been blocked:**
- A contact that has been blocked cannot make a FaceTime call to you. They won't get any alerts that they are blocked, and you won't be able to view their calls or texts.

It should be noted that blocking a contact on FaceTime also blocks them from using other Apple services, such as phone calls and messages.

Frequently Asked Questions

1. How do you enable FaceTime on your iPhone 15 Series?
2. How do you make and receive FaceTime calls?
3. How do you create a link to a FaceTime call?
4. How do you make group FaceTime calls?
5. How do you add someone to a FaceTime call?
6. How do you block unwanted callers on FaceTime?

CHAPTER FIVE
SIRI ON YOUR IPHONE 15 SERIES

Overview

Siri is a voice assistant feature found on your iPhone 15 series and earlier models. With Siri, you can get tasks done easily by just telling Siri to do certain things for you with your voice. This chapter ensures you learn what Siri can do for you and how best to utilize Siri for your daily smartphone tasks.

How to use enable Siri

The steps to enable Siri include the following:

1. To begin, unlock your iPhone by entering your password or using Face ID.
2. To access Settings, tap the **"Settings"** app on the home screen of your iPhone. It resembles a symbol for gears.

3. To find Siri & Search, go to the Settings menu, scroll down, and search for "**Siri & Search**." It should be in the third section, although the precise placement may vary.

4. To make Siri available, press "**Siri & Search**" to open the Siri settings. This toggle will be titled "**Listen for 'Hey Siri**.'" Turn it on to use the voice-activated version of the "Hey Siri" function. Then you may skip this step if it's already on.
5. **Set Up Voice Recognition (if requested):** You could be prompted to teach Siri to recognize your voice if this is your first time configuring her or if you're using a new device. For this procedure to be finished, adhere to the on-screen directions.

6. Make sure the "**Allow Siri When Locked**" option is selected if you want to use Siri while your iPhone is locked. Remember that using Siri while it's locked might cause privacy issues, so proceed with caution.

7. By swiping down to the Siri & Search settings, you can add even more customization to Siri. You have options for language, Siri voice, and other features.

8. To go back to your home screen on an iPhone, either press the home button if your device has one or swipe up from the bottom of the screen if it doesn't.

At this point, your iPhone 15 series device should have Siri activated. You can press and hold the side button or speak **"Hey Siri"** followed by your command to activate Siri. After that, Siri will reply to your query.

How to use Siri

Use these easy methods to use Siri on your iPhone 15 Series:

1. **Wake Siri Up**:

There are several methods to get Siri to work:

- To activate Siri through voice, say "**Hey Siri**" and then provide your demand. Verify that you have this function activated in the iPhone's settings.
- Press and hold the side button, which was once called the sleep/wake button, until Siri appears.

2. **Give your Command**:

- Your screen will display the Siri interface as soon as Siri is turned on. At this point, you may issue a command or pose a query.

3. **Speak Naturally and Clearly**:

- When you talk clearly and naturally, Siri responds best. Aside from giving it orders like "Send a text message to John" or "What's the weather like today?" you may ask Siri a variety of queries.

4. **Listen and Respond**:

- When you ask Siri a question or provide an order, she will answer you both verbally and via text on the screen. Before starting a task, Siri will ask you to confirm that you want it done.

5. **Follow-Up Questions**:
- You can offer Siri other orders or ask follow-up questions throughout the same dialogue. Siri is built with context awareness in mind.

6. **Close the Discussion**:
- You can say "**Goodbye**" or just hit the side button one more time to conclude your chat with Siri.

7. **Customize Siri**:
- You can personalize Siri to suit your needs. Navigate to the settings on your iPhone, choose "**Siri & Search**," then adjust voice feedback, language, and other options.

8. **Security and Privacy**:
- Siri respects your right to privacy. In the privacy settings, examine and control how Siri has access to your information. If you want, you can also completely turn off Siri.

9. **Use Siri for Multiple Tasks**:
- A multifaceted virtual assistant, Siri can assist with a wide range of activities, including checking your calendar, sending messages, making calls, setting reminders, setting alarms, and obtaining directions.

How to edit Siri's response

1. Check that the most recent version of iOS is installed on your iPhone by checking for iOS updates. Updates including new features and enhancements are often released by Apple.

2. You can let Apple know if there's anything wrong with Siri's reaction in any given scenario. Say something along the lines of, "**Hey Siri, send feedback**," and then describe the problem you ran across. Apple can then use this input in the next releases to enhance Siri's replies.

3. Although you cannot directly alter Siri's answers, you can program Siri Shortcuts to carry out certain tasks or deliver personalized replies to your instructions. This is how to make a personalized Siri Shortcut:
- Get your iPhone's "**Shortcuts**" app open.

- If you want to add a new shortcut, tap the **"+"** button.
- When you activate this shortcut, you may personalize what Siri does by using the actions and scripting options offered in the app.
- The shortcut may then be used by asking, **"Hey Siri, [shortcut name]."**
4. **Third-Party applications:** You may be able to create your voice assistant or alter Siri's replies using third-party applications that you may download from the App Store. Look for these kinds of applications in the App Store and check user reviews to determine whether they fit your requirements.

Keep in mind that Apple's privacy and design regulations could restrict how customizable Siri's replies can be. Make sure that any third-party applications or services you use are reliable and safe at all times.

How to change Siri's voice

To change the voice of Siri on the iPhone 15 Series, do the following actions:

1. Start by getting your iPhone 15 Series unlocked.
2. To access Siri Settings, open the iPhone's **"Settings"** app. It usually appears on your home screen and has a gear-shaped symbol.
3. To access Siri settings, scroll down the list of options until you locate **"Siri & Search."** Tap on it.
4. Select the **"Siri Voice"** option from the Siri & Search settings by tapping on it.

5. A list of the available voices may be found here. Siri has a variety of voices with accents and tones. To hear a preview, go down the list and touch each item.
6. Toggle between the voices you prefer by tapping on them. You'll see a checkbox next to the voice of your choice.

7. A pop-up window inquiring whether you want to download the voice will show up. Tap "**Download**" to verify your selection. While the voice data downloads to your device, this can take time.

8. After the download is finished, get out of the settings and launch Siri using the newly chosen voice. To activate Siri, just say "**Hey Siri**." Siri will answer with the voice that you have just chosen.

How to change the way Siri responds

Generally, you can change Siri's replies as follows:

1. First, unlock your iPhone and go to the home screen to access Settings. Find the "**Settings**" app, which is often represented by a gear symbol, and touch it.

2. To customize Siri's actions, scroll down the Settings menu and choose "**Siri & Search**."

3. Tap the "**Siri Voice**" or "**Siri Language & Voice**" option under "**Siri & Search**" to bring up Siri's voice preferences.

4. Select Siri's Voice to get a list of the languages and voices that are available. Choose the voice you'd want Siri to use based on your area and preferred language. Siri will provide a range of voice choices with distinct genders and accents.

5. It's possible that you can alter Siri's voice feedback settings. You can change the volume or amplitude of Siri's answers by adjusting these settings, which include "**Voice Feedback**" and "**Voice Volume**."

6. To further personalize your replies, go to **"Siri & Search" > "Siri Responses."** From here, you can adjust Siri's settings for different kinds of queries, including texts, calls, reminders, and more. Depending on your preferences, you can **pick "Always Speak" or "Control with Ring Switch"** to control when Siri speaks.

7. Your device's settings and the data connected to your Apple ID can also have an impact on Siri's replies. Make sure your contact card is right by going to **"Siri & Search" > "My Information"** to make sure Siri accurately identifies you and responds to you in a tailored manner.

8. You will find settings for both privacy and feedback in the Siri settings. Examine these options to manage the way Siri manages your information and choose if you want to assist Apple in making Siri work better.

How to change the name Siri calls you

On your iPhone 15 Series, changing the name Siri calls you is an easy procedure. You must adjust the name that Siri uses since it is connected to your Apple ID.

How to accomplish it is as follows:

1. Once you are done unlocking your device, navigate to the **Settings app** (it appears as a gear symbol) on your home screen, then press to launch it.

2. Usually located at the top of the screen, touch your Apple ID after swiping down a little in the Settings menu. Your name and, if you've specified one, your profile picture will be there.

3. Tap on the **"Name, Phone Numbers, Email"** section that appears in your Apple ID settings after selecting **"Name, Phone Numbers, Email."**

4. Your name is now visible to you. To modify it, tap on it.

5. Type your new name in the designated space. When addressing you, Siri will use this name.

6. To save the modifications, touch **"Done"** or **"Save"** after inputting your new name.

7. To verify the changes, you may be asked to use Face ID or enter your Apple ID password. Just do as instructed by the on-screen directions.

8. Use the swipe-up motion to quit the Settings app once you've successfully modified your name.

9. Say "**Hey Siri**" or press and hold the side buttons to get Siri to identify your new name. Then, test it by asking a question.

10. Now, Siri ought to address you by your new name. Remember that Siri could need some time to become used to the new name, so if it keeps using your old name at first, give it some time to update.

What Siri can do for you?

As earlier mentioned, Siri is your assistant on the iPhone 15 Series. With the iPhone 15 Series, Siri has advanced significantly and is now more useful and potent than ever. Thanks to developments in artificial intelligence and machine learning, Siri can help you in many ways to improve the efficiency and ease of your everyday life.

1. **Voice Commands**: Siri is still your reliable voice-activated helper. With just a simple "**Hey Siri,**" you can get started. To make your day better, you may ask Siri to make calls, send messages, create reminders, or even crack jokes.

2. **Home automation**: Siri can easily operate your smart home's appliances. Siri can control everything, including the lights, the temperature, and your smart security camera to see who is at your front door.

3. **Multilingual Support:** With the ability to comprehend and react in several languages, Siri has become more user-friendly for people worldwide.

4. **Integration with applications:** Siri easily interacts with a wide range of third-party applications, enabling voice commands for activities like placing restaurant orders, scheduling transportation, and monitoring the weather.

5. **Personalization**: Siri makes suggestions that are unique to you based on your behaviors and interests. It may remind you to get coffee in the morning or recommend your favorite song at the perfect moment.

6. **Navigation**: Siri is a trustworthy guide. It can assist you in locating local sites of interest, provide turn-by-turn instructions, and even recommend other routes to avoid traffic.

7. **Information retrieval:** You may ask Siri questions on a variety of subjects, from basic queries to detailed inquiries. It may include stock market data, sports scores, weather updates, and more.

8. **Accessibility:** For those who need accessibility, Siri is a vital tool. It can make calls, send messages, and set alarms, among other things, so it helps people with impairments keep in touch.

9. **Language Translation**: By translating words and sentences into other languages, Siri can assist you in overcoming communication hurdles while going overseas.

10. **Entertainment:** Depending on your tastes, Siri may suggest films, TV series, songs, and podcasts. It also has volume control and playback control.

11. **Security:** If your device becomes lost or stolen, Siri can help you keep it safe by locking it, finding it, or even remotely erasing it.

12. **Natural Conversation:** Siri has become more adept at having context-aware, conversational conversations, which gives your virtual assistant encounters a more human feel.

How to make corrections in case Siri doesn't get what you say

You should take a few steps to fix Siri's functionality if your iPhone 15 Series device's AI is regularly misinterpreting your voice commands or is having difficulty comprehending you at all.

It may be done as follows:

1. **Speak slowly and clearly:** When giving Siri instructions, be sure you speak slowly and clearly. Steer clear of stuttering or speaking too hastily to avoid giving the wrong impression.

2. **Verify Your Connection**: For Siri to take voice instructions, it has to be connected to the internet. Verify that your iPhone is linked to a reliable cellular data network or Wi-Fi. Siri's functionality may be impacted by loose connections.

3. **Update iOS:** It's critical to keep the operating system on your iPhone up to date. Apple often changes its software, which enhances the general

functioning and speech recognition of Siri. Go to **Settings > General > Software update** to upgrade your iOS device.

4. **Turn on "Hey Siri":** Press the **"Hey Siri"** button if you haven't previously. This enables you to speak **"Hey Siri"** and then your command to activate Siri hands-free. To make it active, go to **Settings > Siri & Search > Listen** and type **"Hey Siri."**

5. **Retrain Siri:** You can improve Siri's ability to recognize your voice. Navigate to **Settings > Siri & Search > Siri Voice Recognition** to do this. To ensure that Siri will correctly identify your voice, follow the on-screen instructions.

6. **Verify Language and Region Settings:** Make sure the language and region settings on your iPhone are set up properly. When these parameters correspond with your location and natural language, Siri works at its best.

7. **Examine Siri Suggestions**: By using them, you can help Siri learn more about your tastes and routines. Navigate to **Settings > Siri & Search**, then turn on the appropriate settings to allow Siri Suggestions for contacts and applications.

8. **Resolve Siri's Misunderstandings**: Saying **"That's not what I said**," followed by the proper command, will prompt Siri to promptly fix any misunderstandings. Usually, Siri will ask for clarification.

9. **Use Commands Wisely:** When providing Siri instructions, try to be as detailed as you can. Don't provide unclear or imprecise directions. Say **"Call John Smith"** to indicate which John you want to contact, for example, rather than just **"Call John."**

10. **Send Apple Feedback**: If you continue to have problems with Siri, you may want to send Apple some feedback. They continue to develop by using input from users. Navigate to **Settings > Siri & Search > Siri Feedback** to do this.

11. **Restart your iPhone**: Occasionally, a simple restart might fix brief issues. To turn off the power, press and hold the side button and slide it. Next, restart your iPhone.

12. **Reset Siri:** You may return Siri's settings to their original state if all else fail. To delete Siri and Dictation History, go to **Settings > Siri & Search > Siri & Dictation History**. By doing this, Siri's speech and language recognition will be reset.

Frequently Asked Questions

1. How do you enable Siri on your iPhone 15 Series?
2. How do you use Siri?
3. How do you change Siri's voice?
4. How do you change the name Siri calls you?
5. How do you edit Siri's response?

CHAPTER SIX
USING THE PHONE APP

Overview

The phone app is a very crucial function and app in every smartphone including the iPhone 15 Series. It allows you to make and receive phone calls from friends, family members, and business partners. Continue reading this chapter to fully explore all the functions of the phone app.

How to make calls via the Contacts list, Keypad, and Favorites

The procedures below can be used to make calls on an iPhone 15 Series using the Contacts list, Keypad, and Favorites:

Making Calls from Contacts

1. First, if your iPhone is locked, unlock it. You can use Face ID or enter your passcode to do this.
2. Look on your home screen for the Contacts app. usually; it features a symbol that looks like a human silhouette. To launch the app, tap on it.

3. To locate the person you want to call, either use the search box at the top of the screen or browse through your contacts.

4. To see the contact's information, tap on their name.

5. You can choose to **"Call"** or **"FaceTime"** the contact (if FaceTime is enabled) from the contact's information screen. Press **"Call"** to initiate a call.

Making Calls from the Keypad

1. Use your Face ID or your password to unlock your iPhone.

2. Go to your home screen and find the **Phone app**. usually; it features a white phone receiver and a green symbol. To open it, tap.

3. Select **"Keypad"** from the tabs located at the bottom of the Phone app, which is labeled **"Favorites," "Recents," "Contacts," and "Keypad."**

4. Enter the phone number you want to call manually using the keypad that displays on the screen.

5. To start the call after inputting the number, hit the green **"Call"** button.

Making Calls from Favorites

1. Use Face ID or your password to unlock your iPhone if it's locked.
2. Locate and press the icon for the Phone app on your home screen.
3. Select **"Favorites"** from the list of tabs located at the bottom of the Phone app, along with **"Recents," "Contacts," and "Keypad."**
4. A list of the contacts you have selected as favorites will appear. To make a call, tap on the desired contact.

5. To initiate a call, touch the green **"Call"** button located on the contact's information screen.

How to make an emergency call

The procedures below should be followed to make an emergency call on the iPhone 15 Series:

1. You are still able to make an emergency call even if your iPhone is locked. To wake up your iPhone, just click the Face ID button (if enabled) or the side button (on the right side).

2. You will see a button on the lock screen with the word "**Emergency**" written in red language. Click on this button.

3. The keypad and dialer interface will now be visible to you. The emergency number in the majority of nations is 911. This emergency number may be different if you are in a foreign nation. Press the emergency number that corresponds to your area.

4. Once the emergency number has been entered, press the green call button. Your iPhone will call emergency services right away.

5. Speak to the emergency operator calmly and as soon as the call is connected. Give them your location, the emergency's nature, and any other details they ask for. Until the operator tells you to hang up, you must remain on the line.

6. Pay close attention to everything the operator says. They could give you advice on how to aid until assistance comes.

7. **Use Emergency SOS If Needed:** The iPhone 15 Series is one of the versions that have an Emergency SOS capability. Press the side button quickly and five times in quick succession to activate this function. This will start a countdown after

which your iPhone will make an automated 911 call. When you are unable to view the screen, this might be useful.

Recall that in most countries, making fictitious or hoax emergency calls are a severe infraction that might have legal repercussions. To guarantee that emergency services can get to those in need as soon as possible, only use these functions in true emergencies. To aid emergency personnel in finding you more quickly, ensure your location services are turned on and that your iPhone is always charged and carried with you.

How to answer or decline calls

With the iPhone 15 Series, accepting or rejecting calls can be done easily. How to accomplish it is as follows:

Answering a Call

1. **Incoming Call Notification:** Your iPhone will alert you with a notice when there is a call coming in. If the caller is listed in your contacts, you will be able to view their name or phone number.
2. **To Answer:** There are two ways you may respond to the call:
- Press "**Answer**" to answer the phone and start a conversation.
- To answer the phone, you can also swipe right on the screen.

3. **During the Call:** Using the on-screen buttons, you can mute, put the call on speakerphone, or terminate the conversation when you're answering it.

Declining a Call

1. **Incoming Call Notification**: You have a few options when you get an incoming call if you choose not to answer it.
2. **To Decline**: There are two ways you may refuse the call:
- Press "**Decline**" to have the call go to voicemail.
- Press "**Message**": Select from pre-written text messages or type your own if you'd like to send the caller a brief note rather than picking up.

3. **Do Not Disturb**: You can activate the "**Do Not Disturb**" mode by sliding down from the top-right corner of your screen to reach Control Center, then touching the crescent moon symbol if you want to refuse calls without being bothered. Calls will only be sent to voicemail unless you are off "**Do Not Disturb**."

4. **Volume Up/Down Buttons:** You can also quickly mute an incoming call by tapping the corresponding button. By doing this, the call will go to voicemail without being rejected.

5. **Auto-Answer Calls:** Activate the "**Auto-Answer Calls**" function in the Accessibility settings if you have certain accessibility requirements or preferences. Once you choose a custom amount of rings, this will automatically answer calls.

How to avoid unwanted phone calls

On the iPhone 15 Series, avoiding unsolicited calls is essential to protecting your privacy and minimizing disruptions.

The following practical advice can assist you in blocking or removing those bothersome calls:

1. **Activate Silence Unknown Callers**:
- Select **Settings**.
- Tap on **Phone** after swiping down.
- Turn on the function to silence incoming calls.
- All calls from numbers that aren't in your mail, messages, or contacts will be sent to voicemail instead of ringing your phone when you do this.

2. **Use Do Not Disturb:**
- Click Settings.
- Select "**Do Not Disturb**."
- Manually activate it or set it for a certain time slot.
- Adjust preferences to accept calls from your preferred callers or recurring calls.

3. **Block Specific Numbers**:
- Get the **Phone app** open.
- Select **Contacts** or **Recents**.

- Next to the contact or number, tap the i symbol.
- After swiping down, choose **Block this Caller**.
4. **Use Third-Party Apps**:
- Get a trustworthy third-party app from the App Store, such as Truecaller or RoboKiller.
- By using a large database of known spam numbers, these applications can recognize and stop spam calls.
5. **Sort Messages by Unknown Senders**:
- Start the Messages application.
- Select **Settings**.
- To distinguish between messages from known contacts and unknown numbers, enable Filter Unknown Senders.
6. **Report Spam Calls**:
- In the Phone app, hit **Recents** when you get a scam call.
- Next to the call, tap the "**i**" symbol.
- Choose **Report as Spam** after swiping down.
7. **Set up Call Forwarding**:
- Calls from certain numbers can be routed to an automated message or another voicemail box.
- To set up this option, go to **Settings**, hit **Phone**, and then choose **Call Forwarding**.
8. **Check with your Carrier**:
- A few mobile service providers give tools to assist in blocking spam calls.
- Speak with your carrier to find out what options are available.
9. **Consistently update iOS**:
- Update the operating system on your iPhone; Apple often releases security and feature updates that may assist in preventing spam calls.
10. **Be Cautious with your Number**:
- Use caution when disclosing your phone number online or while registering for services to lessen the possibility of getting unsolicited calls.

Keep in mind that even though these techniques may drastically cut down on unsolicited calls, some spammers are tenacious.

How to use Emergency SOS

In an emergency, the iPhone 15 Series' Emergency SOS function is an essential tool that may perhaps save lives.

This is how to apply it:

1. **Enable Emergency SOS:**
   - At the same time, press and hold one of the Volume buttons and the Side button, which is on the right side of your iPhone.

2. **Slide to Place an Emergency Call**:
   - You'll experience a vibration and see a slider and emergency call countdown on the screen after holding the buttons for a short while.

3. **Drag the Slider:**
   - To place an emergency call, drag the Emergency SOS slider to the right. This will make an instant call to your local emergency services (911, in the US, for example).

4. **(Optional) Holding the side and volume buttons:**
   - A countdown will start and an alarm sound will play if you keep the Side and Volume buttons depressed. When the countdown is complete, release the buttons if you want to hang up.

5. **Emergency Services through Auto Call (Optional):**

When you move the slider, Emergency SOS will automatically place a call if the "**Auto Call**" function is enabled.

To carry out this:

- Launch the iPhone's Settings app.
- Using the scroll bar, choose "**Emergency SOS.**"
- Turn on "Auto Call."

6. **Alert Emergency Contacts (Optional):**

- When you use Emergency SOS, you can also set up emergency contacts to receive a text message. To accomplish this:
- Launch the iPhone's **Health application**.
- Hold down the top right corner of your profile image.
- After swiping down, choose "**Medical ID**."
- Press the "**Edit**" button in the top right corner.
- Select "**Emergency Contacts**" from the menu and add the people you want to alert.

7. **For SOS, disable Face ID (Optional):**

Activate the "**Call with Side Button**" option if you want to momentarily deactivate Face ID when using Emergency SOS.

To carry out this:

- Select **Face ID & Passcode** under **Settings**.
- Under the "**Allow Access When Locked**" column, scroll down and enable the "**Call with Side Button**" option.

How to block people from reaching you on different call apps

On your iPhone 15 Series, do the following actions to prevent calls from being sent to you using multiple call apps:

1. **Blocking Calls:**
- Launch the iPhone's Settings app.
- Tap on **Phone** after swiping down.
- Then, choose **Blocked Contacts**.
- Click **Add New** to manually input a number or choose a person to ban from your address book.
2. **Blocking FaceTime Calls:**
- Launch the **Settings app**.
- After swiping down, tap **FaceTime**.
- Select **Blocked Contacts** from the "**Call Blocking & Identification**" section.

- Click **Add New**. Then choose the person you want to block.
3. **Blocking FaceTime Calls and Messages:**
- Open the **Settings application**.
- Swipe down and tap on **Messages**.
- Select Blocked Contacts from the "**Message Filtering**" section.
- Tap **Add New** and choose the person you want to block.
4. **Blocking on Third-Party Applications (like Skype, WhatsApp, and others):**
- The specific settings of each third-party app usually determine whether contacts can be blocked.
- Launch the aforementioned app (such as WhatsApp).
- Locate the person you want to block.
- To block or report a contact, you can often view their profile, touch on it, and seek the appropriate option.
- The steps can change significantly throughout applications.
5. **Do Not Disturb Mode:**
- Use the Do Not Disturb function to momentarily block off all incoming calls and alerts.
- To access the Control Center, swipe down from the upper-right corner of your screen.
- Press the Do Not Disturb symbol, which is a crescent moon.
- In your Do Not Disturb settings, you can configure it to accept calls from certain contacts or groups.

Do not forget that banning someone will stop them from contacting you through phone, text, or FaceTime. You can use a similar procedure to unblock them if you ever decide to change your mind.

How to manage blocked contacts

On the iPhone 15 Series, managing banned contacts can help you avoid unsolicited calls and texts.

Here's how to do so:

1. Locate the Settings app on your home screen after unlocking your iPhone. It resembles a symbol of a gearwheel.
2. Scroll down to **"Phone"** in the Settings menu, and then touch on it. The Phone settings will open as a result.
3. To see your list of banned contacts, tap the **"Blocked Contacts"** option found in the Phone settings.
4. A list of the contacts you have previously blocked will now appear. To see a list of the contacts you have blocked, browse through it.
5. All you have to do is touch on the contact's name or phone number to unblock them. This will make their data available on a new screen.
6. When you tap the **"Unblock this Caller"** option on the contact's information screen, the contact will be unblocked and able to contact and message you once again.
7. Tap the **"Add New"** button, which is often found in the upper right corner of the Blocked Contacts page, to block a new contact. After that, you can choose which contact in your address book to block.
8. Your iPhone may prompt you to confirm your decision when you unblock or ban a contact. Verify by choosing **"Block Contact"** or **"Unblock Contact,"** based on what you've done.
9. Make sure your list of prohibited contacts is updated with your current preferences by reviewing it regularly. As needed, you can unblock contacts or add new contacts to the list.

How to use the voicemail function

The voicemail feature on your iPhone 15 Series—which includes the iPhone 15, iPhone 15 Plus, iPhone 15 Pro, and iPhone 15 Pro Max—can be used as follows:

1. **Setting up Voicemail**:
- Verify that your iPhone is linked to the cellular or Wi-Fi network of your carrier.
- On your iPhone, launch the **Phone app**.
2. **Access Voicemail:**

- Press and hold the **"Voicemail"** symbol located in the Phone app's lower right corner. It seems to be a little cassette tape.

3. **Configure a Voicemail Welcome:**
- If you're accessing voicemail for the first time, you'll be asked to customize your voicemail greeting. Record a personalized welcome by following the on-screen directions.

4. **Listen to Voicemail:**
- A list of voicemail messages can be found under the Voicemail tab. To listen to a voicemail, just tap on it. Additionally, you have the option to touch **"Play"** to hear the message, pausing, fast-forwarding, or rewinding as necessary.

5. **Delete Voicemail:**
- Swipe left on a voicemail message and choose **"Delete."** Alternatively, you can select **"Clear All"** in the upper right corner to eliminate all voicemail messages simultaneously.

6. **Save Voicemail:**
- While listening to a voicemail, you can press the **"Keep"** option if you would want to save the message. This will stop it from being removed automatically.

7. **Answer voicemail (if available):**
- The ability to respond to a voicemail using a text message is supported by certain carriers and iOS versions. Listening to a voicemail will display a **"Reply"** option if accessible.

8. **Change Voicemail Greeting:**
- To modify your voicemail greeting, choose the Voicemail tab, press **"Greeting"** in the top left corner, and then record a new greeting by following the on-screen instructions.

9. **Visual Voicemail (Optional):**
- Visual voicemail, which lets you see a list of your voicemail messages with caller IDs and timestamps, is generally supported by iPhones. With visible voicemail, voicemail management is simpler.

10. **Verify Your Voicemail on a Different Phone:**

- In case you need to listen to your voicemail from a different phone, call your number and hit the relevant key (typically * or #) to access your voicemail when hearing your voicemail greeting.

How to view all missed calls

To see all of your missed calls on an iPhone, follow these steps:

1. First of all, use either Face ID or your confirmed passcode to unlock your device.
2. To access the **Phone app**, find it on your home screen. It appears as a green phone symbol. Tap to launch.
3. **View Recent Calls**:
- **Recents Tab**: The "**Recents**" tab at the bottom of the screen will be your default tab. This is a list of all the calls you have made recently, including missed, incoming, and outgoing calls.
- **Missed Calls**: Select the "**Missed**" tab at the top of the screen to examine missed calls in particular. Only the calls you missed will be shown as a result.

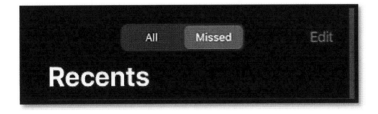

4. Tap on the call item in the list to get further details about a particular call. Call information will be shown to you, including the caller's name or phone number, the length of the call, and the ability to return the call.
5. To remove a call from your history, press "**Edit**" in the upper-right corner, choose the calls you want to remove, and then pick "**Delete**" or "**Clear.**"

How to add contacts to favorites

Add contacts to favorites in the following ways:

1. Use the Face ID or passcode button to unlock your iPhone.

2. Tap the green phone symbol that is usually located on your home screen to launch the Phone app.

3. Generally, the Phone app's tabs are located at the bottom of the screen. Tap **"Contacts"** to open your contact list.

4. To locate the contact you want to add to your favorites, either browse through your contacts or use the search box at the top.

5. To see the contact's information, select the contact and tap on their name.

6. You ought to notice an **"Add to Favorites"** option or a star symbol on the contact's information page. Squeak it.

7. If the contact has numerous phone numbers or email addresses, you can choose which one to add to your favorites. Select your favorite.

8. Tap **"Done"** or **"Save"** to add the contact to your Favorites list and confirm.

9. Return to the Phone app and choose the **"Favorites"** option to view your favorites. The contacts you added ought to be shown there.

Frequently Asked Questions

1. How do you make calls via the contacts, keypad, and favorites list on your iPhone 15 Series?

2. How do you make an emergency call?

3. How do you answer or decline calls?

4. How do you avoid unwanted phone calls?

5. How do you manage blocked contacts?

6. How do you add contacts to favorites?

CHAPTER SEVEN
USING THE SAFARI APP

Overview

The Safari app allows users to browse the internet and visit their favorite and preferred webpage whenever they like. Although this isn't possible if there is no access to the internet, it is still a sophisticated app that ensures you are at the forefront of the happenings around the world.

How to view websites in Safari

Here are the methods to view webpages in Safari on an iPhone 15 Series:

1. To begin, unlock your iPhone 15 Series. You can enter your passcode or use Face ID to do this.
2. Check your home screen for the Safari icon. It's a white background with a blue compass icon. To launch the Safari web browser, tap on it.
3. **Navigate to a Website**:
- To access the website URL, tap the address bar located at the top of the screen.
- If you have a particular website in mind, use the on-screen keyboard to enter its URL.
- Another way to use Siri is to say, **"Hey Siri, open [website name]."**

- By touching the grid symbol in the lower right corner of the screen and choosing a website from your Favorites or regularly Visited list, you can easily access websites that you visit regularly.

4. **Navigate within a Website**:

- Swipe up or down on the screen to navigate the page after the webpage is loaded.
- You can squeeze a section of a website with your fingers to enlarge or reduce its size. To zoom in or out, pinch out or pinch in.
- You can use your finger to touch buttons or links on the page to interact with them.

5. **Use Safari's Features**:

The following Safari features are located at the bottom of the screen:

- The arrows to the left and right go between pages that you have already viewed.
- The share button (seen as a square with an arrow) to share the page that is now shown or carry out other operations like printing, making a shortcut, or adding a page to your favorites.
- The bookmarks button, which is symbolized by an open book, allows you to see your reading list and stored bookmarks.
- The tabs button is two overlapping squares that you may use to see and control open tabs.

6. **Search Using Safari**:

- Type your search phrase into the search box at the bottom of the screen after tapping it to conduct an online search. Both search recommendations and search results will be shown by Safari.

7. **Open Several Tabs**:

- Press the tabs button in the lower right corner of the screen, then press the "+" button to start a new tab if you want to see numerous websites at once. Tapping on tabs allows you to navigate between them.

8. **Adjust Safari Settings**:

- Go to the iPhone's settings app and scroll down to discover "**Safari**." From here, you can change several options, including search engine preference and privacy settings.

How to translate a webpage or image

You can use Apple's built-in translation tools and applications for the iPhone 15 Series to translate a website or picture.

Translating a Web Page

1. First of all, open your iPhone 15's Safari web browser.
2. Go to the website that has to be translated.
3. Tap the "**aA**" symbol that shows up in the upper address bar's left corner while you're on the site.
4. Select a language from the menu that appears at the bottom of the screen. Select **"Translate to [your preferred language]."**

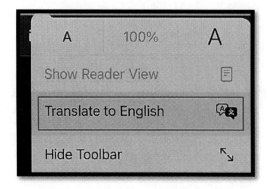

5. The site will be translated into the language of your choice. The translated version of the text is now readable.

Translating an Image

1. Turn on your iPhone 15 and open the **Camera app**.
2. Grab a photo of the text you want to translate using the camera. Ensure that it is well-lit and readable.
3. Open the **Photos app** after capturing the photo.
4. Locate and choose the picture you just snapped.
5. Press the **Share button**, which resembles a square with an upward-pointing arrow.
6. Select "**Translate**" by navigating through the sharing sheet's choices and looking for "**Translate**" among the possible actions. Squeak it.
7. Decide the language you want to translate into and from by selecting the "**Select Languages**" option.
8. The rendered text shall manifest on the display. At this point, the translated text is readable.

How to preview website links

The steps:

1. From your iPhone's home screen, find the Safari app and press to open it. The built-in web browser on iOS devices is called Safari.

2. Tap on a link to preview a message or app, or use the address box at the top to input the URL of the website you want to visit.

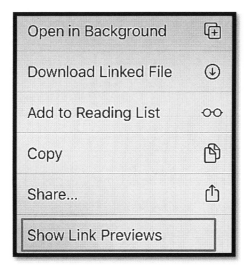

3. **Swipe and Hold**:
- Preview links by touching and holding them. "**Preview**" will be one of the options on the menu that displays. Tap "**Preview**" to see a screen grab of the website that is connected.

4. **Full-Screen Preview (Optional):**
- Touch the preview to open the website in full-screen mode if you need to interact with it first or if you would like a bigger preview. You can swipe from the left side of the screen or hit the "**<**" arrow in the upper left corner to return to the previous page.

How to use a reading list

Using a reading list on an iPhone is done as follows:

1. To access Safari, launch your iPhone's Safari web browser.
2. Open a website or article that you want to save for subsequent read-through.
3. Tap the "**Share**" button, which is usually found at the bottom of the screen and resembles a square with an arrow pointing up, to add the article to your reading list.

4. Select "**Add to Reading List**" from the Share menu by tapping on it.

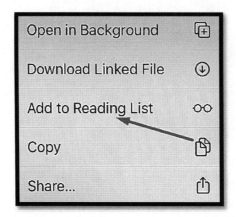

5. At the bottom of the Safari screen, there is a "**Bookmarks**" symbol that resembles an open book. Tap this icon to see your reading list at a later time.

6. From the Bookmarks menu, choose "**Reading List**." By tapping this option, you can access content that you have saved.

7. The articles you've added to your reading list are now available for you to peruse. To read an article, tap on it. If it's cached, it will load in Safari so you can read it even when you're not connected.

8. Swipe left on an item in your Reading List, then press the "**Delete**" option if you've finished reading it or decide you no longer want to retain it.

9. Your Reading List ought to sync between Apple devices if you're logged in with the same Apple ID on each of them. Accordingly, you can store an item on your iPhone and see it on your Mac or iPad at a later time.

How to change between dark and light theme

Here's how to switch between Safari's bright and dark themes:

1. Launch the "**Settings**" app. It is often located on your home screen.
2. Locate the "**Display & Brightness**" option by swiping down.
3. There should be two options under the "**Appearance**" section: "**Light**" and "**Dark**."
4. Tap "**Dark**" to go to the dark theme or "**Light**" to get to the light theme.

5. In the Appearance section, there is an option labeled **"Automatic"** or **"Auto"** on certain iOS versions. If you turn this on, your iPhone will automatically flip between bright and dark themes according to the ambient light levels and the time of day.
6. Click **"Exit"** to close the **"Settings"** app after making your choice.

At this point, Safari ought to use the theme that you choose in the device settings. Safari will show online sites in a dark color scheme when you switch to the dark theme, making it easier on the eyes in low light. Safari will utilize a light color scheme when you switch to the light theme.

How to carry out a safe and advanced search

You can take the following actions to conduct safe and sophisticated searches in Safari on the iPhone 15 Series:

1. Make sure the iPhone operating system and Safari browser are current. New features and security improvements are often included in updates.
2. Safari has a function that helps shield you from dangerous websites called **"Safe Browsing."** Activate it:
- Launch the iPhone's **"Settings"** application.
- After swiping down, tap **"Safari."**
- Turn on **"Fraudulent Website Warning"** and **"Warn About Harmful Websites"** under **"Privacy & Security."**
3. **Use Private Browsing**: You can use Safari's Private Browsing mode to protect the privacy of your browser history and data.
- Launch **Safari**.
- To launch a new tab, tap the square symbol located in the bottom-right corner.
- To activate Private Browsing, tap **"Private"** in the bottom-left corner. The UI will become dingy gray.
4. **Manage Cookies and Website Data**: For more sophisticated privacy options, you can decide how Safari manages cookies and website data.
- Upon accessing the **"Safari"** area of your iPhone's settings, choose **"Privacy & Security."**

- Choose "**Block All Cookies**" or "**Prevent Cross-Site Tracking**" based on your favorite option.

5. **Advanced Search Techniques**: By efficiently using search engines, Safari provides sophisticated search capabilities. This is how to apply them:
- Click the top search bar while Safari is open.
- Enter the search term and press the "**Go**" key on the keyboard.
- Use targeted keywords or phrases to refine your search results.
- Use symbols like "+" to require a term, "-" to exclude a term, or quote marks for a specific phrase to use sophisticated search operators.
- Voice search is also supported by Safari. Once you've tapped the microphone icon, voice your search.

6. **Search Engines**: You can change the Safari default search engine to personalize your search experience:
- Select "**Search Engine**" from the Safari settings.
- Make a selection from DuckDuckGo, Bing, or Google.

7. **Content Blockers**: Install content filters to improve privacy and security:
- Access **"Settings" -> "Safari" -> "Content Blockers."**
- To avoid intrusive advertisements and tracking, use your favorite content blocker.

8. **Use Reader Mode**: Using Reader mode may make websites simpler to read by simplifying their content. When available, tap the **Reader symbol** in the address bar.

9. **Verify Website Certificates**: Make sure websites are using HTTPS at all times for safe transactions. For safe websites, Safari will show a lock symbol in the address bar.

10. .**Report Suspicious Websites**: Use Safari to report a suspicious website that you find. Click "**Report a Concern**" in the Settings menu's "**Safari**" section.

How to change language in Safari

Here's how to change the language in Safari on iPhone 15 Series:

1. To access Settings, find and touch the **Settings app** on your iPhone's home screen. Usually, the Settings app displays a gear symbol.
2. Using the Settings option, get to the list of installed apps on your iPhone by scrolling down. Find **"Safari"** in the menu and press on it.
3. To change the language settings for Safari, tap the "**Language & Region**" option located within the settings.
4. A list of languages is now shown to you. When displaying online pages, Safari employs these languages. Press "**Preferred Language Order**" to change the language order.
5. Tap the "**Add Language**" button and choose the desired language from the list to add a new language. A language can be eliminated by swiping left on it and selecting "**Delete**."
6. By dragging and dropping languages, you can change the sequence in which they are used. The language that appears first in the list will be Safari's default language.
7. To ensure that your modifications are saved, make sure to press "**Done**" or "**Save**" in the top right corner of the screen after you have added, deleted, or rearranged the languages as desired.
8. To make sure the language settings take effect, it's a good idea to close and restart Safari. This may be accomplished by swiping up from the bottom of the screen. To end the Safari app preview, swipe up. Next, open **Safari** again.

Safari will now provide web material in the language you have selected as the default language, or in the sequence you have chosen. Safari will automatically show webpages in the language you've selected if they are available in that language.

How to view saved tabs

Here's how to view saved tabs:

1. To launch **Safari**, find the Safari symbol on the home screen of your iPhone and press it to launch the Safari web browser.
2. To display the overview of your open tabs in Safari, just hit the square icon located in the lower right corner of the screen. The **"Tab Overview"** or **"Tabs"** button is represented by this icon.
3. Check for a section in the Tab Overview named **"Saved Tabs," "Reading List,"** or something similar if you have any saved tabs that you would want to examine.
4. To see the list of tabs you've saved, tap the **"Saved Tabs"** or corresponding area. You may choose which saved tab to see from this point on.
5. When you click on a saved tab, Safari opens that website so you may browse or use it. As with normal tabs, you can browse through your saved tabs.

How to bring back Safari to the home screen

Use these easy steps to get Safari back to the home screen on your iPhone 15 Series. Be aware that although the overall procedure is the same, the steps may differ significantly based on the iOS version you are using. iOS 17 is the new and updated OS for iPhone users including iPhone 15 Series users.

The steps:

1. If your device hasn't been unlocked before, start by doing so. Your home screen should display a variety of app icons.
2. Swipe right on your home screen to reach the App Library if you're having trouble finding Safari on your screen and think it could be there. Using the search box at the top of the screen, you can also look for Safari.
3. Search for the Safari icon, which is usually a white backdrop with a blue compass. It might be on one of the pages on your home screen or in the App Library.

4. Locate the Safari icon and press and keep your finger down on it to do a long press. Your home screen's app icons will all begin to jiggle after a short while, and a menu will show up.

5. You can drag the Safari icon to an existing folder or a space on your home screen while the icons are jiggling. Drag it to the left or right side of the screen until the appropriate page appears if you want to put it on an already-existing home screen page.

6. After positioning the Safari icon on the home screen where you want it, release your finger from it.

7. Swipe up from the bottom of the screen to end edit mode and halt the jiggling symbols.

How to use tab groups

To use tab groups in Safari, follow these steps:

1. Make sure that iOS 17 is installed on your iPhone. To verify and update your iOS device, go to **"Settings"** > **"General"** > **"Software Update."**

2. To launch the web browser, tap the **Safari icon** located on your home screen

3. To open more than one tab in Safari, press the square icon with a number within it that is situated in the lower-right corner of the screen, if you haven't already. The number of open tabs is shown by this indicator.

4. **Create a Tab Group**:
   - Swipe up on the tab bar to expose the tab view to create a new tab group.
   - The **"New Tab Group"** button should be tapped. It seems to be a square stack.
   - Although it's not required, you are welcome to give your tab group a name.

5. **Add Tabs to the Tab Group**:
   - Tap the **"+"** button in the tab view to add tabs to your newly formed tab group.
   - Tapping on the tabs will choose the ones you want to add to the group.
   - Touch **"Add [X] Tabs"** to include them in the collection of tabs.

6. **Manage Group Tabs**:
   - Tap the name of the tab group at the bottom of the Safari window and choose the one you want to use to transition between tab groups.

- You can change, dismiss, or create new tab groups by tapping and holding the name of the group.
7. **Remove/Delete Tabs from a Tab Group**:
- To remove a tab from a collection of tabs, swipe left on the tab inside the tab view and choose "**Remove**."
8. **Exit Tab Groups**:
- In the tab view, press the "**X**" that appears next to the tab group name to dismiss the tab group.

How to change the name of tab groups

Here's how to rename tab groups:

1. To use the web browser, unlock your iPhone and hit the **Safari icon** located on the home screen.
2. **The following actions can be used to form a new tab group:**
- To access numerous tabs, click the square icon with a number in Safari's upper-right corner. This will display every tab you have open.
- Press and hold a tab that you want to add to the group.
- Pick "**Add to Tab Group**" from the menu that displays then pick an already-existing group or start a new one.

To access an already-existing tab group:

- Press and hold the square symbol with a number in Safari's top-right corner.
- Locate your tab groups by scrolling down, and then press the one you want to open.
3. **Change the Tab Group Name**:
- When asked, you can provide the preferred name when establishing a new tab group.
- Tap on the tab group to open it and change its name if it already exists.
- Press the "**Tab Group**" name located at the screen's top.
- Upon making necessary edits to the name, press the "**Done**" key on the keyboard.

How to change how tab groups are arranged

On your iPhone 15 Series running a current version of iOS, you can change the way tab groups are structured as follows:

1. To open the Safari browser on your iPhone, tap the **Safari icon** located on the home screen.
2. Tab Groups can be created or accessed by touching the square icon located in the lower-right corner of the Safari screen if you haven't previously. The tab view is now open. Next, you can add a new tab group by tapping the '+' symbol. Swipe down to see the address bar, then hit the "**Tabs**" icon (it looks like two overlapping squares) to access existing tab groups.
3. **Rearrange Tab Groups**:
- **Drag and Drop**: The drag-and-drop technique may be used to reorganize tab groups. To move a group of tabs in the list to the appropriate location, press and hold on the group.
- **Use the Edit Button**: The tab group view has an "**Edit**" button in various iOS versions. By using this button, you can move or remove tab groups.
4. You can touch on any tab group to view its contents after rearranging the tab groups.
5. Slide a tab group to the left or right, then hit the corresponding "**Close**" or "**Delete**" option to make it disappear.

How to delete a tab group

Remove a tab group as follows in Safari:

1. To unlock your iPhone, either uses a passcode or Face ID.
2. To launch the Safari browser, tap the Safari icon located on your home screen.
3. Tap the square symbol in the Safari browser's lower-right corner to examine the tabs you currently have open. Your current tab count is shown by this symbol.
4. The tab view's top list of tab groups is shown if you have them configured. Small sets of tabs with titles are often used to symbolize tab groups.

5. Tap and hold the tab group you want to remove to delete it. It should take time for a menu with choices for that tab group to emerge.
6. Tap the "**Close Tab Group**" or "**Delete Tab Group**" option provided in the menu that opens.
7. You may be prompted to verify the removal. Verify that you want to remove the tab group if asked.

How to view all the tabs in a tab group

Follow these basic instructions to examine every tab in a tab group:

1. To open Safari, press the **Safari app icon** on your iPhone to bring up the web browser.
2. To access a tab group that you've made, press the square icon located in the lower-right corner of the Safari window. Your tab groups are represented by this symbol.
3. All of the tabs that are presently grouped should be visible to you when you've opened the tab group. To navigate through the list of open tabs inside that group, swipe up or down on the screen.
4. **Select a Tab**: Just touch on any tab in the group to go to that particular tab.
5. **Manage Tabs**: The "..." (Three dots) button, which is often situated in the lower-right or upper-right area of the screen, can also be used to manage the tabs in the group. You can then choose various options, such as adding a new tab to the group or shutting certain tabs.

How to bookmark a page

The procedures listed below can be used to bookmark a page in Safari on the iPhone 15 Series:

1. To start using Safari, first unlock your iPhone and locate the symbol for the app, which resembles a blue compass. To open the Safari browser, tap on it.

2. Type the URL of the page you want to bookmark into the address box at the top of the page. Alternatively, you can click on a link from another app or does a search engine query to access the website.

3. **Access the Bookmarks Menu**:

- Tapping the action button, which resembles a square with an upward-pointing arrow, in the toolbar at the bottom will bring up the bookmarks menu.

4. **Add a Bookmark**:

- Select "**Add Bookmark**" from the bookmarks menu. Usually, it has the appearance of an open book symbol.

- Change the bookmark's name and choose where you want it saved (in the bookmarks bar or a folder) by navigating via a pop-up window that appears.

5. If you want the bookmark to be more easily recognizable or descriptive, you can change its name. You can also arrange your bookmarks in a separate folder.

6. Select the "**Save**" button located in the upper right corner of the pop-up window after you've made any necessary adjustments. To save the bookmark, do this.

7. To retrieve your stored bookmarks in the future, just press the bookmarks icon (the square with the upward arrow) once again and choose the bookmark you want to see.

How to add a bookmark

These are the steps to add a bookmark in Safari on an iPhone 15 Series:

1. If your iPhone hasn't been unlocked before, start by doing so.

2. Find the Safari app icon on your home screen to open Safari. It resembles a blue rose on a compass. To launch the Safari browser, tap on it.

3. To browse the site you want to bookmark, use the address bar located at the top of the screen. To reach the site, you can either input the URL manually or use a search engine.

4. **Bookmark the Page**:

- Select the "**Share**" button located at the bottom of the screen when you've reached the site you like to bookmark. It seems to be a square with an upward-pointing arrow.

- A menu with many options will appear. Navigate this menu until you come across **"Add Bookmark**." Press it.
- A new window with the bookmark's information will open. You have the option to modify the bookmark's name and store it in a different location (the bookmark bar or a designated folder, for example).
- Upon reaching contentment with the information, choose **"Save"** located in the upper-right corner.

5. **Accessing Bookmarks**:
- Tap the book icon located at the bottom of the Safari screen to see your bookmarks at a later time. The bookmarks menu will then appear.
- Your newly added bookmark and any other bookmarks you've saved will be shown here.

How to open a bookmark

The procedures below can be used to access a bookmark in Safari on the iPhone 15 Series:

1. Unlock your iPhone by using Face ID or your passcode.
2. On your home screen, look for the Safari app icon. It resembles a blue rose on a compass.
3. To launch the Safari web browser, tap the **Safari icon**.
4. To access your bookmarks, look for a few icons at the bottom of the Safari screen. Press the icon that resembles a book open. Your bookmarks will open when you click on this bookmark symbol.
5. The websites you have bookmarked are now visible to you. If you have many bookmarks, swipe up and down to browse.
6. To open a bookmark, choose it by tapping on it. You will be sent to the chosen website via Safari.
7. If necessary, you may pinch or zoom in to change how the site appears.
8. After the website loads, you can use it in the same way as any other webpage. You can scroll, tap links, and do other necessary activities.

9. When on a site, press the address bar at the top of the screen, then hit the bookmarks symbol (which resembles an open book) once more to access your bookmarks.

How to edit a bookmark

Editing a bookmark in Safari is as easy as you can imagine. Here's a detailed how-to:

1. To begin, unlock your iPhone and find the Safari application on your home screen. It's the symbol that has a blue compass-like appearance.
2. To access bookmarks, tap the open book-shaped symbol at the bottom of the screen. You can access your reading list and bookmarks by doing this.
3. Navigate through your bookmarks until you come to the one you want to modify. To open it, tap on it.
4. **Edit the Bookmark**:
- **Change the Name**: Tap the name box at the top of the screen to make changes to the bookmark's name. Now you can use the keyboard that displays to change the text.
- **Change the URL**: Click on the website address located under the name of the bookmark to make changes to the URL. Here, you can change or remove the URL.
- **Change the Folder**: Tap the "**Folder**" section and choose the new folder from the list if you want to transfer the bookmark to a different folder.

5. After completing the required adjustments, touch "**Done**" or "**Save**" to save the modifications.
6. Return to the bookmarks list and find the bookmark you just updated to make sure your modifications have been saved. Now, it should show the modifications you made.

How to delete a bookmark

Here's how to remove a bookmark from Safari on your iPhone 15 Series:

1. To launch Safari, find the **Safari symbol** on the home screen of your iPhone and press it to launch the Safari web browser.

2. A toolbar with many icons is located at the bottom of the screen. Press the icon that resembles an open book to access your bookmarks. You can access your internet history and bookmarks by doing this.

3. Select **Bookmarks Folder** to exit the "**Favorites**" area by default. To see your bookmarks folders if it's in a different folder, touch "**Edit**" in the lower-right corner of the screen. Choose the folder containing the bookmark you want to remove.

4. Look through the folder you've chosen to see a list of bookmarks, and then choose the one you want to remove. In case you are unsure which one it is, just tap on it to open it.

5. Tap the address bar at the top of the screen after opening the bookmark. The URL of the website will be highlighted for you. To remove the URL, click the "**X**" symbol located on the address bar's right side. A "**Edit**" button will show up in the lower-right area of the screen after the URL's removal. The bookmark's name will now have a red circle with a minus sign next to it. Give this circle a tap.

6. You'll get a notification asking you to confirm the deletion of the bookmark. To confirm your selection, press "**Delete**."

7. To close the edit mode after you've finished organizing your bookmarks, press "**Done**" in the lower-right corner.

How to view search history

Take the following actions to access your search history in Safari:

1. Launch **Safari** from your home screen.

2. Tap the bookmarks symbol at the bottom of the screen to access your search history. Looks like an open book.

3. The "**History**" option is located at the top of the bookmarks menu. To see your browsing history, tap on it.

4. This brings up a history of the websites and searches you have lately visited. You may locate the exact items you're searching for by scrolling through this list.

5. Using the search box at the top of the History page, you can look for a certain phrase inside your browser history. With only a keyword input, Safari will filter your history to provide just the most relevant information.

6. Tapping the "**Clear**" button at the bottom of the History page will allow you to delete your browser history. The last hour, today, today, and yesterday, or the whole period may all be cleared from your history.

How to clear browser search history

Follow these steps to delete your browser's search history:

1. To access Safari, touch the **Safari symbol** (a blue compass) on the home screen of your iPhone.

2. An icon that resembles an open book may be found in the lower-right corner. To access your bookmarks, tap on it.

3. To see your browsing history, hit the "**Clock**" symbol in the bookmarks menu.

4. Press "**Clear**" (or, if you're using an earlier version, "Clear History and Website Data") at the bottom of the history screen.

5. You'll be prompted for confirmation before being able to remove website data and browsing history. Select "**Clear History and Data**" to be sure.

Deleting your browser history may also erase cookies, stored website data, and other data associated with your surfing. Once these procedures are finished, Safari should have no more browsing history.

Frequently Asked Questions

1. How do you view websites in Safari?
2. How do you translate a webpage or image?
3. How do you view saved tabs?
4. How do you preview website links?
5. How do you use tab groups?
6. How to bookmark a page?
7. How to clear browser search history?

CHAPTER EIGHT
USING THE CAMERA APP

Overview

Chapter eight talks about the camera app. The camera app on the iPhone 15 Series is even more sophisticated as the camera is capable of taking much more stunning photos and recording much more beautiful videos. Learn all about the camera app here.

How to launch the camera app

Take these easy steps to open the iPhone 15 Series camera app:

1. First, use Face ID or your password to unlock your iPhone.
2. Swipe down from the top-right corner to visit the home screen if you're not already there.
3. On your home screen, look for the **Camera app icon**. Usually located in your app library or on the first page of your home screen, it is a straightforward camera lens symbol.

4. After locating the icon for the Camera app, tap on it. This will launch the camera app right away.

5. You'll be in the default picture mode when you launch the camera app. You can swipe left or right to switch between several camera settings, including Photo, Video, Portrait, and more.

6. At this point, you can now take pictures or record videos by simply touching the shutter button (typically a white circle) or the video record button (usually a red circle) on the screen after the camera app is open and in the correct mode.

7. Tapping the buttons or symbols on the camera interface will give you access to a variety of camera capabilities, including the flash, timer, filters, and more.

How to launch the Camera app using Siri

The basic steps to use Siri to open the Camera app on an iPhone are as follows:

1. Siri may be woken up by saying "**Hey Siri**" if this functionality is enabled, or by pressing and holding the side buttons of your iPhone until Siri appears on the screen.
2. You may instruct Siri to launch the Camera app after it's turned on and listening. For example, you can say, "**Open the Camera app**," or "**Launch the Camera**."
3. The order will be carried out by Siri, who will process it and launch the Camera app on your behalf.

How to change the Camera aspect ratio

Generally, you can adjust the iPhone's camera aspect ratio as follows:

1. To access the Camera app, tap its icon.
2. The camera app often opens in Photo mode by default. If it doesn't, slide the screen left or right to enter photo mode.
3. Examine your screen for the aspect ratio options. This option is often shown on earlier iPhones as an icon that resembles a rectangle with arrows pointing in or out. To see other camera choices, you may need to slide up or down or hit the icon.
4. Depending on the type of your iPhone 15 Series, you can usually select from choices like 4:3, 16:9, or others after you've reached the aspect ratio settings. Decide which aspect ratio is your favorite.

5. Your camera will now take pictures in the selected aspect ratio once you have selected it.

Note: Adjusting the aspect ratio might have an impact on your photographs' quality and field of vision.

How to set the flashlight to be on always

You can usually turn on the flashlight in the camera app as follows:

1. To unlock your iPhone, press the power button and choose between using Face ID or a password.
2. To get access to the Control Center, swipe down from the upper-right corner of the screen.
3. There are several quick-access icons in the Control Center. Search for the flashlight icon, which resembles a little sign for a flashlight. To activate the flashlight, tap on it. When the flashlight turns on, its preset brightness will be used.
4. To quit the Control Center after turning on the flashlight, either presses outside of it or swipe up to open it again. Launch the Camera app now.
5. After launching the Camera app, you may make any necessary adjustments to the camera's settings. While you use the camera, the flashlight will continue to function, adding extra light to your pictures and movies.
6. To return to the Control Center, just swipe down from the upper-right corner of the screen to turn off the flashlight. Click the symbol of the flashlight to turn it off.

How to enter into Live Mode

Use these basic methods to access Live Mode in the iPhone camera app.

Here are the steps:

1. First of all, if your iPhone is locked, you can use Face ID or your password to open it.

2. To open the camera, find the Camera app icon on your home screen and press it.

3. Choose a camera mode from the options available in the Camera app, which are located at the bottom or sides of the screen. To choose between "**Live**" and "**Live Photo**" mode, swipe left or right, or press the relevant mode.

4. Press the shutter button to capture a picture as usual while in Live Mode. Before and after the picture is taken, the camera will record a few seconds of video, which is called a "**Live Photo**."

5. Open the Photos app and find the Live Photo you just took to view your Live Photos. The picture can be pressed and held to bring it to life with music and action.

How to take steady shots with your Camera timer

Using the iPhone 15 Series camera timer to take steady shots is a terrific technique to make sure your pictures are clear and crisp.

Here's how to do so:

1. Make sure that the iPhone 15 Series is powered on. Verify that there are no smudges or dirt particles on the camera lens since this might lower the quality of your images.

2. Locate the **Camera app** on your home screen after unlocking your iPhone. To open it, tap on it.

3. Locate the camera mode you want to use by swiping through the options at the bottom of the screen. The "**Photo**" setting works best for stable photos.

4. To guarantee that your iPhone stays still during the picture, place it on a sturdy surface or use a tripod. You can hold your phone against a sturdy item if you don't have a tripod.

5. Press the symbol for the timer at the top of the screen. It seems to be a clock. There is a 3-second and a 10-second timer available. Use a 10-second timer to achieve the steadiest photos since it gives you more time to bring the camera into focus and stabilize.

6. Modify the camera's location and angle to compose your shot. Make sure the background is visually pleasing and your topic is placed correctly.

7. Make sure your iPhone is perfectly steady before the timer begins to count down. Try to keep your hands calm and don't make any rapid movements if you're holding it.

8. On the screen, tap the shutter button, which is represented by a big circle. Ten seconds will pass before the timer begins to count down. Make use of this opportunity to center yourself and get ready.

9. When the countdown hits zero, your iPhone will snap the picture on its own. To prevent blurriness, try to stay as steady as you can during this procedure.

10. Check the photo in the Photos app once it's taken to make sure it lives up to your expectations. You can always try again until you get the intended outcome if it's not flawless.

How to take pictures and videos using the Camera app

Use the following procedures to snap images and movies with your iPhone 15 Series' Camera app:

1. To unlock your iPhone, either press the power button or use Face ID.

2. To open the Camera App, find its icon on your home screen. On your screen, it is usually located at the bottom and resembles a camera.

3. **Select the Camera Mode:**

- **Photo Mode**: When the Camera app launches by default, it is in Photo mode, which enables you to snap still pictures.
- **Video Mode**: To switch to video mode, swipe to the right. It is possible to capture videos in this mode.
- **Portrait Mode**: To add a depth-of-field effect to your images, slide left to activate Portrait mode, if your iPhone model supports it.
- **Panorama Mode**: To take broad, sweeping pictures, swipe to the right once again to get Panorama mode.

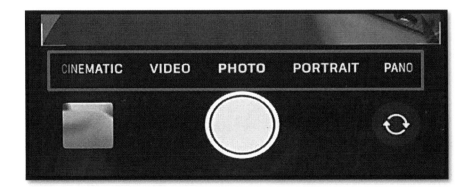

4. **Adjust Camera Settings (optional):**
- Touch the screen to concentrate on a particular item or region before taking a picture or recording a video. By swiping up or down on the screen, you may also change the exposure.
- Depending on the type of your iPhone, you can access more options like the flash, timer, and filters by touching the arrow or icons on the top or side of the screen.

5. **Capture a Photo:**
- To snap a picture in photo mode, just press the shutter button, which is often a circle at the bottom of the screen. A shutter sound will ring, and your Photos app will store the picture.

6. **Record a Video:**
- To start video recording when in video mode, press the **red or white record button**. You can press the button to halt recording when it changes to a stop button. You'll save your video to the **Photos app**.

7. **View and Edit Photos and Videos:**
- Open the photos app, and go to the **"Photos"** and **"Videos"** areas to see and edit your recent photographs and videos.

- The Photos app allows you to immediately edit your media, including brightness adjustments, cropping, filter additions, and more.

8. **Access Additional Camera Features**:

- As for the type of iPhone, you can use other camera functions such as Time-Lapse, Slo-mo, and Night mode. Investigate these options to improve your filmmaking and photography.

9. **Use the Front-Facing Camera**:

- Tap the camera symbol with arrows on the top or side of the screen to switch to the front-facing (selfie) camera.

10. **Save and Share**:

- After taking pictures and videos, you can save them in your iCloud or share them with others via social media applications, email, messages, and other compatible services.

How to change between the rear and front camera

With your iPhone 15 Series, you can use the Camera app to alternate between the front and back cameras by doing the following steps:

1. Use either Face ID or your passcode to unlock your iPhone.
2. Locate the Camera app icon on your home screen. It resembles a camera lens. Tap this symbol to activate the app.
3. The camera viewfinder appears when the Camera app is launched. You can swipe horizontally (left or right) on the screen to switch between the various camera modes. To move between other modes, such as Photo, Portrait, Video, etc., swipe to the right until you reach the **"Photo"** option, which is the default rear camera mode.
4. Press and hold the camera symbol with curving arrows in the upper-right corner of the screen to turn on the front camera, often referred to as the selfie camera. By doing this, the front camera will be shown instead of the back camera.

5. **Adjust Camera Settings (Optional):** By pressing on the icons or settings wheel, which are often situated on the top or sides of the camera interface, you can change many camera settings, including flash, HDR, timer, and more.

6. You can now snap pictures or record videos by hitting the shutter button, which is often a big circle at the bottom center of the screen, after switching to the front camera and adjusting any preferred settings.

7. To return to the rear camera, just touch the camera symbol with the curved arrows once again. With this, you can switch between the front and back cameras.

8. Keep using either camera to take pictures or record movies, switching between them as necessary to capture the moments you desire.

How to disable image mirroring for the front camera

On the other hand, you can take the following general actions to disable picture mirroring for the front camera:

1. Find the **Camera app** on the home screen of your iPhone, and then press to launch it.

2. To switch to the front camera, touch the camera flip symbol. This icon is usually shown as a circle with two arrows creating a circle or as a camera icon with circular arrows. This will cause the front camera to swap.

3. Locate the settings icon on the camera screen, which is often found at the top or bottom of the screen. It resembles an icon of a gear or slider.

4. You should be able to locate an option about front camera settings or image mirroring inside the camera settings. The name **"Mirror Front Camera," "Flip**

Front Camera," or a similar one can be on it. To stop picture mirroring, toggle this setting.

How to adjust color and light in the Camera app

The procedures below can be used to modify the color and light settings in the iPhone 15 Series Camera app:

1. After unlocking your phone, swipe left from the lock screen or select the app's icon on the home screen to launch the **Camera app**.

2. Choose the option you want to use based on your requirements while taking photos. Options such as Portrait, Night, Photo, and any other mode that is offered are yours to choose from.

3. Locate the settings menu or choices icon, which is often found at the top or bottom of the screen, to access the camera settings. It is shown as a set of gear-shaped symbols or sliders.

4. **Adjust Brightness**: The exposure slider allows you to adjust the exposure as well as the overall brightness of your picture. To adjust the exposure level, swipe up or down on the exposure slider. Your picture will seem brighter if you move it up; it will appear darker if you move it down.

5. **Adjust Color (White Balance)**: Tap the white balance icon (often a sun or lightbulb image) to change the color temperature of your picture. After that, you may use the slider to manually adjust the color temperature or choose from presets like **"Auto," "Incandescent," "Fluorescent," "Daylight," or "Cloudy"** to fit the lighting circumstances.

6. **Use Filters (Optional):** Filters can be used to further modify the color or add creative effects. Choose your preferred filter by tapping on the filter symbol, which often resembles three overlapping circles. To change the strength of the filter, swipe left or right.

7. **Adjust the High Dynamic Range (HDR):** In settings with strong contrast, HDR can assist in balancing exposure. If your mode supports HDR, you can turn it on or off in the options.

8. Tap and hold the desired location on the screen to lock focus and exposure if you want to keep the focus and exposure settings for that particular portion of

your picture. There will be a yellow AE/AF lock indication, and unless you press somewhere else or remove the lock, nothing will change in the settings.

9. After adjusting the lighting and color to your preference, compose your picture and press the shutter to start taking a picture.

10. After shooting the picture, you can use the Photos app to adjust the lighting and color settings by choosing the image and hitting the **"Edit"** option.

How to edit photos and videos

Editing Photos

1. From your home screen, press the camera symbol to open the Camera app.
2. Press the shutter button to take a picture.
3. To use the Edit feature, click the picture. A thumbnail of the photo will appear in the bottom-left corner of the screen. To use the editing tools, tap this thumbnail.

4. By touching the corresponding icons at the bottom of the screen, you can make simple adjustments like cropping, rotating, or auto-enhancing.

5. To make more complex changes, hit the "**Edit**" button located in the upper-right corner of the screen. The editing interface will then appear, allowing you to change the color, lighting, and other aspects. To adjust exposure, brightness, contrast, saturation, and other factors, use the sliders.

6. Tap the symbol with the three overlapping circles to add filters to your shot. You can swipe left or right to choose from a variety of filters and change how strong they are.

7. Press the "**Revert**" button to return to the original image if you make a mistake or want to reverse a change.

8. Select "**Done**" in the lower right corner of the screen when you're happy with your changes. Your altered picture will be saved to your Camera Roll as a result.

Editing Videos

1. Open the Camera app, then swipe right on the camera screen to enter video recording mode, or choose "**Video**" from the available camera modes.

2. Press the **red record button** to begin recording your video.

3. To use the Edit feature, click the video thumbnail in the lower-left corner of the screen once it has finished recording. To access the editing tools, tap on it.

4. To pick the part of the video you want to save, drag the handles on the timeline at the bottom. Next, choose "**Trim**."

5. Tap the "**Edit**" button located in the upper right corner of the video to see further editing options. The video may be cropped, exposure adjusted, filters used, and more.

6. Tap the **play button** to get a preview of your modified video.

7. Click "**Done**" in the lower right corner of the screen if you're happy with the changes you've made. The altered video may be saved as a new clip or overwritten, depending on your preference.

8. You can share your modified video straight from the Photos app or other social networking sites after saving it.

How to rotate, flip, and crop images

Here's how to use the iPhone Camera app to crop, rotate, and flip images:

1. Find and launch the iPhone's Camera app.
2. Press the shutter button on the Camera app to take a picture.
3. To view the picture that you just took, touch the thumbnail preview that appears in the lower-left corner of the Camera app.
4. **Rotate an Image:**
    -   In the image viewer, touch the **Edit icon** (often a pencil or slider symbol) to rotate a picture.
    -   Seek alternatives for rotation. You can usually find a rotation icon that lets you turn the picture in either a clockwise or counterclockwise direction. To rotate the picture as required, tap this symbol.
    -   Tap **"Done"** or **"Save"** to save the modifications once you've made the required rotation.
5. **Flip an Image:**
    -   In the editing options, there's usually a horizontal flip icon (which looks like two arrows pointing in opposing directions) that you can use to flip a picture.
    -   To turn the picture horizontally, tap this symbol.
    -   Once again, ensure that you hit **"Done"** or **"Save"** to save the altered picture and apply the flip.
6. **Crop an Image:**
    -   In the editing options, press the **Crop icon** (often a square or rectangle) to crop a picture.
    -   Next, you can move the corners or edges of the cropping frame to change it. To choose the area of the picture you want to preserve, you can also adjust the frame.

- Tap "**Done**" or "**Save**" to save the cropped picture if you're happy with the crop.
7. After adjusting the picture as you see fit (rotation, flipping, or cropping), remember to save it by selecting "**Save**" or a related menu item.

How to undo and redo edits

The steps:

1. Turn on your iPhone and open the "**Photos**" app.
2. Tap the image that you want to modify.
3. To enter Edit Mode, find the "**Edit**" button or icon, which is often found at the bottom of the screen or in the upper-right corner. To access the editing interface, tap on it.
4. **Undo an Edit**: The ability to reverse changes may exist, depending on the design of the updated editing interface. An "**Undo**" button or an undo arrow

might be used to symbolize this. To go back to the previous edit, tap this option.

5. **Redo and Edit**: In the same way, to go back and make changes, search for a "**Redo**" button or a redo arrow in the editing tools. To modify it again, tap on it.

How to adjust and straighten the perspective

The basic procedures to modify and align the viewpoint in the Camera app are as follows:

1. Find the iPhone's Camera app and launch it.
2. Just make sure you are in the "**Photo**" mode since that's where perspective changes are usually made—not in the video mode—when shooting pictures.
3. **Turn on the Gridlines (Optional):** Using the gridlines will aid in correctly aligning your photo. Toggle on the "**Grid**" or "**Gridlines**" option in the Camera settings, which are often located in the Settings app under "**Camera.**"

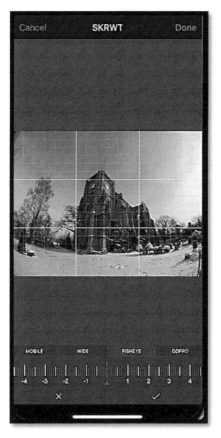

4. Use the viewfinder to compose your shot. Particularly when capturing architecture or other subjects where perspective is important, make an effort to get as straight of an alignment as you can with the lines and objects in your picture.

5. To ensure that your camera is always absolutely level, many iPhone models come with a level indicator. If this is a function on your iPhone, ensure the indicator is showing a level horizon.

6. Press the shutter release button to capture the image after it is framed the way you want it.

7. The Photos app has built-in editing capabilities that you may use to modify perspective after you've taken the picture.

8. Open the Photos app and find the image that needs editing.

9. To edit a picture, first open it and then choose the "**Edit**" button.

10. Find options such as **"Crop," "Straighten," or "Perspective"** modifications when you crop and modify. As necessary, use these tools to correct and alter the perspective.
11. To save the modified image, touch **"Done"** if you're happy with the changes.

How to apply filters

The steps to apply filters on an iPhone using the Camera app are as follows:

1. To access the camera on your iPhone, find and hit the **Camera app icon** on the home screen.
2. Make sure you are in photo mode since that's where filters are usually applied—to images, not videos. On the camera screen, you can swipe left or right to choose between modes.
3. Seek for the filter icon, which often takes the form of a wand or three overlapping circles. Usually, it may be found in the upper or lower corner of the camera screen. To see the available filters, tap on them.
4. The screen will provide a list of the available filters. Swiping left or right usually allows you to navigate through the available selections. To pick a filter, tap on it.
5. After deciding on a filter, compose your image and push the big circular shutter button to snap a picture with the chosen filter applied.
6. After clicking the picture, you may press the preview thumbnail located in the camera app's lower-left corner to examine it. To save the image to your Camera Roll, touch **"Done"** when you're happy with it. You may snap another picture or use a different filter if not.

How to take portrait images

Here's how to take portrait images:

1. To start, first unlock your iPhone and go to the home screen.
2. To access the app, find the Camera app icon on your home screen. It resembles a camera lens. Tap on it.
3. The Camera app opens and several shooting options appear at the bottom of the screen. It usually contains an icon of a person's silhouette, so swipe left or right to locate and pick "**Portrait**."

4. Locate your subject and compose your picture. Make sure the topic is positioned inside the frame and has enough lighting. To adjust the focus and exposure point, touch the screen. This aids in the camera's understanding of the subject's location.
5. If you want to change the composition, you can zoom in or out using the pinch-to-zoom action.
6. Choose from a variety of Portrait Lighting effects on certain iPhone models, including Natural Light, Studio Light, Contour Light, and more. These are located at the screen's bottom. Choose the one that best meets your needs.

7. When everything is ready, take a portrait picture by pressing the shutter button, which is often either on the side of your iPhone or at the bottom of the screen. To prevent blurriness, try to keep your hands steady.

8. Once the picture has been taken, you can examine it by touching the thumbnail preview located in the camera app's lower-left corner. If necessary, change the picture by cropping it, adding filters, or improving it using the built-in photo editing tools.

9. After you're happy with the portrait shot, save it to your Photos app by tapping the **"Done"** button. After that, you can upload it to social media or share it with friends and family.

10. Portrait photography has the potential to be an art form; therefore to become better at it, you must experiment with various lighting setups, subjects, and perspectives. To acquire the ideal portrait, don't be scared to take many photographs.

How to take panorama images

Use the following easy steps to take beautiful panoramic photos with your iPhone 15 Series Camera app:

1. Find the Camera app on your home screen after unlocking your iPhone. To launch the Camera app, tap on it.

2. Navigate the camera modes by swiping until the **"Panorama"** option appears. It often coexists with other modes, such as Video, Portrait, and Photo.

3. Make sure you are in a favorable position before you begin to capture the panoramic. Rotate your iPhone to the landscape position while holding it vertically in portrait mode.

4. Decide on the starting point for your panorama. Depending on your taste, it's a good idea to begin at either the left or right edge of the scene.

5. Press the shutter button to begin taking pictures of the panoramic. Move your iPhone steadily and gently in the direction indicated by the on-screen arrow or guideline, either from left to right or right to left.

6. Be careful you move your iPhone at a steady, fluid speed while taking the panoramic. Avoid jerky motions since they might lead to mistakes in the sewing.

7. Once you've got the full scene you want in the panoramic, keep moving your iPhone. When the Camera app determines that the panorama is long enough, it will automatically cease taking pictures.

8. Once you've completed taking the panoramic, the picture will be processed by the Camera app. After that, you may see the whole panorama by swiping left or right on the screen. To save the outcome of your Photos collection, hit **"Done"** if you're happy with it.

9. Using the Photos app's integrated editing tools, you can make further edits to your panoramic view. Use filters, color correction, or cropping to make your panoramic better. Once you're happy, sharing it on social media or with friends and family is simple.

10. Try experimenting with various settings and viewpoints to get some unique panoramic photos. Wide-angle views of expansive landscapes, cityscapes, or even group shots may be achieved with the use of panoramas.

How to record a time-lapse video

Here's a broad overview:

1. Locate the Camera app on your home screen after unlocking your iPhone. To open the camera, tap on it.

2. Swipe left or right on the camera modes at the bottom of the Camera app until you see **"Time-Lapse."** A clock indicator indicates the location of this option.

3. Be sure your shot is steady and framed before you begin filming. The greatest results are obtained from time-lapse recordings when the camera stays still the

whole time. To secure your iPhone, either locate a sturdy surface or use a tripod.

4. Wherever you want the camera to focus and adjust exposure, tap the screen. This will assist in ensuring that the exposure and focus of your time-lapse movie are correct.

5. You can change your time-lapse recording with extra settings, depending on the version of your app. This may include modifying the time between frames or the time-lapse's pace.

6. Press the **red record button** to begin the time-lapse recording if you're happy with your settings. At regular intervals, the Camera app will take a series of pictures automatically.

7. Press and hold the red record button one more to end the time-lapse recording.

8. The Camera app will process the photos into a time-lapse movie when you stop recording. Using the Photos app, you may inspect it and make any required adjustments.

9. After you're satisfied with your time-lapse film, use the Photos app's Share option to send it to friends and family.

How to revert an edited video or image

1. Open your iPhone's **"Photos"** app. All of the pictures you've taken and processed are kept here.

2. To locate the modified picture you want to go back to, browse through your photo collection. The **"Edit"** symbol (three sliders) is usually seen in the upper right corner of edited photographs.

3. Tap on the altered image to see it. Press the **"Edit"** button that appears in the upper right corner of the screen after it has opened. You'll reach the editing interface by doing this.

4. A variety of editing tools and choices should be visible in the editing interface. One way to undo the edits done to the picture is to use the **"Revert"** button, which is often indicated by a curving arrow symbol. By using this button, you can restore the image to its unaltered original form.

5. The app will prompt you to confirm that you want to remove the adjustments and return to the original image when you hit the **"Revert"** button. To verify the action, press **"Revert to Original."**

6. Your picture will be returned to its original condition and the edited modifications will be removed after you have approved the reversion. You can either hit **"Done"** or just close the editing window to save this version. At this point, you can now see your original picture again.

How to copy and paste edits to images

Here's how to copy and paste edits to images:

1. First, launch the iPhone's **"Photos"** app.
2. Look through your photo collection and choose the picture you want to modify or alter.
3. In the upper-right corner of the screen, tap the **"Edit"** button. This will cause the chosen image's editing interface to open.
4. To make the necessary edits to your picture, use the several editing options at your disposal, including tweaks, filters, cropping, and more.
5. To leave the editing mode after applying the adjustments you want to duplicate, touch the **"Done"** button.
6. You must save the changed picture as a copy before you can paste these changes to another image. To make a copy of the modified picture with all the modifications made, tap the **"Save as Copy"** option.
7. Return to your photo library and choose the picture you want to use for the same editing.
8. To begin modifying the second picture, use the "Edit" button once again. As soon as you enter editing mode, a **"Paste"** option ought to appear. If you choose **"Paste,"** the changes made to the earlier modified picture will be applied to the current one.
9. If necessary, you may adjust the applied modifications. When you're happy, hit **"Done"** to save the second image's altered version.

How to edit time, location, and date in the Camera app

The general steps you should take are as follows:

1. To access the "**Photos**" app on your iPhone, hit its icon.
2. To alter the time, location, or date for a picture, go to it and press to open it.
3. Press the "**Edit**" button located in the upper-right corner of the screen.
4. **Edit Time and Date**:
- **Date**: Tap the "**Adjust**" button (sometimes shown as a clock symbol) to change the date.
- **Time**: To change the time, enter the required amount using the numeric keypad or the slider.
- **Location**: You may need to use a third-party program or piece of software that enables geotag editing if you want to alter the photo's location. This may not be a capability that the iPhone's Camera app has built-in.
5. After making the required adjustments, touch "**Done**" or "**Save**" to keep the modified picture.

How to record a slo-mo video

The methods below can be used to shoot a slow-motion film using the iPhone 15 Series' Camera app:

1. To begin, unlock your iPhone and press the icon of the Camera app. It is usually located on your home screen and has a little camera-like appearance.
2. "**Slo-Mo**" is often symbolized by an icon with the letters "**Slo-Mo**" or a slow-motion symbol. Swipe the screen to flip between camera settings until you discover "**Slo-Mo**."

3. Make some changes to your slow-motion video's parameters before you begin recording. Tap the "**Settings**" or "**Options**" icon to do this. Here, you can adjust the frame rate, resolution, and other parameters. Select a higher frame rate, such as 120 or 240 frames per second (fps), to get the greatest slow-motion effect.

4. Ensure that the subject is properly framed in the viewfinder of your camera. To get the smooth slow-motion film, think about using a tripod or stabilizer.

5. Click the **red record button** to start a slow-motion video recording. A timer that indicates how long you've been filming will appear on the screen.

6. Capture the scene or activity that you want to slow down. Keep in mind that the greatest way to capture quick movements or action scenes is in slow motion.

7. Press the red stop button to end the slow-motion video recording. You'll save your video to the Photos app.

8. Your slow-motion film is available to watch in the Photos app. To play your video, open the Photos app, locate it, and touch on it. To improve the slow-motion effect, you may also modify your movie by pressing the "**Edit**" option and making changes to the speed, trim, and other aspects.

9. Share your slow-motion film with friends and family if you're happy with it. Select the sharing platform or method (typically indicated by an upward-pointing arrow) by tapping the share symbol. You can share the file over iMessage, share it on social media, or save it to your iCloud Drive.

How to share photos and videos

Using the iPhone 15 Series Camera app, sharing images and videos can be done easily. Your friends and family may simply get your recorded moments through email, social media, or iMessage, among other means.

Here's how to do so:

1. **Capture the Video or Photo**:
- Launch your iPhone 15 Series **Camera app**.

- The shutter button (white circle) on the screen may be tapped, or you can use the physical volume buttons to snap a picture.
- To begin recording a video, press and hold the **red record button**; to end recording, touch the button once more.

2. **View your Captured Media**:

- You can see a picture or video that you have taken by pressing the little thumbnail icon in the Camera app's lower left corner.

3. **Sharing Pictures and Videos**:

Through Text Message or iMessage:

- On your iPhone, launch the **Photos app**.
- Locate the image or video that you want to share.
- To open, tap on it.
- Press the **share button**, which is a square in the lower left corner with an upward-pointing arrow.
- Type in the phone number of the person you want to send it to or choose them.

- If you see a blue bubble with an upward-pointing arrow, tap the send button.

Through Email:

- Launch the **Photos app**.
- Find the image or video that you want to share or send.
- To open, tap on it.
- Press the share button, which is a square in the lower left corner with an upward-pointing arrow.
- From the list of sharing choices, choose the **Mail app**.
- Write your email, including any message you want to include, the recipient's email address, and the subject line.
- In the email composition box, tap the **send button**.

Through social media:

- First of all, launch the **Photos app**.
- Locate the image or video that you want to share.
- To open, tap on it.
- Press the share button, which is a square in the lower left corner with an upward-pointing arrow.
- Select the social networking app (such as Facebook, Instagram, or Twitter) that you want to share to.
- To personalize your post and share it with your followers, adhere to the instructions.

Using AirDrop:

- Launch the **Photos app**.
- Find the image or video that you want to share.
- To open, tap on it.
- Tap the share button, which is a square in the bottom left corner with an upward-pointing arrow.
- Choose the device that is closest to you to transmit it to via AirDrop.

Basic Camera settings

They include the following:

1. **Camera App:** Swiping right from the lock screen or touching the camera symbol on your home screen will launch the Camera app on your iPhone 15 series.
2. **Photo Mode:** This is the default option that you will often start in. This is the setting for taking regular still images.
3. **Zoom:** Adjust the zoom level by either touching the "1x" or "2x" buttons on the camera interface or by using the pinch-to-zoom motion.
4. **Flash:** The lightning bolt symbol on the screen can be tapped to adjust the flash. Options such as Auto, on, and off are available for selection.
5. **HDR (High Dynamic Range):** In difficult lighting situations, HDR enables you to take pictures with superior exposure. Even though it's usually set to **"Auto,"** you can manually turn it on or off.
6. **Live Photos:** This function records your snapshot and a little video clip. You can use the concentric circle symbol to turn on or off Live Photos.
7. **Timer:** To start a countdown before the camera snaps a photo, use the timer icon. Timer options usually consist of 3 and 10 seconds.
8. **Filters:** By pressing the symbol with the three overlapping circles, you can instantly add filters to your images. To choose from a variety of filter choices, swipe left or right.
9. **Exposure Control:** After focusing your shot with a press on the screen, manually change the exposure (brightness) by swiping up or down.
10. **Portrait Mode:** The bokeh effect, or blurred background effect, is achieved in images taken in portrait mode. To get the best results, swipe to activate this mode and then follow the on-screen directions.
11. **Panorama:** To take wide-angle, panoramic pictures, swipe to the Panorama mode. Use the screen's arrow to direct your panning movements.
12. **Video Mode:** To record video, swipe to the Video mode. In the options, you can change the frame rate and video resolution.
13. **Slo-Mo:** Swipe to enter the slow-motion video recording mode. In the options, you may choose the recording speed (such as 120 or 240 frames per second).

14. **Time-Lapse:** To record a time-lapse movie, swipe to the Time-Lapse mode. The camera will record a sped-up movie by taking pictures at regular intervals.

15. **Night Mode:** Using the night mode improves your low-light photos. In low light, it often turns on automatically, but you can also manually adjust how bright it becomes.

Frequently Asked Questions

1. How do you launch and use the Camera app?
2. How do you enter into live mode?
3. How do you change between the rear and front cameras?
4. How do you edit images?
5. How do you apply filters?
6. How do you take panorama, portrait, and record slo-mo videos?
7. How do you share photos and videos?

CHAPTER NINE
USING THE CALENDAR APP

Overview

The calendar app is another important built-in application in the iPhone 15 Series that allows you to view the dates and weeks of different years and months. Learn all there is to know about using the calendar app in this chapter.

Downloading the iPhone Calendar App

Your iPhone 15 Series should arrive with the iPhone Calendar app installed. It is located on your home screen.

Don't worry if it was removed for whatever reason! By going to the App Store, you can reinstall it on your phone.

Here are the steps:

1. On your iPhone's home screen, tap the **App Store icon**.
2. In the search box, type "**calendar**."
3. Tap "**Get**" after swiping down until you reach the Calendar icon. It will indicate "**Open**" if it is already installed on your phone. To launch the app on your phone, just touch that.)

The App Store has a wide selection of calendar applications. Verify that you are installing the calendar app for your iPhone. A white symbol with black numerals and red text should be on it.

iPhone Calendar App Views and Icons

The five perspectives available inside the iPhone Calendar app are among its many wonderful features. It's simple to switch between viewpoints whether you want to gaze forward many months or just a week. Using the different calendar views might be compared to zooming in and out. To see the full year, zoom out. To see the schedule for a specific day, you can zoom in.

1. **List View**

To see an organized schedule of your appointments and activities.

- Always start by touching the iPhone Calendar icon on your home screen to browse the various calendar views.
- To see a month, tap on it.
- Select the day you want to view.
- Press the list icon located at the screen's top. It has three lines and three dots.

This is the app's list view. It's simple to see what you have planned for the day thanks to this.

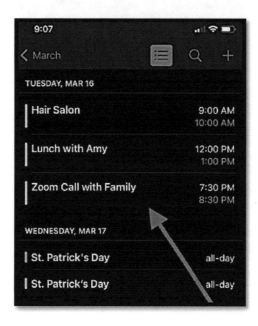

2. **Daily View**

When it's useful: To see the items on your daily agenda.

- In the app, tap the month you want to see.

- To view a certain day, tap it.

Today's perspective is as follows. What's scheduled for the day is visible to you hour by hour.

3. **Weekly View**

When it's useful: To review your week and determine your busy and spare times.

To fully use the weekly view on your iPhone, be sure you tilt it horizontally. To do this, open the Control Center and make sure the lock on your portrait orientation is off.

- Swipe down from the top-right corner of your screen to access the Control Center.
- Press the lock button that has an arrow around it. After you touch it, confirm that it reads **"Portrait Orientation Lock: Off."**
- Tap the screen or slide up from the bottom to shut the Control Center. You're now prepared to see the weekly view! To begin, hit the calendar icon located on the home screen of your iPhone.
- To display a certain month, tap it.
- To display a certain week, tap it.

You can see the complete week when you turn your phone horizontally. You can also swipe left to see the week that's coming up or right to see the week that's coming up.

4. **Monthly View**

When it's useful: To see your monthly obligations and forthcoming holidays.

- To see a month, tap on it inside the app.
- Press the top-level list view.
- On a given day of the month, a gray dot indicates that there is an event to be seen. Keep in mind that a few of these are preset events.
- To get a list of the events for each day, tap.

5. **Yearly View**

It's useful for swiftly paging through the months. It's easy to find out what day of the week your birthday or Christmas falls on this year.

- The software allows you to see years in the past or future by swiping up and down.

For the record:

The iPhone Calendar app comes preloaded with the main holidays and observances in the United States. Thus, all you have to do is check your iPhone Calendar to find out when a holiday is approaching.

How to Create an Event

The steps:

1. Tap the red + symbol located in the upper-right corner of the iPhone Calendar app.

2. Tap the box at the top to enter the event's title. This can be an event, meeting, appointment, etc. By tapping "**Location**," you can even enter the address if you'd like. To adjust the start time, choose "**Starts**" next.
3. Enter the start time by typing the digits on the keyboard.

4. After you're done, choose **"Ends"** from the menu if you want to add an end time. Enter the end time by typing on your keyboard.

5. Scroll down to **"Alert"** and press it.

6. This is where you configure the app to remind you of the event at a certain time. This implies that a sound will be heard on your phone to notify you of the impending event.

7. Finally, choose **"Add."**
8. The event ought to now appear on your calendar.

How to Edit an Event

The steps:

1. Tap the event you want to change in your calendar app.
2. Select **"Edit"** from the left upper corner.
3. From this point on, you may modify the event's time, title, location, and alerts. Remember to hit **"Done"** in the upper-right corner to save your modifications!
4. After modifying, tap Done to save your changes.

How to Delete an Event

The steps:

1. In the Calendar app, tap the event that you want to remove.
2. Press the **"Delete"** button at the bottom of the display.
3. Next, choose **"Delete Event."**

How to Search for an Event

The steps:

1. Open the **iPhone Calendar app** and tap the magnifying glass button at the top.
2. Type the title of the event into the search field to find it.
3. Based on the term you provide, it will display all of your relevant appointments from the past and present.
4. To see or change the event's information, tap it.

View and Manage Calendars

The instructions below can be used to access and control the Calendar app on the iPhone 15 Series:

Viewing the Calendar

1. From your iPhone's home screen, find the Calendar app icon. Iconically, it resembles a plain calendar with a date on it.
2. To launch the Calendar app, tap its icon. It will show the current month by default.
3. Swipe left or right to flip between months, and then tap a date to see what's happening on that day.
4. There are many view options, including **"Day," "Week," "Month," and "Year,"** at the bottom of the screen. You can adjust the calendar display according to your preferences by tapping on them.

Managing Events

1. **Adding Events**:
- Press the **"+"** button in the upper-right corner of the screen to create a new event.
- Complete the event information, including the name, location, time, and date.
- You can also choose which calendar to add the event to, if you have numerous, and configure notifications.
2. **Editing Events**:
- To make changes to an already-confirmed event, just touch on it.
- To modify the event information, use the **"Edit"** button.
3. **Deleting Events**:
- Tap on an event to see its information and remove it.
- At the bottom, choose **"Delete Event"** by scrolling down.
4. **Sharing Events**:

- Upon hitting the event and using the "**Add Invitees**" option, you can share it with additional people.
- Invitations may be sent by email or message, and recipients can mark the occasion on their calendars.

5. **Enabling iCloud and External Calendar Sync**:
- Verify that iCloud synchronization is turned on in **Settings > [your name] > iCloud > Calendars** to guarantee that your calendar is synchronized with all of your devices.
- To add more calendar services (like Google Calendar), go to **Settings > Passwords & Accounts > Add Account**, and then choose the appropriate service.

6. **Setting Reminders**:
- In the Calendar app, you can create reminders by touching the "**+**" button, choosing "**Reminder**," and entering the necessary information.

7. **Search for Events**:
- Use the Calendar app's search box at the top to locate certain events. Enter keywords, and the app will display events that match.

8. **Viewing Several Calendars**:
- In the Calendar app, press "**Calendars**" in the bottom center of the screen to flip between your different calendars (e.g., work and personal).

9. **Adjust Calendar Preferences**:
- Select **Settings > Calendar** to personalize your calendar's settings. This is where you change settings for things like the default calendar, support for different time zones, and notifications.

How to Use Siri to Create Events

Siri can set up appointments in your calendar using only your voice if you'd rather avoid typing and tapping and save some time. It is comparable to having a personal assistant.

1. Hold down the Power button to bring up Siri. You might also just say, "Hey, Siri." A colorful sphere will show up at the bottom of your iPhone's screen. This indicates that Siri is waiting for your instructions.

2. Make a plan to get coffee with William at 7 a.m. tomorrow. Siri will plan (enter your event, place, date, and time here!).
3. To add it to your calendar, you'll next need to speak or press "**Confirm**."

Frequently Asked Questions

1. How do you use the calendar app?
2. How do you use Siri to create events?
3. How do you view calendars?
4. How do you manage calendars?
5. How do you delete an event?

CHAPTER TEN
NOTES APP

Overview

Chapter 10 talks about the Notes app found on the home screen of the iPhone 15 Series. It allows you to pen down a to-do list or things you want to do at a particular point in time.

How to Access the Notes app

On your iPhone 15 Series, opening the Notes app is an easy and clear procedure.

Here's how to access the Notes app:

Using the Home Screen

1. First, unlock your iPhone 15 Series by using Face ID or entering your passcode.
2. Locate the **"Notes"** app icon once you're on the home screen. Usually, it resembles a yellow notepad with a white pen on it.

3. Hit the "**Notes**" application icon. You can then read, add, or modify your notes in the Notes app that opens.

Using Siri

1. Saying "**Hey Siri**" or pressing the side button will activate Siri.
2. You can say things like "**Open the Notes app**" or "**Launch Notes**" after Siri has started to listen.
3. Siri will launch the Notes app for you.

Using Spotlight Search

1. To reach the Spotlight Search bar, swipe down from the center of your home screen.
2. Enter "**Notes**" into the search field, and then check the search results for the "**Notes**" app.
3. To launch the Notes app, tap the "**Notes**" app icon in the search results.

Using Control Center

1. To access the Control Center, slide down from the upper right corner of your iPhone, or swipe up from the lower part if your iPhone is older.
2. You can find the search bar at the top of the Control Center. Press "**Notes**" in the search field.
3. To launch the Notes app, tap the "**Notes**" app icon in the search results.

Using whatever way you like, you can easily access and manage your notes, create new ones, and maintain organization on your iPhone 15 Series thanks to the Notes app.

How to create a new note

Using the Notes app on an iPhone from the 15 Series, you can do the following actions to create a new note:

1. First of all, unlock your iPhone. You can do this by entering your password or using Face ID.

2. To discover the "**Notes**" app, either slide left on the home screen or use the search function. It has a symbol that resembles a white pen on a yellow notepad.

3. Click the "**Notes**" app icon to launch the Notes app.

4. **Create a New Note**:

- You'll see a list of your previous notes if you're using the default view. There is a circular button with a pencil icon in the bottom-right corner. To add a new note, tap on it.

- As an alternative, you can hit the back arrow (often in the top-left corner) to go back to the main Notes screen and then tap the circular pencil symbol if you are in a particular folder or have a note open.

5. **Write Your First Note**: The screen will display a blank note. You may use the on-screen keyboard to begin entering your message.

6. **Formatting and Options**:
- The formatting toolbar located above the keyboard can be used to format your writing. This lets you add headers, bullet points, numbers, and more, as well as alter the text style.
- The toolbar's icons can be used to include checklists, drawings, and photos in your notes.

7. As you type, your note is automatically stored. It does not need you to save manually.

8. **Organize your Notes**:

● In the Notes screen, touch "**New Folder**" to create a folder to help you manage your notes.

● It is also possible to work together on a note with others by using the "**Add People**" option.

● The search box at the top of the primary Notes screen makes it simple to find notes later.

9. To close and return to the list of notes after finishing the creation or modification of your note, just click the back arrow in the upper-left corner.

10. If you're logged in with the same Apple ID, your notes should sync across all of your Apple devices, including additional iPhones, iPads, and Macs. You can view your notes on any of these devices by launching the Notes app.

How to type and format your note

Here's how to type and format your note:

1. Use Face ID or input your password to unlock your iPhone 15 Series.

2. On your home screen, find the "**Notes**" app. It appears as a yellow symbol with a white notepad.

3. Open the "**Notes**" app by tapping on it.

4. If you have any existing notes, you will see a list of them within the Notes app. The "**+**" (plus) button is often found in the top right or bottom left corner. Tapping it will open a new note. This will open a blank note. You may use the on-screen keyboard to begin entering your message. All you need to do is touch the spot where you want to start typing.

5. To format text, select it by touching and holding it until it is highlighted.

6. The chosen text will have a menu with many formatting options displayed above it. In this case, you can:

● **Bold**: To make the text bold, tap the "**B**" symbol.

● **Italics**: To make text italic, tap the "**I**" symbol.

● **Underline**: To make the text underlined, tap the "**U**" symbol.

- **Font Color**: To adjust the font color, tap the "**A**" symbol.
- **Highlight**: To give the chosen text a background color, tap the highlighter symbol.
- **Font Size:** To adjust the font size, hit the "**Aa**" symbol and choose a size from the available possibilities.

7. Create Lists Type your list items and they will be formatted as a list automatically. To make a list, hit the "**Aa**" button in the formatting menu (next to the font size choice) and choose "**Bulleted**" or "**Numbered List**."
8. Insert photos from your device by tapping the "**+**" button above the keyboard and choosing "**Take Photo or Video**" or "**Photo Library**" to attach images.
9. To save your note when you've completed entering and formatting it, touch the "**Done**" button located in the upper left corner.
10. Reorganize your notes by moving them into folders and creating new ones by touching the "**Back**" button in the Notes app's upper left corner and choosing "**New Folder**."
11. Your iPhone's notes immediately sync with iCloud, allowing you to access them on other Apple devices—like an iPad or Mac—that are logged in with the same Apple ID.

How to add media to your note

With the Notes app on your iPhone 15 Series, you can generally take the following actions to add media (such as pictures, videos, drawings, or scanned documents) to your notes:

1. On your iPhone, find and open the **Notes app**.
2. You have the option of either selecting an existing note to edit or creating a new note by touching the "**+**" button.
3. Locate and tap the addition symbol (+) in the message by looking for it. Usually, you use this symbol to add text to your message.
4. Tap the plus icon (+) to bring up the options menu.
5. When you choose **Media**, your iPhone's media gallery or picture library will open. You can then peruse and choose the images, movies, drawings, or scanned papers you like to include in your letter.

6. If necessary, add subtitles or descriptions to the media after choosing it. Additionally, you can resize or rearrange the media within the memo.

7. To save the note with the media included, touch **"Done"** or **"Save"** once you've added the media and made any required adjustments.
8. To avoid data loss, make sure your notes are backed up and synchronized to iCloud or another chosen backup solution.

How to sort notes

Organizing notes on the iPhone Notes app:

1. Tap the **"Notes"** app icon on the home screen of your iPhone to launch the app.
2. A list of your notes will appear once you're in the Notes app. To see your notes, you can tap on a certain folder or account (such as iCloud or On My iPhone).
3. Tap on the note that you want to arrange or categorize. The chosen note will open as a result.
4. To enter edit mode if you haven't previously, hit the **"Edit"** button or the pencil icon in the note's upper right corner. You will then be able to edit the note.
5. Press and hold a note to drag it to the correct location in the list if you want to manually arrange your notes. This allows you to reorganize notes within a folder or account.
6. The Notes app allows you to create folders if you want to group your notes into folders. To do this, return to the main notes list by selecting "\ Notes" in the upper left corner. Next, choose **"New Folder,"** give it a name, and begin transferring notes into it.
7. To get back to the main notes list and sort notes by date, hit the **"Notes"** button in the upper left corner. Next, choose **"Sort By"** from the menu at the top. Notes can be sorted either ascending or descending depending on when they were produced or changed.
8. Use the search box located at the top of the main notes list if you have a lot of notes and need to locate anything fast. Notes just have to be typed in to see results that match the entered keyword.

How to view attachments in notes

The typical steps to see attachments in notes on an iPhone using the Notes app are as follows:

1. Firstly, unlock your iPhone with your Face ID or a password.
2. On your home screen, look for the Notes app icon. Usually, it resembles a yellow notepad with a white pencil emblem on it.
3. The Notes app can be opened by tapping on its icon.
4. A list of your notes will appear once you're in the Notes app. To see the attachment, tap the message containing it.
5. Tap on any attachments to view or interact with them if there are any included with the message. Documents, drawings, pictures, and other file formats may all be attached. To open and see the attachment, tap on it.
6. Take different actions with different kinds of attachments. If it's a picture, for instance, you may share it, modify it, and zoom in or out. If it's a document, you can share it or open it using an app that works with it.
7. Look for options like the **share button**, which is often represented as a square with an upward arrow, or the save/download option if you want to save or share the attachment.
8. Generally, you can use the back arrow or close button, which is found in the upper-left corner of the screen, to go back to your message.

How to organize and search notes

The notes app has several features to assist you in keeping your notes accessible and well-organized.

Here's how to do so:

1. To access the **Notes app**, find its icon on the home screen of your iPhone and touch it.
2. Press the "**Compose**" button in the lower right corner of the screen to start a new note. If you are using the list view, you may also touch the "**+**" symbol.
3. **Organize Notes:**

To arrange your notes, you can create folders. To carry out this:

- To access the Notes screen's primary navigation, tap the "**Back**" button located in the upper-left corner.
- In the upper-left corner, tap the "**Edit**" button.
- Press "**New Folder**."
- After naming your folder, choose "**Save**."
4. **Organize Notes into Folders**:

Transferring a note to a folder:

- Touch the note you would like to move.
- At the top of the screen, there is a square with an arrow pointing up. Tap this symbol to share content.
- To transfer the note, choose "Move to Folder" and choose the desired folder.
5. **Search for Notes**:
- To access the search bar, swipe down from the center of the Notes app's screen.
- Enter the search term. As you type, the app will show you relevant results.
6. **Use Tags (Optional):**
- To make your notes more accessible, you can also tag them.
- After making changes to a note, hit the **share button**.
- Select "**Add Tags**" and type in pertinent keywords.
- Using these tags, you can then look for notes.
7. **Sort Notes**:
- You have the option to arrange your notes by title, date created, or date changed.
- Go back to the Notes screen's main screen.
- Press the "**Options**" button (three circles surrounded by horizontal lines) in the upper-left corner.
- Decide on the sorting strategy you like most.
8. **Lock Notes (Optional):**

Use Face ID or a password to secure individual notes for extra privacy.

- Launch the note that you want to lock.
- Press the sharing icon.

- Press "**Lock Note**" to configure your security settings.
9. **Collaborate on Notes (Optional):**

If you'd want to work on a letter with someone else:

- Open the letter that you want to share.
- Press the sharing icon.
- Select the note's distribution method (e.g., email or Messages).
10. Go to the "**Recently Deleted**" folder, pick the note, and hit "**Recover.**" To remove a note, swipe left on it and tap "**Delete.**"

How to view notes in folders

Here's how to use your iPhone 15 series' Notes app to read notes within folders:

1. To launch the Notes app, locate its icon on the home screen of your iPhone and press it.
2. The primary screen of the Notes app usually displays a list of your notes or folders. You may need to press "**Notes**" in the upper-left corner or "**Back**" to see the main folder view if you don't see folders right away.
3. Tap the folder you want to see the notes in. When the folder opens, you'll get a list of notes included in that particular folder.
4. To see notes, tap the particular note that you want to view. Depending on your requirements, you can read the note's contents, make changes, or take other actions after it opens.

5. Tap the "**Back**" button located in the upper-left corner of the screen to go back to the folder view. You can use the same way to navigate and choose additional notes in the folder or to switch to other directories.

6. Use the search box at the top of the Notes app to locate a particular note if you have a lot of it and need to locate it. To find the note fast, just enter keywords or the title of the note.

How to create a smart folder

To create a folder on your iPhone's Notes app:

1. Open the Notes app by tapping on it after finding it on your home screen.

2. If you don't currently have notes in your Notes app, you can skip this step and create a new note if necessary. If not, hit the "**+ New Note**" button located in the lower right corner of the screen to start a new note. Put a heading in your letter.

3. Press "**Done**" to save the updated note.

4. To access the main Notes screen, tap the back arrow located in the upper-left corner of the screen.

5. Your notes should be listed on the Notes screen. Tap "**Folders**." You should see a "**Back**" button and "**Folders**" in the upper-left corner.

6. The "**+**" button or "**New Folder**" option, which is often found at the bottom of the folder list, can be tapped to create a new folder.

7. Give your folder a name. Give it a name that corresponds with the kind of notes you want to keep in it.

8. Begin arranging your notes after the folder has been created. If you tap on a note, it opens. Next, press the share icon, which is often a box with an upward-pointing arrow. Select "**Move to Folder**" from the sharing menu, then picks the newly created folder.

9. You've just arranged your notes within a folder that you made in the Notes app. Return to the Notes page and touch the newly created folder to open your smart folder.

How to share and collaborate on your note

Using the Notes app on the iPhone 15 Series to collaborate and exchange notes is a practical method to share information with friends and coworkers or work on projects together.

1. Locate the **"Notes"** app on your home screen after unlocking your iPhone. To launch the app, tap on it.

2. Tap the **"+ New Note"** button to start a new note that may be worked on collaboratively. You can skip this step if you already have a message that you would want to share.

3. Write your note or open the draft that you want to work on together. To your message, you may text; attach images, drawings, and more.

4. Tap the share icon to share your message. Depending on your device's settings, it usually appears as a box with an arrow pointing up at the top of your screen or in the bottom toolbar.

5. **A selection of sharing options for the note will now appear. Here are a few typical sharing techniques:**

- **Message**: One or more contacts may receive the note as an iMessage.
- **Email**: Attach the message to an email.
- Use **AirDrop** to share the note with Apple devices that are in close proximity.
- **Add People**: This feature enables you to work with other people on the note. Choose it if you want to work together in real time and share the letter with certain people.

6. You can ask other people to work with you on the note if you select the **"Add People"** option. If you would like, provide a note along with their phone numbers or email addresses. An invitation to see and update the letter will be sent to them.

7. You can provide collaborators the ability to modify the note or just see it. By pressing the **"Add People"** button once again, you may modify these preferences whenever you'd like.

8. Your colleagues may see the note by launching the Notes application and selecting the **"Shared with You"** folder once you've shared it. They may read

and modify the note in real-time here, which makes it an effective tool for exchanging information or working on projects together.

9. You'll be notified when there are revisions to the note by collaborators. To ensure continued productive cooperation, you may examine these modifications and take appropriate action.

How to delete or archive notes

On your iPhone 15 Series, to remove or archive notes in the Notes app:

1. On the home screen of your iPhone, find the Notes app and press it to launch it.
2. A list of your notes will appear once you're in the Notes app. To remove or archive a note, tap the folder or account that contains it. If you have numerous accounts, this may be "**Notes**" for iCloud notes or a particular account.
3. Press on the note you want to open or remove from the archive.
4. **Delete a Note**:
- Tap the **trash can icon**, which is often found at the top or bottom of the note display, to remove a note. The note will be moved to the "**Recently Deleted**" folder as a result.
- Locate the note in the "Recently Deleted" folder, and choose "**Delete All**" or "**Delete [Note Name]**" to completely remove it.

5. **Archive a Note**:
- To archive a note, touch the share symbol in the note's upper-right corner, which is often shown as a box with an arrow going up.
- Under Sharing, choose "**Archive**." This will transfer the note to the archive part of the "**Notes**" folder.

6. **Access Archived Notes**:
- Return to the main note list to see archived notes.
- An "**Archive**" folder or a comparable choice could be visible to you. For access to your stored notes, tap on it.

Frequently Asked Questions

1. How do you access the Notes app on your iPhone 15 Series?
2. How do you create a new note?
3. How do you view notes in folders and attachments?
4. How do you add media to your note?
5. How do you organize and search notes?
6. How do you sort notes?

CHAPTER ELEVEN
MAPS APP

Overview

The maps app allows you to view your current location and gives you the function of locating another far away distance so that you won't get lost. Chapter eleven talks about how you can fully explore the maps app on your iPhone 15 Series.

How to access the maps app

Take these actions to open the Maps app on your iPhone 15 Series:

1. First of all, unlock your iPhone by entering the passcode or by using Face ID.
2. Find the Maps app icon from your home screen. Usually, it has a red location pin on a map icon.
3. To launch the Maps app, just give it a single press on the icon.
4. When you use the Maps app for the first time, it can request permission to access your location. Depending on your preferences, you can decide whether to provide access when using the app or at all times.
5. After the app opens, you can explore and make use of its many capabilities, which include location search, directions, traffic monitoring, and more.
6. Hit the search box at the top of the screen, type the address, location, or phrase you're searching for, and then hit the search button (often a magnifying glass symbol) to find the location.
7. Choose between driving, walking, or public transportation instructions when you input your location in the search field, touch it when it shows up in the search results, and then press "**Directions.**"
8. Tap the location icon (often a blue dot) in the lower-left corner to view your current position on a map. This will make your present location the center of the map.
9. The Maps app has several features, including satellite view, 3D mapping, and the capacity to save favorite places. Tap on various menu items and app icons to explore these possibilities.

10. Return to the home screen by swiping up from the bottom of the screen after you're done using the Maps app.

How to get your current location

Using the Maps app on the iPhone 15 Series, do the following actions to get your present location:

1. If your iPhone is locked, you can use Face ID or your password to unlock it.
2. To reach your home screen, slide up from the bottom of the screen.
3. Locate the Maps app icon on your home screen to find the Maps app. usually, it has an arrow pointing to a spot on a map.
4. To start the Maps app, just press and hold the icon.
5. You'll be requested to give location access if you're using the Maps app for the first time or if you haven't permitted it to access your location. Take care to choose **"Always Allow"** or **"Allow While Using App"** to activate location services.
6. Using GPS and other location services, the Maps app will need some time to pinpoint your exact position. Once it's identified, you'll see a blue dot on the map that represents your position.

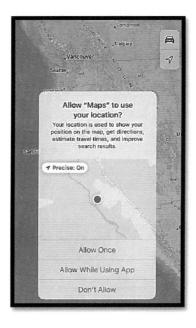

7. Your current location should now be shown on a map, indicated by a blue dot. To get a better perspective, you may zoom in or out of the map. You can also use the Maps app's capabilities to identify local locations and get directions.

8. Tapping the blue dot will reveal choices to share your location with contacts or via applications like Email or Messages if you would want to let someone know where you are right now.

9. To discover particular destinations, get directions, or look up neighboring points of interest, use the search box at the top of the Maps app.

How to search for a location

Using the Maps app on an iPhone 15 Series is a simple way to find a place.

The steps:

1. If your iPhone hasn't been unlocked before, start by doing so. You can enter your passcode or use Face ID to do this.

2. The Maps app can be accessed by locating its symbol on your home screen, which resembles a map with a red location pin. To launch the app, tap on it.

3. If you haven't given the Maps app location access, you may be asked to do so the first time you use it. To get accurate results, let the app access your location.

4. The Maps app has a search bar at the top. To open the search box, tap on it.

5. Type the name of the place, address, or attraction you're looking for using the on-screen keyboard. The Maps app will provide recommendations as you write, depending on the data you've supplied.

6. Tap the appropriate place when you see it listed in the search results to make it your destination. The selected place will then be magnified on the map.

7. Tap the "**Directions**" button at the bottom of the screen to get instructions to this place. If your beginning place hasn't been identified by the app, it will ask you to do so before giving you turn-by-turn instructions.

8. Swipe to pan around, pinch to enlarge or reduce the size of the image, and press any point on the map to get additional details. Additionally, you can use the "**Search Nearby**" function to locate eateries, petrol stations, lodging facilities, and other attractions close to the place you've chosen.

9. Tapping on the name or marker on the map will bring you more choices if you want to save this location for later or share it with someone else. It may be added to a collection, shared using Messages or other applications, or saved to your favorites.

10. Press the "**Start**" button in the Directions pane when you're prepared to go to the chosen place. You can get detailed directions for navigating using the Maps app.

How to view search results

To display search results on the iPhone Maps app, follow these basic steps:

1. Firstly, proceed by unlocking your iPhone by using Face ID or your passcode.

2. To open the Maps app, find it on your home screen. A symbol with a map and a location pin serves as its representation.

3. Press and hold the map app's icon to bring it up.

4. **Search for Location**:

- There's usually a search

- Type in the name of the place, address, or item of interest you want to look up. You should see recommendations as you write.

- Click "**Search**" on the keyboard or tap the suggestion that corresponds with your search term.

5. **View Search Results**:
- The Maps app will show you a list of search results on the screen once you've typed your query.
- In general, the locations, companies, and attractions associated with your search query will be included in these search results.

6. **Choose a Result**:
- Use the list's scroll feature to look through the search results.
- Tap on the location or area you want to see when you've located it. This will cause the location's information to open.

7. **Explore Details**:
- Following your selection of a result, you may examine further information including the location, contact information, website, reviews, images, and more.
- Tapping the "**Directions**" button will also provide instructions to the chosen destination.

8. **View on Map**:
- If available, touch the "**View on Map**" button or the map preview to display the location on a map. This will put a marker at the spot on the map.

9. **Zoom and Interact with the Map**:
- You can zoom in and out on the map using the typical pinch-to-zoom motions.
- To explore the environment, you can also swipe and pan.

How to get directions

Here are the steps to get directions:

1. Ensure you unlock your device by using Face ID or your passcode.
2. On your iPhone, look for the **Maps app icon** (typically a map with a location marker) on the home screen. To launch the app, tap on it.
3. One of the screen's main features is a search bar. Press and hold it to begin inputting the destination's name or address. Suggestions will show up below as you write. If one of these recommendations corresponds with your destination, you may touch on it.

4. Once you input your destination, a map with many possible routes will appear in Maps. You have the choice of driving, walking, or using public transit. Choose the one that best fits your requirements by swiping through it and tapping on it.

5. After you've decided on your favorite path, press the **"Start"** button, which is usually indicated by a blue arrow. Turn-by-turn navigation will then start, and while you go, your iPhone will give you voice directions and on-screen instructions.
6. Your iPhone will navigate every curve and give you an estimated time of arrival whether you are driving or walking. Along with your path, a map will also be

shown to you on the screen. If you follow the instructions exactly, Maps will automatically redirect you if you miss a turn or need to make adjustments.

7. The Maps app will notify you when you've arrived at your location. To end the navigation session, you can then touch the "**End**" button.

Tips:

- By touching on the settings symbol (sometimes shown as a gear or three lines) while navigating, you can change settings including speech volume, preferred routes, and avoidances.
- Tap the arrow symbol in the bottom left corner of the screen to display an overview of your complete trip, or you can pinch to zoom out on the map.
- Hit the search box and type in your query if you need to identify local places of interest (restaurants, petrol stations, etc.) or make stops along the route.

How to choose a transportation mode

Follow the steps below using the iPhone Maps app to choose a method of transportation:

1. Since the Maps app depends on data, start by unlocking your iPhone and making sure you have a functional internet connection.
2. To open the Maps app, find its icon on the home screen of your iPhone. It seems to be a map with a place marking on it.
3. **Search for your Destination**:
- Touch the top search bar on the screen.
- The destination's name or address should be entered. Landmarks and other well-known locations may also be used as search phrases.
4. Tap the location you want to go to from the search results. This will cause the place to appear on a map.
5. Press the "**Directions**" button at the bottom of the screen, which often has an arrow or an automobile symbol. The instructions choices will then appear.
6. **Choose your Mode of Transportation**:
- You will see symbols for many modes of transportation, including automobile, pedestrian, cycling, and public transportation, in the instructions selections.

- Press the option that best fits your demands when it comes to transportation. For instance, press the automobile symbol if you're operating a vehicle.

7. You may have to manually input your current location if the program doesn't recognize it as the starting point automatically.

8. **Examine and Launch the Navigation**:

- The route that the Maps app shows you depends on the method of transportation that you have chosen. You'll see an estimated trip time and distance.

- Initiate navigation by tapping "**Start**" or "**Go**". Voice advice and turn-by-turn instructions will be available via the app.

9. **Optional Features**:

- Depending on your preferences, you can also change your route by excluding roads, ferries, or fees and adding waypoints instead.

- Enabling elements such as satellite view and traffic information will provide you with a more thorough navigating experience.

10. To get to your location, adhere to the voice-guided and on-screen instructions.

How to begin navigation

The methods below can be used to start using the Maps app on the iPhone 15 Series for navigation:

1. Before you proceed to start navigation, you need to unlock your device using your passcode or Face ID.
2. To open the Maps app, find its icon on your home screen. Imagine a map with a location pin on it. To launch the app, tap on it.
3. You could be asked to allow the Maps app access to your location if you haven't previously. To ensure precise navigation, make sure the app has location services enabled.
4. **Search for your Destination**:
- Enter the name or address of your destination in the search box located at the top of the Maps app. You'll get ideas that correspond with your input as you write.
- Select the option that corresponds to your intended location. The destination marker will then appear when the map zooms in on the specific spot.
5. **Get Directions**:
- After deciding where to go, press the **"Directions"** button, which is often found at the bottom of the screen. It seems to be an arrow.
- The optimal path to your location will be determined by the Maps app and shown on the map. Also, information like the distance, several route alternatives, and expected time of arrival (ETA) will be shown.
6. **Launch the navigation**:
- Press the **"Start"** button to begin turn-by-turn navigation. Voice-guided instructions may be obtained from your iPhone, and the map will display both your present position and the path to your intended destination.

- During navigation, you can also change settings like notifications and speech volume by pressing on the speaker icon.

7. To navigate to your location, heed the voice and on-screen directions. In addition to turn-by-turn instructions, traffic updates, and alternative routes if needed, the app will provide real-time assistance.

8. Tap the "**End**" button on the screen to stop navigation when you get to your location.

9. You will see other routes, avoid tolls, and get more trip information by tapping on the search symbol or ETA information while traveling.

10. If you would rather navigate without using your hands, you can speak to Siri by saying "**Hey Siri**" if it is enabled or by pushing the side button if your iPhone has this capability. After that, you can ask Siri to lead you to your destination or to give you directions to a certain place.

How to zoom in and out on the map

The fundamental instructions for using the iPhone Maps app to zoom in and out of a map are as follows:

1. Locate the **Maps app icon** on your iPhone's home screen, and then press it to launch the application.

2. Enter the address you want to see on the map using the search box at the top of the screen. An address, landmark, or place of interest can be typed in.

3. To view the map after entering the desired location, touch the search result or use the "**Search**" key on the keyboard.

4. **You can use one of the following techniques to enlarge a portion of the map:**

- **Pinch Gesture**: Press two fingers together on the screen, preferably your thumb and index finger, and then release them. By doing this, you can enlarge and enhance the shown region of the map with greater information.

- **Double-Tap**: To enlarge a screen, double-tap with one finger. You can zoom in even further by double-tapping again.

5. **Zoom Out**: Use one of the following techniques to enlarge the map:

- **Pinch Gesture**: Start with two fingers apart from one another on the screen, then move them closer together. By doing this, the map will zoom out and display a bigger, less detailed region.
- **Double Tapping with Two Fingers**: To zoom out, double-touch the screen with two fingers. You can zoom out even more by double-tapping again.

6. Use your finger to swipe across the screen to explore the map after zooming in or out to the appropriate degree. For further information, you can also touch on certain locations of interest or use the search box.

How to rotate the map

Use the following procedures to rotate the map on an iPhone 15 Series using the Maps app:

1. To open the Maps app, first activate your iPhone and then hit the "**Maps**" app icon, which appears on your home screen and resembles a map marker.
2. Enter the address you want to see on the map using the search box at the top of the screen. You can enter a city name alone, an address, or even a landmark.
3. The map will zoom in and show the place you've selected by tapping on it. This will put you in the "**North Up**" position by default, with the map centered at the top of the screen.
4. **Rotate the Map**:
- Touch the screen with two fingers to rotate the map.
- Using those two fingers, spin them in either a clockwise or counterclockwise direction. The map will begin to revolve following your actions.
- Continue turning he map with your fingertips until it is aligned the way you want it.
5. You can use your two fingers to precisely adjust the rotation angle. As you move your fingers, the map will revolve in real-time.
6. Press the compass symbol in the top-right corner of the screen to lock the map's orientation and stop unintentional rotations. The map will revert to its original "**North Up**" orientation as a result.

7. When the map is in the rotatable view, you can also squeeze in or out with two fingers to increase or decrease its size. This enables you to see the area you're investigating from a closer or more expansive angle.

8. Just press the compass symbol in the upper-right corner of the map once more to bring it back to its original orientation.

How to end navigation

If you want to stop using the Maps app on your iPhone 15 Series, do the following:

1. On your home screen, search for the Maps app icon, which resembles a map with a location marker. To launch the app, tap on it.

2. Verify that you are in the midst of a navigation session by checking Navigation. You ought to see the map with your path and navigational directions if you are using GPS to go there.

3. **End Navigation**:

- **Swipe Up from the Bottom**: To reach the app switcher, swipe up from the bottom of the screen.

4. Look for the Maps app in the app switcher or frequently used applications list. It needs to show up as a card or thumbnail that symbolizes the application.

5. Tap the Maps app card and slide it up or off the screen to the left or right using the app switcher. You will now have ended your navigation session and closed the Maps app.

6. A confirmation window asking whether you'd want to finish navigation may appear. Verify your selection by selecting **"End"** or a related menu item.

7. Your iPhone's home screen will appear after the navigation has ended.

How to bookmark a map

Here's how to bookmark a map:

1. Locate the Maps app icon on your iPhone's home screen, and then press it to launch the application.
2. Type the name or address of the place you want to bookmark into the search box at the top of the Maps app. By pressing the microphone icon and saying the location, you may also use voice commands.
3. After locating the location on the map, touch it to get further information about it.
4. **Add to Bookmarks or Favorites**:

    *   If the feature is still referred to as "**Favorites**," you should see a heart-shaped symbol or an "**Add to Favorites**" option. When you tap on it, you'll be able to save the location and give it a name.
    *   If there have been any modifications, you may want to search for "**Bookmark**" or "**Save**" rather than "**Favorites**."

5. To make the bookmark simpler to find later, you may be able to give it a unique name or label.
6. To save the location to your favorites or bookmarks, confirm the information and then press the "**Save**" or "**Done**" button.
7. Generally, you can return to the Maps app, hit the "**Search**" box, and seek a section like **"Favorites," "Bookmarks," or "Saved Places"** to retrieve your bookmarked destinations in the future.

How to see the overview of your route

Use the Maps app on your iPhone 15 Series to obtain an overview of your journey by following these steps:

1. First things first, unlock your iPhone and make sure you have internet access. The Maps app needs an active data connection to function.
2. Find the Maps app icon on your home screen to open the app. It resembles a map with a direction arrow on it. To launch the app, tap on it.

3. To find your destination, tap the top search bar on the screen. You can provide the location, place name, or even a generic description such as **"coffee shop."**

4. Tap the location you want to go to when you see it in the search results.

5. A route with a blue line showing the way will appear on the map after you've chosen your location. Look for choices like **"GO"** and **"Details"** at the bottom of the screen. Tap on **"Details**."

6. A summary of your path is shown in the **"Details"** section. This contains the approximate trip time, the distance, and a detailed set of instructions. To see the whole course, just scroll through the instructions.

7. Tap the **"Route Options"** button to change your route or look at other options. Depending on your preferences, you can choose options like avoiding highways, ferries, or tolls here.

8. Press the **"GO"** button at the bottom to begin your trip. You'll start receiving turn-by-turn instructions to your location via the Maps app. The audio instructions and on-screen directions are easy to follow.

9. You can also get an overview of your path by hitting the **"Overview"** button, which is usually found in the lower left or right corner of the screen, while you are in navigation mode. This will give you a quick overview of the whole journey.

10. All you have to do is hit the **"End"** or **"X"** button on the screen to put an end to your navigation session. You will then be able to see the map again.

How to customize map settings

Use the Maps app on your iPhone to change the map settings by following these basic instructions:

1. Locate the Maps app icon on your iPhone's home screen, and then press it to launch the application.

2. The first thing you should do is use the search box at the top of the Maps app to find a place or input an address.

3. After you've chosen your location or destination, press **"Directions"** to get instructions to that address.

4. **Customize Map Settings**:

- **Type of Route**: By pressing on the respective icon, you can choose between **"Driving," "Walking," and "Transit"** as your route type.
- **Steer clear of Tolls and Highways**: Press **"Options"** (often located under the route description) and adjust the **"Tolls"** or **"Highways"** settings as necessary.
- **Turn-by-Turn speech advice:** Touch the sound icon or modify the speech preferences in the app's settings menu to activate or disable turn-by-turn voice advice.
- **Satellite View**: Tap the symbol that looks like stacked squares, which are often in the bottom left corner, to convert between the conventional map view and satellite view.
- Real-time **traffic information** is often available through the Maps app. Toggle the **"Traffic"** option by tapping the "i" button located in the upper-right corner of the app to see the current traffic conditions.
- **Location Services**: Verify in the iPhone's settings that location services are turned on for the Maps app. Go to **"Settings" > "Privacy" > "Location Services"** and make sure **"Maps"** is selected as **"While Using the App"** or **"Always."**

5. You can bookmark the page or save the route to save these customized settings for later use.
6. Tap **"Start"** or **"Go"** to start navigation after adjusting your map's settings.

How to report an issue

The iPhone 15 Series Maps app has an easy-to-follow method for reporting problems, which enhances the program's dependability and accuracy.

To report a problem, do the following steps:

1. To open the Maps app, tap the **Maps icon** located on the home screen of your iPhone.
2. Enter the address or place for which you want to file a report using the search box at the top. The location will then be shown on the map.

3. To see the specifics of the problem you want to report, tap on the designated area.

4. To see further details and options, swipe down on the details card for the place.
5. Tap the "**Report an Issue**" button located towards the bottom of the location info.

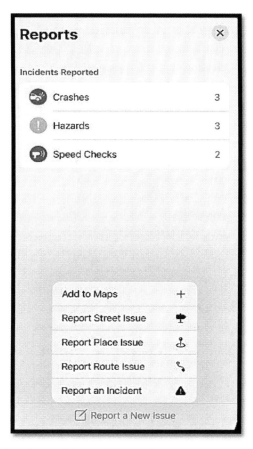

6. You will see a selection of issue kinds that you may report on the app. Typical errors include a mistaken address, inaccurate company details, or difficulties following instructions. Choose the one that addresses your issue.
7. You'll be asked to elaborate on the nature of the problem. Ensure you describe the issue in as much detail as you can. For example, if the location is inaccurate, supply the right location; if the problem is business-related, provide proper information.
8. If you would like to provide visual proof of the problem with your complaint, you can also attach photographs. This is particularly useful for things like misplaced road signs or building numbers.

9. Click "**Submit**" when you have entered all the required data. We'll forward your problem report to Apple for consideration.

10. You can choose to "**Report an Issue**" in the Maps app's settings or you can check your email for updates from Apple if you want to inquire about the progress of your complaint or give further details.

How to mark my location

The methods below can be used to indicate your location using the iPhone 15 Series Maps app:

1. To begin, use your password or Face ID to unlock your iPhone 15 Series.

2. Find the Maps app on your home screen to open it. The typical symbol for it is a map that resembles a folded map.

3. Make sure Location Services is enabled for the Maps app by going to "**Settings**" on your iPhone, scrolling down to "**Privacy**," and then tapping on "**Location Services**." Depending on your preferences, you may agree to enable location access "While Using the App" or "**Always**."

4. In the Maps app, type the name of the place you want to mark into the search box at the top. You can type in a location's name, landmark, or address.

5. After inputting the address, you can see further details about it on a map by tapping on it in the search results.

6. Press and hold the exact position you want to indicate on the map to mark it. A red pin will drop at that spot in a minute.

7. Your selected location is shown by the red pin. To get further details about the location, you can touch on the pin. After tapping the pin once again to display the information card, choose "**Add to Collection**" or "**Save**" to preserve the location. By pressing the share symbol, you may also decide to share the location with other people.

8. The pin can be customized by touching on it and choosing "**Edit Location**" or "**Change Pin Color**" if you'd want to add remarks or make it stand out more.

9. Return to the Maps app and choose the "**Saved**" option located at the bottom to see your saved destinations. All of the places you've noted and saved are listed here.

10. Touch the location and then touch the share symbol to let someone know where you've marked. It may be sent using Mail, Messages, or other compatible applications.

How to create a new guide

Whether you're visiting a new location or just searching for things to do in your area, the Maps app on the iPhone 15 Series makes it easy to plan and organize your travels. Just create a new tour using this app.

The steps to make your guide are as follows:

1. If your iPhone 15 Series is locked, unlock it to see the Maps app icon on the home screen. The appearance resembles a map with a place marking on it. To launch the app, tap on it.
2. To find the place for which you want to make a guide, use the search box at the top of the Maps app. A city, a particular location, or even simply a category like "**coffee shops**" or "**parks**" might be entered.
3. To access additional information, touch the place after you've located it that interests you.
4. On the location's website, scroll down until you find the "Add to Guide" button. Squeak it.
5. You will be requested to create a new guide if you haven't already done so. Assign a name and brief description to your guide to aid in recalling its purpose.
6. Once a new guide has been created, you can begin adding locations to it. To do this, search for other places and click the "**Add to Guide**" button next to each one. We'll include them in the guide you wrote.
7. Tap the guide's name at the bottom of the screen to modify it. This is where you can change the title, description, or location order of the guide. If necessary, you can also take locations out of your guide.
8. To see your guide once you've added all the locations you want to, touch on its name one more time. Every location will be mapped out on a map, and you may touch on any location to get additional details.

9. To share your guide with friends or family, press the share symbol (often shown as an upward-pointing arrow) and choose the appropriate sharing method, such as email, Messages, or other applications.

10. Use your guide to find your way to the locations you've added while you explore. To receive turn-by-turn instructions using Apple Maps, just press on a location inside the guide and then hit the **"Directions"** button.

How to explore nearby areas

With the iPhone 15 Series, exploring neighboring locations with the Maps app is a snap. Apple makes constant improvements and upgrades to its Maps app to provide people with a smooth and entertaining navigation experience.

Here's a detailed guide on using your iPhone 15 Series' Maps app to explore neighboring areas:

1. Find the Maps app icon on the home screen of your iPhone. Usually, it's a white backdrop with a vibrant map symbol. To open the app, tap on it.

2. The Maps app may ask you to activate Location Services if you haven't previously. This is necessary for the app to locate you right now and provide precise instructions and data. By heading to **Settings > Privacy > Location Services** and turning it on, you may enable location services.

3. Verify that you let the app access your location while you're using it, once you've enabled Location Services. Navigating to **Settings > Privacy > Location Services > Maps** will reveal this option. Assign to **"While Using the App."**

4. A map with your current position in the middle will appear while the Maps app is active and has access to your location. A blue dot will appear, showing you where you are.

5. Use the search box at the top of the screen to find neighboring locations. Type in a place's name or just a term like **"coffee," "park," or "gas station"** to get a list of possibilities that are close by.

6. A selection of pertinent places will appear after you type in your search query. To get additional information about a place, tap on it in the list.

7. Tap the "**Directions**" button to get instructions to the chosen place. Depending on your choices, you can get instructions for walking, driving, or using public transportation.

8. You can also use the map's zoom and panning features to explore neighboring places. Streets, sites of interest, and other pertinent data will be shown on the map.

9. Use filters to focus your search for locations that are close by. In the search results, you can choose parameters like ratings, open now, and more by tapping the "**Filters**" button.

10. By clicking the "**Save**" or "**Add to Favorites**" option, you can save a location to your favorites so you can revisit it at a later time. This will facilitate future navigation to the place.

11. Select your favorite sharing option, such as Messages, Email, or AirDrop, by tapping the "**Share**" icon and sharing a place with friends or family.

12. Swipe down on the location's page to read reviews and look up ratings for establishments.

Frequently Asked Questions

1. How do you access the maps app?
2. How do you get directions and get to your current location?
3. How do you zoom in and out on the map?
4. How do you search for a location on the map?
5. How do you begin navigation and rotate the map?

CHAPTER TWELVE
NEWS APP

Overview

Chapter twelve discusses the news app where you can get access to all of the latest happenings around your area and the world in general.

How to access the News app

Here are the steps:

1. To start, use Face ID or your password to unlock your iPhone.
2. The News app icon can be seen on your iPhone 15 Series' home screen. With a red "**N**" on a white background, it resembles a newspaper.

3. Use the search function or slide left or right on your home screen pages to find the News app icon. You can access the search bar at the top of your screen by swiping down from the center of your home screen.
4. Enter "**News**" into the search field, and the News app icon ought to appear in the list of results.

5. After you've found the News app icon, press it to launch the application.
6. You need to set up the News app by choosing your favorite news sources and interests if this is your first time using it. The application will ask you to sign in using your Apple ID if you have previously used it.

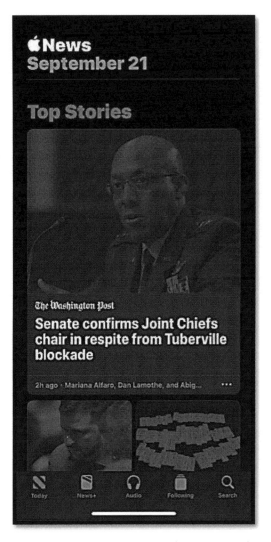

7. Following your setup or sign-in, you can begin to take advantage of the most recent news articles and stories from a variety of sources, tailored to your tastes.
8. Swipe up and down or touch on portions that catch your attention to peruse through various news categories and topics.

How to set up Apple News

The procedure of configuring Apple News on the News app on your iPhone 15 Series is simple.

To get started, do these actions:

1. Make sure that your iPhone is signed into your iCloud account before attempting to view Apple News. If you haven't already, go to **"Settings" > [your name] > "iCloud"** and log in with your Apple ID.
2. Find the News app on your home screen to open it. It seems to be a white **"N"** on a blue symbol. To open it, tap on it.
3. The News app will prompt you to choose your area when you initially launch it. This helps in localizing the news items to your area. Choose your nation or area from the list.
4. The app will prompt you to choose the news sources and subjects that you find most interesting to customize your news feed. You can choose how many or how few you want. You can see news on Apple News that is most relevant to your interests thanks to this.
5. A variety of periodicals, magazines, and newspapers are available via Apple News. Subscribing to your preferred newspapers allows you to have a more customized news experience. Just choose the **"Following"** link at the bottom and go through the various alternatives to become a subscriber. To confirm your subscription, tap on the magazine of your choice and follow the on-screen instructions.
6. You can turn on alerts if you want to be informed when articles or breaking news from the newspapers you have subscriptions appear. Toggle notifications on and off by going to **"Following"** and tapping the bell symbol next to the name of the publication.
7. After the basic setup is finished, you may begin investigating the News app. Look through the **"Today"** tab to see the most recent news, choose **"Favorites"** to see news that is tailored to you, and select **"Following"** to view the most recent articles from the magazines to which you have subscriptions.

8. To find news articles or specific subjects, hit the magnifying glass icon located in the app's lower right corner. After you type in your search term, Apple News will show you relevant results.

9. When you come across an article that you would want to read later, you have the option to store it by hitting the share symbol and choosing "**Save Story**."

10. By pressing the share button, you can also send articles to your friends or relatives. Explore the app's options to further personalize your news experience. Change the font size, activate dark mode, and manage your subscriptions, among other things.

How to navigate the news app

On the iPhone 15 Series, navigating the news app is simple and easy.

Here's how to do so:

1. To begin, use Face ID or your password to unlock your iPhone 15 Series.
2. Scan your home screen for the News app icon. Usually, it's a red "**N**" on a white symbol. If that doesn't help, you may slide down on the home screen and enter "News" into the search field.
3. Press the icon of the News app to make it open.
4. Go through the "**For You**" tab.
- The "**For You**" option serves as the News app's default home page. A customized selection of news stories based on your reading preferences, hobbies, and sources you follow may be found in this area.
- Use the up and down arrows to navigate the articles. To read an article in full, tap on it.

5. **Navigate the News Article**:
- You can swipe up and down to navigate through the text of an article as it opens.
- You can swipe from the left side of the screen or hit the "**Back**" button in the upper-left corner to return to the main "**For You**" feed.

6. **Browse the Following Tab**:

- To examine news from certain sources or subjects you've been following, use the **"Following"** option located at the bottom.
- Articles from the sources and subjects you've chosen are available here. To read any of them, swipe across them and touch on them.

7. **Search for News**:
- Use the magnifying glass icon located at the bottom of the screen to look for articles or news subjects that interest you.
- When you type your search term into the search field, a list of relevant results will appear.

8. **Explore Other Tabs**:
- You can also see trending news, browse topics, and control your alerts by navigating via the News app's tabs including **"Today,"** **"Browse,"** and **"Notifications."**

9. **Customize your News Preferences**:
- You can adjust the news that appears to you by tapping on your profile symbol, which is often situated in the upper-right corner.
- You can manage your reading history, change your notification preferences, and alter your channels and subjects here.

10. To save an article or share it with others, just press the share symbol, which is often a square with an arrow pointing up. This will give you access to options like **"Save," "Copy Link," and "Share."**
11. Swipe up from the bottom border to close the News app and go back to your home screen or open another app.

How to read articles on the news app

The steps:

1. To begin, unlock your iPhone by entering your password or using Face ID.
2. On most iPhones like yours, the News app is pre-installed, so it's normally located on your home screen. The symbol for it is a blue icon with a white **"N."**
3. To access the News App, just tap its icon.

4. Your preferences and past surfing activity are used to tailor the news feed that the news app offers you. You can see the most recent news by scrolling through this stream. As an alternative, you may browse other news sources and subjects by tapping on the "**Channels**" option located at the bottom.
5. To access an article that piques your curiosity, just tap on its title or thumbnail picture.
6. Read the complete story by scrolling up and down after it has opened. If the article is lengthy, swipe from right to left to get to the next page.

7. Pinch your fingers together to make the text larger or smaller, or apart to make it smaller, if you feel the text to be too tiny. You can also change the font size that all applications, including News, use by going to **Settings > Display & Brightness > font Size** on your iPhone.

8. To share or store an article for later, just touch the share icon, which is often a square with an arrow pointing up, or the bookmark symbol, which is typically a flag icon, located at the bottom of the page.

9. Just hit the back arrow or swipe from left to right in the upper-left corner of the screen to go back to the main news feed or the list of articles from the source or subject you were reading.

10. By going back to steps 4 through 7, you can read and explore other articles.

11. Use the News app's search feature to find news on a particular subject or phrase. Enter your search term, tap the magnifying glass icon at the bottom, and peruse the results.

12. By favoriting or unliking stories and sources, you can make changes to your news choices using the News app. The app will adjust your news stream over time to more closely align with your preferences.

How to share and save on the news app

Sharing an article

1. To access the News app, find it on your iPhone's home screen and press on it.

2. Look through the news stories until you come to the one you want to share.

3. To spread the word about this article, find and tap the share icon. You can normally locate it near the top or bottom of the page; sometimes, you may need to touch the article to display this choice. It usually appears like a square with an arrow going up.

4. A menu including several sharing options will show once you hit the **share button**. The article may be saved to your Notes app and shared through Messages, Mail, or social networking applications like Facebook and Twitter. Decide which approach you like most.

5. To share the article, you may need to adhere to the on-screen directions, depending on your selection. If you pick Messages, for instance, you will have to choose a contact and email the article link.

Save an article

1. On your iPhone, launch the **News app** as you would have before.
2. Look for the article you want to save for subsequent use.

3. In some versions of the News app, there is a separate "**Save**" button; in other iterations, you may need to press the share button and choose "**Save to Reading List**" or a similar choice. Locate the relevant menu item or button.

4. The News app's "**Saved**" or "**Reading List**" sections are usually where you can locate the items you've saved for later access. This might be found in a specific tab or the app's main menu.

How to follow channels and publications on the news app

Generally, you can use the Apple News app to follow publications and channels in the following ways:

1. On your iPhone 15 Series, find the Apple News app. It often has a symbol that looks like a newspaper.
2. To open the Apple News app, just tap its icon.
3. Use the app's content search to locate magazines and channels that pique your interest. To find new information, use the search box at the top or browse the **"For You," "Following," or "Browse" sections**.
4. **Keep Up with a Publication or Channel**:
- **For Channels**: Tap the channel you want to watch to get it open. Locate and touch an option such as **"Follow" or "Add",** if available. The channel will now be included in your list of channels to follow.

- **Regarding Publications**: To adhere to a certain publication, find an article inside it and touch on it to see the content. To follow the publication, tap the **"Follow" or "Add"** button that may be located near the publication's name at the top.

5. Open the Apple News app and choose the **"Following"** option to see and modify the channels and publications you follow. A list of every channel and publication you have followed can be seen here.

6. You could get alerts for new content and updates from the channels and journals you subscribe to, based on your preferences. The **"News"** section of the iPhone's settings app is where you may modify these alert settings.

How to customize your newsfeed

One excellent approach to keeping updated about the subjects that are most important to you is to personalize your news feed on the iPhone 15 Series news app.

Here's how to customize your news feed:

1. Find the News app on the home screen of your iPhone 15, and then press to open it.
2. **Select your Interests:**
- Where the **"Today"** tab is located on the screen is at the bottom. Select it.
- If you scroll down, you'll see a section titled **"Topics,"** which contains the subjects the app believes you would find interesting based on your use.
- Scroll through the recommended subjects and choose the ones that catch your attention. This will improve the app's comprehension of your preferences.
3. **Look for Specific Topics**:
- Use the search box located at the top of the **"Today"** tab if you have particular interests that aren't covered by the recommendations.
- Go into the app and type in terms that are relevant to your interests, such as **"technology," "politics," or "travel."** Relevant subjects and channels will appear.

4. **Follow Channels**:

- To customize your experience, choose a subject or channel to follow by tapping on it.
- A "**Follow**" button will appear. You can add the subject to your News app feed by tapping it.

5. **Unfollow Channels or Topics**:
- Unfollow a subject or channel if you later decide you're no longer interested in it.
- Tap the "**Following**" button at the top of the "**Today**" page to get to the "**Following**" section.
- Locate the channel or subject you want to unfollow, and then hit the "**Following**" icon once again.

6. **Change the Notifications**:
- In the "**Following**" area, tap on the subject or channel you want to get alerts for.
- Depending on your preferences, you can choose to allow or disable alerts for that particular subject or channel.

7. **Personalize your Feed**:
- The News app will adjust your feed based on its growing understanding of your preferences.
- Remember to interact with the stories you like by sharing, liking, or reading them to aid the app in improving the news suggestions it makes.

8. Check out the "**For You**" tab in addition to the "**Today**" page. This section selects news and articles according to your reading preferences and areas of interest.

How to view notifications on the news app

Use the steps below to display alerts on the iPhone 15 Series News app:

1. If your iPhone is locked, start by unlocking it. You can do this by entering your password or by using Face ID.

2. The News app icon appears as a white "**N**" surrounded by a blue newspaper. Usually, your App Library or one of your home screens will have it. If it's not there, you can search for it using the smartphone by sliding down on the home screen and entering "**News**."

3. Tap the News app icon to launch the application.

4. To access the Notification Center, slide down from the top edge of the screen (or from the top-left corner if your iPhone has a notch). A collection of your most recent alerts, including those from the News app, can be seen here.

5. Look for alerts from the News app in the Notification Center to see your news alerts. Usually, they will show the news story's title or the name of the publisher. To read the whole article, tap the notification.

6. To get rid of all of your alerts, slide them to the right and choose "**Clear**" or "**Clear All**" from the Notification Center dropdown menu.

7. The iPhone's settings allow you to alter how alerts from the News app operate.

- Choose "**Settings**" from the iPhone menu.
- Swipe down to choose "**News**."
- Within "**Notifications**," you can change several aspects of the notice, such as the sound and appearance.

How to use the search bar on the news app

The steps:

1. To begin, open the iPhone and go to the home screen.

2. To use the News App, find its icon on your home screen. With a blue symbol and the phrase "**News**" beneath, it resembles a newspaper. To launch the app, tap on it.

3. To use the search bar, touch on the "**Search**" tab, which is often symbolized by a magnifying glass icon. Once you're within the News app, you'll be provided with numerous tabs at the bottom of the screen, such as **"Today," "News+," "Following," "Search," and "Browse."**

4. A search bar will now appear at the top of the screen. Press and hold it to bring up the keyboard, and then enter your search term. To get news items regarding **"technology,"** for instance, just put the word **"technology"** into the keyboard.

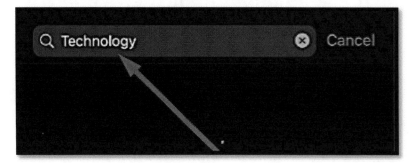

5. Once your search term has been entered, you have two options: either hit **"Go"** on the keyboard or touch the **"Search"** key.
6. Following that, the app will show you a list of search results associated with your query. To locate the news stories or subjects that pique your interest, just browse through these results.

7. Hit the search bar once more and change your query if you want to focus your search even further. To filter the results, for example, you may add additional keywords or provide a date range.

8. To read the whole text of an article you've found interesting, just touch on it. With the app's features, you can share articles or save them for later reading.

9. All you have to do is use your iPhone's back button or motion to go back to your search results.

10. Use the back button or the "**Cancel**" or "**X**" buttons in the search bar to end the search and go back to the News app's main interface.

How to use the news audio feature to listen to news

Generally, you would take the following actions to use an iPhone's news audio capability to listen to the news:

1. Find the "**News**" app on your iPhone and launch it. The application could come pre-installed, but if not, you can get it from the App Store.

2. To locate the news you're interested in, search through a variety of news sources and themes on the News app. Depending on how the app is designed, you may see categories like **"For You," "Today," "Browse," or "Following."**

3. Tap on a story or article that catches your attention. Text, pictures, and sometimes audio or video are all combined in news pieces.

4. If the article has an audio section, there ought to be a way to listen to it. A "**Listen**" button or speaker icon can be used to signify this.

5. To begin listening to the news, choose the audio option. While listening, you may change the volume and pause/play as necessary.

6. Using arrows to swipe or press to go to the next or previous article is a navigation feature of several news applications.

7. You may be able to customize your news stream, share stories with friends, and save articles for later, depending on the news app and version you're using,

8. To improve the user experience for those with visual or hearing impairments, iPhones often come equipped with accessibility features. If necessary, look for accessibility options in your device's settings.

Frequently Asked Questions

1. How do you access and set up the Apple News app?
2. How do you read articles on the News app?
3. How do you share and save on the News app?
4. How do you customize your news feed?
5. How do you view notifications on the news app?
6. How do you use the news audio feature to listen to news?

CHAPTER THIRTEEN
REMINDERS APP

Overview

Simple tasks like reminding you to give your dog a prescription at supper or to give your grandmother a call at a certain time every week are the focus of the Reminders app. Even if you haven't used the app in years, it has been on your iPhone, iPad, and Mac; yet, you may want to start using it. This chapter reveals everything there is to know about the Reminders app.

Using the Reminders App

In recent years, Apple has completely redesigned the Reminders app, offering it additional features, an updated interface, and Siri integration. Moreover, it synchronizes flawlessly with all of your Apple devices, making it an extremely potent productivity aid. Furthermore, the Reminders app doesn't need a charge to maximize its benefits, in contrast to many other **"to-do list"** applications. The first thing you need to know if you haven't used the Reminders app is how to make a reminder; it's very easy. Simply launch the app, choose **"+ New Reminder"** from the bottom-left corner, then complete the form to set up a reminder. You only need to plan when (and how frequently) you want to get reminders after that. Is that all? At the scheduled reminder time, a push notification will be sent to you by the app.

However, it is only an essential feature, since the Reminders app is a powerful and practical instrument. You can highlight some reminders as particularly essential, attach images to certain reminders to provide more contexts, and even provide connections to a particular website or app so that, when you are reminded, you can quickly do the tasks at hand.

How to make a list

Lists are used to organize the Reminders app. But you can create multiple lists for your various activities - **"Planning Grandpa's Birthday"** or **"School work"** - and then populate those lists with reminders to get that activity done. When you create a reminder, it gets populated into your default list, either titled "Reminders" or "My Day." It's an orderly and straightforward method of grouping all the similar reminders.

To make a list:

1. Launch the **Reminders** app.
2. In the lower-right corner, click the "**Add List**" button.

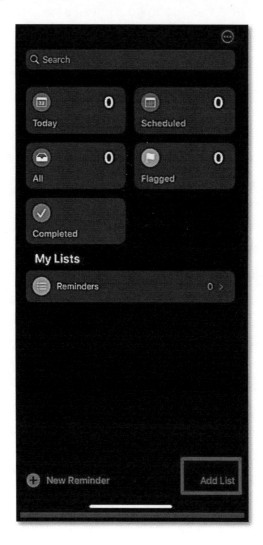

3. Give it a name.

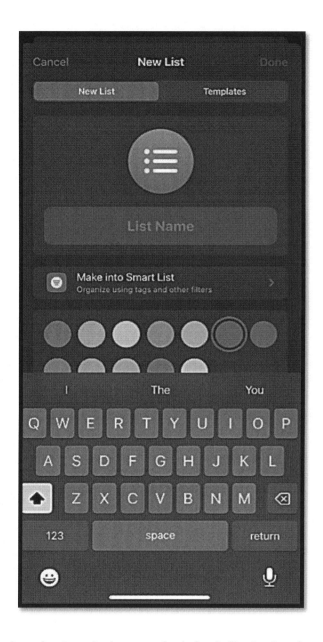

Additionally, changing the Reminders app's default list is simple:

1. Launch the Settings app.
2. Choose **Reminders**.
3. Choose "**Default List.**"
4. Select the list you want to use as your new default by checking it.

How to Create a Smart List

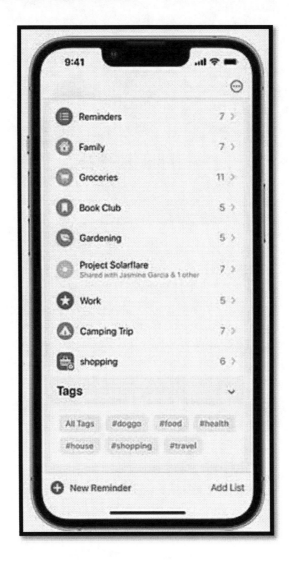

Smart List is a list that gathers all of your reminders from all of your other lists and automatically organizes them into a single **"smart"** list based on unique factors that you provide. The reason it's regarded as a **"smart"** list is because it automatically organizes all past and future reminders that meet those specific specified specifications. For instance, you may make a Smart List with all of your reminders that are based on a place, overdue, or due within a certain window of time, and those reminders will then be added to that particular Smart List.

Creating a Smart List:

1. Launch the Reminders app.
2. In the lower-right corner, click the "**Add List**" button.
3. Give it a name.
4. Opt for "**Make into Smart List**."

Next, you can choose the list's specifications, such as a time or date range, a different place, or a particular tag.

Organize your reminders with Tags in the iPhone Reminder app

It might be challenging to remember them all if you have a lot of different reminders. Apple added its tagging mechanism to the Reminders app for just this reason. Reminders may have hashtags added to them in both their title and description, much like the Notes app. When this happens, all of the other reminders with the same hashtag will be grouped. (When creating or modifying a reminder, you can also add a tag by using the Tag (#) option.) To make several reminders, such as those for picking up the kids, heading to the dry cleaners, and sending a box to the post office, you may add the #Errands hashtag, and those reminders will all show up in the same Errands tag.

How to use subtasks

Can you create a reminder inside of another reminder? The Reminders app refers to this as subtasking. You can, for instance, make your reminder to "Bring ski helmet" a subtask of your main reminder to "Pack for ski trip."

Drag and drop the "Bring ski helmet" reminder into the "Pack for ski trip" reminder to do this. Alternatively, you can swipe right on a reminder to make it a subtask for the reminder that's just above it. Subtask push alerts will then be sent to you through the Reminders app, exactly like ordinary reminders.

How to use Siri commands

Voice commands using "**Hey Siri**" now function well with the Reminders app thanks to Apple. Simply say to Siri, "**Hey Siri**, remind me to call my dad at 7pm tonight." Siri can also recognize recurring commands, such as, "Hey Siri, remind me to set my fantasy lineup every Saturday morning at 7:30 a.m."

This isn't very hard to do, but the most recent software updates have made it function incredibly well. You can also have Siri broadcast your reminders as they occur if you're using AirPods (or Beats headphones with Apple's W1 or H1 processors).

To turn this functionality on:

1. First, launch the **Settings app**.
2. Choose the "**Siri & Search**" option by swiping down.
3. Choose "**Announce Notifications**."
4. Lower your screen and confirm that the Reminders tab is set to "**On**."

How to set location-based reminders

You can set up location-based reminders with the Reminders app, which does exactly what its name suggests: it will remind you of things based on where you are. For example, you can set a reminder to turn on the air conditioning when you get to work in the morning or to turn on the sprinklers when you get home in the evening. Both granting your iPhone permission to track your location (**Settings > Privacy > Location Services > On**) and adding your home and work addresses (as well as any other addresses you wish to have location-based reminders for) to your card in the Contacts app (My Card (under your name) > Edit (top-right corner) > scroll down to add address) are prerequisites for these location-based reminders to function.

Then, in the Reminders app, go to a specific task, choose the "**i**" icon next to it, choose "**Remind me at a location**," and then select a location to establish a location-based reminder for each time you arrive at a location.

How to set reminders that use the Messages app

You likely use the Messages app, also known as iMessage, a gazillion times a day. You can also integrate the Reminders app with the Messages app. For instance, you can create a reminder to alert you whenever you message a specific person in the Messages app. This way, the Reminders app can remind you to send a picture of your grandchild every time you open a message with your parents.

To do this, launch the **Reminders app**, choose the task you want to be reminded of, click the "**i**" icon next to it, choose "**Remind me when messaging**," and then select the contact's name.

How to view your "completed" reminders

The Completed section is a new feature that Apple added to the Reminders app. You can access the Completed section directly from the main view of the Reminders app, and it arranges your completed tasks according to when they were completed: the previous day, week, month, or year. This allows you to see what you completed previously, which may be a good way to remind yourself of new tasks you might need to complete again in the future. Additionally, you may see your completed tasks from a specific list by opening that particular list, tapping the more (three dots) icon in the top-right corner, and choosing "Show Completed" from the drop-down menu.

What can we expect from iOS 17?

The Reminders app will get many new features when Apple releases iOS 17 in September along with the iPhone 15.

Here's everything you need to know:

- **Early Reminders**: With the latest software update, you can now set up an **"Early Reminder"** for particular tasks that you may need more time to prepare for. As long as the task has a deadline, you can set up a notification for an Early

Reminder, and you can even customize it to be set a few minutes, hours, days, weeks, or even months in advance of the task in question.

- **Interactive Widgets**: iOS 17 introduces interactive widgets, which enable you to interact with certain widgets directly from the Home screen without having to open the app. The Reminders app will be launched with support for this new feature, which will let you cross off chores that you've finished more quickly.
- **Sections**: One of the features that will make the Reminders app much more robust is iOS 17's ability to let you create sections within lists to help you better organizes tasks. You can also drag and drop specific tasks between sections and expand or collapse individual sections to see more or less of your tasks.

10 Key Tips to Get More from the Apple Reminders App

When it comes to managing your calendar, Apple Reminders is an excellent tool for remembering appointments, birthdays, deadlines, and much more. If you struggle with forgetting things, the Reminders app may help you avoid missing important events or turning in assignments after the deadline.

Here are the tips:

1. **Add a Location to a Reminder**

Whether you're using the Reminders app on an iPhone, iPad, or Mac, you can add a location to it. Reminders will remind you depending on where you are. On the Reminders toolbar, tap the **Place** button. It will provide a few alternatives, such as **"Getting in the car"** and **"Getting out of the car,"** and you can set it to whatever place you like. You need to enable exact location access to establish your current location. To accomplish this, go to **Settings > Privacy > Location Services > Reminders > Exact Location**.

2. **Add URLs and Notes to a Task**

By swiping from the right and selecting Details, or by pressing the little Info (i) icon next to a reminder while updating it, you may additionally add URLs and Notes to Reminders. Alternatively, you can add Notes to further clarify your reminder, in case it isn't clear enough on its own; the little space designated for adding a URL could come in handy, for instance, if you're planning to order a bouquet at a flower shop and want to jump right to the product you're interested in. Your reminders are kept more organized with the notes, which are shown in tiny font under the headline.

3. **Organize Reminders with Subtasks**

Making subtasks to create a list of items you need to buy is a great way to organize the flow of your Reminders. For example, if you have a reminder to go to the store, you can use subtasks to make a list of items you need to buy. If you're the kind of person who needs sub-lists under a general list, doing this on an iPhone, iPad, or Mac is simple. You can use Apple Reminders to continue working productively while you're not in the office by using subtasks.

There are three methods to establish a subtask:

- To access the Indent button, swipe left to right. This may be done on any list, and it will automatically make a subtask of the task that's above it.
- To see the task details, press the Info (**i**) symbol. Next, scroll down to subtasks and tap this. From here, you can change and add new subtasks.
- Reach out and drag one reminder onto another, causing the one you transferred to become a subtask of the reminder you originally put it on.

4. **Create Reminders with Siri**

Not surprisingly, Siri works well with Reminders. You can ask Siri to make reminders for you by saying things like "Siri, remind me to take my medicine at 7 in the morning." After that, Siri will make a reminder for you and offer you the chance to edit it with any additional information. Try using Siri to set reminders for you if you have a full handbag or are unable to write the reminder yourself. It's also considerably quicker than typing the information by hand, so give it a go if you want to save time.

5. **Share Reminders with Others**

Sharing your lists with others is another fantastic feature of Reminders. Rather than creating a fresh text each time you need to inform someone about your task plans, you can cooperate by sharing your lists from Reminders. From the Reminders main page, touch a list under My Lists. Then, hit the Share icon in the upper right corner. You can then share your list by social media, text message, or email. Upon accepting an invitation, the invitee can only see the shared list; all of your other Reminder lists will be private. The invitee may only edit the reminders in that particular list.

6. **Use Safari or Another App to Add a Reminder**

Add a new reminder directly from inside an app on your iPhone. For example, you can use the Share button in any app to make a reminder to read an item in a news app or watch a movie on Netflix. This is particularly useful for bookmarking URLs on a Mac since it will create a task for you with an automatically generated URL that links to the location from where you shared it.

7. **Try the "When Messaging" Feature**

Like adding a location to your reminders, this function is really helpful if you want to be reminded of something the next time you're messaging a friend—perhaps you want to urge them to bring something when they visit. When editing, hit the Info (**i**) icon, or slide left to right and choose **Details**. In the resulting menu, select When Messaging to enable Reminders to notify you the next time you start a Messages thread with that user.

8. **Add Attachments to Reminders**

As previously mentioned, you can attach files to a reminder to store all task-related information in one location. For instance, if you have an appointment and need to bring a document, you can attach the file to the reminder. Edit the reminder and choose the Camera icon from the Reminders app's bottom toolbar. From there, you may scan a document, snap a fresh picture, or select a document from your collection.

9. **Flag a Reminder**

Another tool in your organizing toolbox is the ability to flag reminders. If you have a lot of reminders lying about, you may flag the most important ones first. To flag a reminder, either tap the toolbar's Flag icon or swipe left to right and select Flag. The flagged reminder will then show up in the Flagged list on the Reminders main screen, allowing you to view all of your most important tasks in one location. Priority tags are another useful tool in Apple Reminders for organizing particularly important tasks.

10. **Move a Reminder to Another List**

If you add a reminder by accident to the incorrect list, you may change it to the proper list using this final Apple Reminders option, which will save you time. To do this, long-press on any reminder in any list, hold it down and then use a second finger to touch **Lists** in the upper-left corner to bring up the main screen. Drop the long-pressed reminder to the appropriate list. Now that you've dropped your reminder in the list, it will appear with all of the attachments, notes, and other information.

Frequently Asked Questions

1. What is the Reminders app all about?
2. How do you make a list with the Reminders app?
3. How do you create a smart list?
4. How do you use subtasks?
5. How do you use Siri commands in the Reminders app?

CHAPTER FOURTEEN
ITUNES STORE

Overview

The iTunes store is where you can search for content, purchase and download content, stream content, and so much more. Chapter fourteen talks about how you can easily achieve all these and more.

How to launch and sign in to iTunes Store

To open and log in to the iTunes Store on an iPhone, follow these basic instructions:

1. Use your password or Face ID to unlock your iPhone.
2. Locate the **"App Store"** icon on your home screen. Usually, it's a blue symbol with the letter **"A"** in white writing. On tapping it, the App Store will open.
3. Using the search box at the bottom of the screen, look for **"iTunes Store"** in the App Store. In the search field, type **"iTunes Store"** and choose **"Search."**
4. You will need to download and install the iTunes Store app from the App Store if it isn't already pre-installed on your iPhone. To download and install the iTunes Store app, tap the **"Get"** or **"Install"** button next to it.
5. To open the iTunes Store app, press the **"Open"** button once it has been installed.

6. You'll need to check in using your Apple ID if you haven't previously. You can create an Apple ID if you don't already have one. This is how to log in:

- Tap the "**Account**" or "**Sign In**" button, which is often found at the bottom or upper right of the iTunes Store screen.
- Type in your password and Apple ID.
- Select "**Sign In**."

7. Use the iTunes Store's many services, including buying and downloading music, movies, TV series, and more, after logging in.

How to browse and search for content

Here are the procedures to browse and search the iTunes Store on an iPhone 15 Series:

1. Unlock your iPhone 15 Series smartphone to start. You need to enter your passcode or use Face ID to make sure this happens.

2. On your iPhone 15 Series, find the "**iTunes Store**" app. It's symbolized by an emblem of a musical note. To launch the app, tap on it.

3. The home screen of the iTunes Store often showcases material that is in high demand, including music videos, albums, and new releases. You may peruse this material to find recently released films, TV series, songs, and other stuff.

4. By tapping on the corresponding category at the bottom of the screen, you may explore certain categories, such as Music, Movies, TV Shows, or Podcasts. You may then look through the information in that category.

5. **Search for Content**:

- To find a certain item, hit the "**Search**" icon, which is often a magnifying glass in the lower right corner.

- Type relevant terms into the search box located at the top of the screen. You have the option to search for actors, genres, albums, songs, movies, and more.
- The iTunes Store will provide recommendations based on your search query as you write. You can quickly find similar material by tapping on a recommendation.

6. You can refine your search results by using the filters and sorting options after entering your query. Depending on what you're looking for, these filters can include categories like **"Music," "Movies," "TV Shows,"** and more.

7. Tap an item to explore its information when you discover one that interests you. This is where you can examine more details about the product, such as the price, reviews, ratings, and description.

8. To acquire or get an object, use the relevant button (such as "Buy," "Rent," or "Get"). It may be necessary for you to use your Apple ID or, if set up, Face ID to verify your transaction.

9. Select the **"Library"** tab located at the bottom of the iTunes Store app to see the stuff you've downloaded or bought. Your favorite music, films, TV series and more are all available here.

10. The iTunes Store app allows you to modify your account settings and payment details by tapping your profile icon in the top-right corner and choosing "Account." You may then modify your account information and settings from there.

How to view content in the iTunes Store

To see what's available in the iTunes Store:

1. Find the **"iTunes Store"** or **"Apple Music"** app icon on your home screen. It is a purple symbol with a white musical note enclosed in a white circle. To launch the app, tap on it.

2. You can browse through categories like Music, Movies, TV Shows, and more while you're within the iTunes Store (or Apple Music app). The main screen displays prominent content as well.

3. Use the search box at the top of the screen to find particular content. Press the magnifying glass-shaped search button, type the name of the material you're searching for, and then choose **"Search."**

4. Tap on an item of content to get additional information when you find it appealing. You may see details about the material, such as user ratings and pricing.

5. You could be able to read more about an app, hear a song sample, or have a sneak peek at a film or television program, depending on the kind of material.

Tap the pricing button (such as **"Buy,"** **"Rent,"** or **"Get"**) to purchase content, then follow the on-screen instructions to complete the transaction.

6. Depending on the kind of media, you can watch or download content straight to your device after buying or renting it. If you have a membership to Apple songs, you can stream songs via it.

How to purchase and download content

Use these procedures to buy and download media from the iTunes Store to your iPhone 15 Series:

1. Find the **"iTunes Store"** app on your iPhone 15 Series. Usually, it features an emblem of a colorful musical note. To launch the app, tap on it.
2. You'll need to enter your Apple ID and password to log in if you haven't previously. You will need to create an Apple ID if you do not already have one.
3. To locate certain information, either use the search box at the bottom or go through the highlighted things. Songs, albums, films, TV series, novels, and more may all be found via searches.
4. Tap on the content to access the details page when you've located the item you want to buy and download.
5. The price is shown on the content's details page. To buy it, just tap the price or the **"Buy"** button. If the item is free, a **"Get"** button will appear. If it's an album, you can purchase each track or the whole thing.

6. To verify the transaction, you could be asked to enter your Apple ID password, use Face ID, or enter the passcode on your iPhone. Watch the directions on the screen.

7. Immediately after the completion of the transaction, the content will begin to download. Tapping the "**Downloads**" icon (which appears as a downward arrow) at the bottom of the screen allows you to keep track of the status of your downloads. To ensure quicker downloads, particularly for bigger files, make sure you are linked to Wi-Fi.

8. After the download is finished, open the relevant app on your iPhone to access the content you've bought. For instance, the Apple TV app will house movies and TV series, the Apple Books app will house books, and the Apple Music app will house music.

How to access purchased content

Here's a broad overview:

1. The Apple Music app is used to access paid music and content. The Apple Music app can be accessed by finding and tapping the symbol, which is usually a white icon with a musical note on it.

2. You will need to check in with your Apple ID if you haven't previously. Press "**Sign In**" and provide your password and Apple ID. You could be asked to use Face ID for authentication if you use it.

3. The "**Library**" tab ought to appear at the bottom of the screen once you've logged in.

4. There should be several categories in your library, such as **"Playlists," "Artists," "Albums,"** etc. You can discover your bought content by scrolling down to the **"Purchased" or "Purchased Music"** section. Tap on it.

5. A list of all the songs and other media you've bought from the iTunes Store can be seen here. To access and play certain songs, albums, or other material, just touch on them.

6. You could see a cloud symbol with a download arrow if the content hasn't previously been downloaded to your device. To download the material to your iPhone for offline usage, tap on this symbol.

How to download and stream content

Use these procedures to get content from the iTunes Store to your iPhone 15 Series for download or streaming:

1. On your iPhone 15 Series, find the iTunes Store app. usually; it features an emblem of a colorful musical note. To launch the app, tap on it.

2. You'll need to check in using your Apple ID if you haven't previously. You will need to create an Apple ID if you do not already have one.

3. **Browse or Search for Content**:

- **Browse**: By navigating the home page or touching on other categories such as Music, Movies, TV Shows, etc., you may discover highlighted content.

- **Search**: Use the magnifying glass-shaped Search icon to locate a particular material by typing in the title, artist, or keyword of your choice.

4. **Choose the Content**:

- Tap on the content to see its information once you've found it to download or watch.

- You can buy individual tracks or albums of music. Renting or buying movies and TV programs is an option.

5. **Purchase or Rent Content**:

- The price of a song or album will be shown next to it if you are purchasing it. After you tap it, use your Face ID or your Apple ID password to authenticate the transaction.

- You have the option to purchase (to own) or rent (for a certain period) movies and TV series. To finish the transaction, adhere to the on-screen directions.

6. **Download Content**:

- Your music collection will instantly include any songs you have bought. Navigating to the "**Library**" area of the Music app will allow you to hear it.

- You can download TV series and movies to your device so you can watch them offline. Locate and press the download button, which is often represented by an arrow on a cloud. The content will be available in the "**Library**" area of the Apple TV app when the download is finished.

7. **Stream Content**:

- If you want to watch content without downloading it, just touch on the title. As long as your internet connection is active, the video will begin to stream. With Apple Music in particular, this is helpful since it allows you to stream music without using up storage space on your smartphone.

8. Use the iTunes Store app's "**Downloads**" area to manage the material you've downloaded. To clear up storage space, you can see and remove downloaded items here.

Keep in mind that although downloaded material may be viewed offline, streaming content needs a steady internet connection. Additionally, make sure your iPhone 15 Series has adequate storage space for you to download and save the stuff you choose.

How to access your account settings

Here are the steps:

1. Open the Home Screen on your iPhone after unlocking it.
2. Click the "**Settings**" application. This app icon is usually located on your Home Screen and resembles a gear or cogwheel.
3. Scroll to the bottom and choose "**iTunes & App Store**." Normally, it's located close to the top of the Settings menu.
4. Your Apple ID will be shown at the top of the screen. To see your account settings, tap on your Apple ID.
5. A window that pops up will show up. Pick "**View Apple ID**" from the list of choices.

6. You could be asked to use Face ID for identification or enter your Apple ID password. Give the necessary details to continue.
7. You can control your account's payment details, subscriptions, and other features by going into your Apple ID settings.
8. You can go down and search for **"iTunes & App Store"** options to get certain iTunes Store settings. Also control options about downloads, purchases, and in-app purchases are here.

How to redeem gift cards or codes

Generally, gift cards and vouchers can be redeemed as follows:

1. Initially, confirm that your iPhone is either connected to Wi-Fi or has a mobile data connection.
2. Find and press the **"App Store"** icon on the home screen of your iPhone. If it's not on your home screen, you can use the search function by swiping down.
3. Tap on your initials or profile image in the upper right corner of the screen on the App Store. You can access your Apple ID settings by doing this.
4. Locate and touch the **"Redeem Gift Card or Code"** option in your Apple ID settings.
5. A request to input your gift card or code will appear. Gently remove or expose the code, then type it into the designated space. Make sure the code is entered correctly.
6. Click **"Redeem"** after the code has been entered. The gift card's credit will be transferred to your Apple ID balance if the code is valid.
7. A confirmation notice stating that your gift card has been successfully redeemed and that the money will be credited to your Apple ID balance should appear.
8. You can now use the balance in the iTunes Store, App Store, and other Apple services like iCloud and Apple Music.

Frequently Asked Questions

1. How do you open and sign in to the iTunes store?
2. How do you view content in the iTunes store?

3. How do you browse and search for content in the iTunes store?
4. How do you purchase and download content?
5. How do you access purchased content?
6. How do you redeem gift cards or codes in the iTunes store?

CHAPTER FIFTEEN
APPLE APP STORE

Overview

Chapter fifteen discusses the Apple App Store where you can access your favorite and preferred applications, install apps, update apps, manage app subscriptions, and so much more. Learn everything about the Apple App Store on any of your new iPhone 15 Series in this chapter.

How to access the App Store

Use these easy methods to get into the Apple App Store on an iPhone 15 Series:

1. To begin, use Face ID or your password to unlock your iPhone 15 Series.
2. Search for the App Store icon on the home screen of your iPhone. Typically, it has a white letter **"A"** on a blue background. Usually, you may discover it in the App Library or on one of your home screens.
3. Once the App Store icon is in position, tap it to launch the App Store.

4. You'll be asked to log in with your Apple ID if you haven't already. In addition to entering your Apple ID and password, you also need to use a Face ID or a verification number delivered to your trusted devices to confirm your identity.

5. After logging in, search for individual applications using the bottom search box or browse through categories and highlighted apps. Additionally, you may scroll down to get suggestions for customized apps.

6. Examine additional information by tapping on an app when you discover one you want to download. Information about the app, user reviews, and ratings are shown. Tap the **"Get"** or **"Download"** button to begin the app's download. You may be prompted to enter your password or use Face ID to authenticate your download.

7. In some situations, particularly if it's been a while since you entered your Apple ID password, you could be prompted to use it to confirm your identity.

8. Your iPhone will start to download the app. The app's icon on your home screen allows you to monitor your progress.

How to explore the app store

On the iPhone 15 Series, you can find and download a huge selection of applications, games and other entertainment by exploring the Apple App Store.

Exploring the app store can be done below:

1. To unlock your iPhone, use Face ID or your passcode.
2. Find the icon for the App Store on your home screen. It's a pencil-shaped "**A**" on a blue symbol.
3. To access the App Store, just touch its icon.

4. Usually, the **"Today"** page is where you'll start when you first access the App Store. Featured applications, app and game-related content, and more are available here. You may see the fascinating and fresh content by scrolling down.

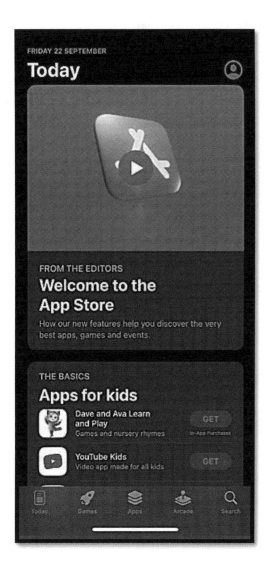

5. To find the exact app you're looking for; choose the **"Apps"** button located at the bottom and browse through several categories such as **"Games," "Health & Fitness," "Productivity,"** and many more. To locate certain applications or app categories, you may also use the search box at the top.

6. In case you are aware of the app's name or have certain terms in mind, just touch on the magnifying glass-shaped search button located in the lower right corner of the screen. Input your search settings and peruse the outcomes.

7. To discover additional information about an app you find interesting, touch on its icon. You can check the app's ratings, read user reviews, see screenshots, and read a description here.

8. If you choose to download an app, just touch the **"Get"** button (or, if it's a paid app, the pricing button). To verify the download, you may be asked to use Face ID or enter your Apple ID password. Watch the directions on the screen.

9. Your home screen will display the app's icon after the download is finished. Via there, you can launch it, or swipe to the right of the home screen page to access it via the App Library.

10. Frequently check the "**Updates**" tab at the bottom of the App Store for updates to ensure your applications are up to date with the newest features and security patches. If updates are available, choose "**Update All**" or press the "**Update**" icon next to each app.

11. If you have any app subscriptions, you may check, edit, or cancel them by pressing on your profile image in the upper right corner of the App Store and choosing "**Subscriptions**."

How to search for an app in the Apple App Store

Use these easy methods to look for an app in the Apple App Store on an iPhone 15 Series:

1. To unlock your device, you must use Face ID or your device passcode.
2. Find the icon labeled "**App Store**" on your home screen. It resembles a blue "**A**" constructed with a paintbrush, ruler, and pencil. On tapping it, the App Store will open.

3. The App Store has five tabs at the bottom: Today, Games, Apps, Arcade, and Search. On the far right, there is a **"Search"** option that resembles a magnifying glass. Tap on it.

4. There will be a search box at the top of the screen if you choose the Search option. Press and hold it to reveal the keyboard. Next, enter the name of the application or a relevant search term associated with it.

5. The App Store will start to provide search results underneath the search box as you write. Apps that fit your search criteria will be included in these results.

6. Navigate through the search results to locate the desired app. To get further information about the app, such as screenshots, reviews, and ratings, you can touch on each result.

7. Once the desired software has been located, touch it to bring up its software Store page. There will be an **"Install"** or **"Get"** button on this page, depending on whether the software is free or not. To download and install the app, tap this button.

8. Depending on your device's settings, you may be asked to verify your download using your Apple ID password or Face ID.

9. The application will begin to download, and when it's finished, its icon will show up on your home screen.

10. Now, you can touch the app's icon on your home screen to launch it.

How to install an app

Here's how to install an application:

1. Depending on your settings, you can either push the side button or touch the screen to wake up your iPhone. If your iPhone is locked, you can unlock it using Face ID or by entering your password.

2. On your home screen, look for the App Store icon. The App Store may be accessed by tapping on the blue symbol with the white letter "**A**."

3. There are many methods to locate the software you're looking for in the software Store:

- **Search Bar**: Type the name of the desired app in the top search bar after selecting the Search tab, which appears like a magnifying glass, at the bottom of the screen.

- **Browse**: By pressing on the Explore or Categories buttons at the bottom, you can easily peruse through different app categories.

- **App Recommendations**: The Today tab on Apple often features applications that are well-liked and highly recommended. You can see whether the desired app is listed there.

4. Once the desired app has been located, touch it to see its information page. This section contains details about the app, such as reviews, descriptions, and screenshots.

5. You will notice a button that either reads "**Get**" or shows the app's pricing on the details page. The word "**Get**" will appear if the app is free, and the price will be shown if it is purchased. Give this button a tap.

6. You will be required to authenticate with your Apple ID, which may require you to use Face ID or enter your Apple ID password if requested.

7. The app will begin downloading and installing after successful authentication. A progress circle will be seen on the app icon. When it's finished, the **"Get"** symbol will become **"Open."**

8. Locate the newly installed app on your home screen and touch on its icon there, or you can press the **"Open"** button next to its icon to launch it.

9. When using particular applications for the first time, you may need to give them special rights or configure their settings. Use the on-screen instructions to adjust the app's settings as necessary.

How to manage your downloads

Follow the steps below:

1. With any of your iPhone 15 Series smartphones, open the **App Store**. Tapping the App Store icon on your home screen will enable you to do this.

2. You can identify your account profile by looking for the symbol in the App Store's lower right corner.

3. You'll need to sign in using your Apple ID and password if you haven't previously done so.
4. You will further be redirected to your Account page after logging in. You may access several Apple ID-related settings here.
5. Select **"Purchased"** by tapping on it. When you click on this, a list of every app you've ever downloaded or bought using your Apple ID will appear.
6. Opt to restrict your downloads by choosing categories like **"Not on This iPhone," "Family Purchases," or "Not on This iPad"** if you have several Apple devices. By default, your app downloads are organized by **"All."**
7. Locate the app you want to re-download by using the search box at the top or by simply scrolling through the list of previously downloaded apps. Once you've located it, press the download symbol (an arrow-shaped cloud) that appears next to the app's name. Your smartphone will begin to download the app.
8. Return to the Account page and scroll down to manage app updates. Below the **"Updates Available"** column, a list of applications that need updates will be shown. Select **"Update"** to update each app individually, or select **"Update All"** to update every app that is currently accessible.
9. You may **"Offload"** applications from your smartphone to clear up space while retaining the app data. Navigate to **[Your Device] > Settings > [Your Name] > iCloud > Manage Storage > Backups**. You can also **"Offload Unused Apps"** under **"Recommendations,"** which will delete the app but save its files and information. When necessary, you can re-download the program from the App Store.
10. To fully delete an app along with all of its data, touch and hold the icon until it begins to jitter on your home screen, and then hit the **"Delete" (X) button**.

How to update apps

Update applications as follows:

1. If your iPhone is locked, use Face ID or enter your password to open it.
2. On your home screen, find the App Store icon, which resembles a blue "A" surrounded by a white circle. On tapping it, the App Store will open.

3. The App Store should have five tabs at the bottom: Today, Games, Apps, Updates, and Search. The **"Updates"** tab, which looks like a downward arrow within a circle, should be tapped. You can examine the available updates in the Updates area after doing this.

4. A list of applications with awaiting updates can be found here. Apps may be updated individually by pressing **"Update"** next to each one, or all at once by tapping "Update All" in the upper right corner.

5. To authenticate the update process, you could be asked to enter your Apple ID password or use Face ID. This is to guarantee safety.

6. One by one, the applications will begin to download and install. Each app's icon has a progress bar that shows you how far along the download and installation are.

7. After all the updates are finished, you can either go back to your home screen and start the updated applications from there, or you'll see an **"Open"** option next to each updated app, enabling you to begin it immediately.

8. Updates for apps may bring in new features or call for additional permissions. After upgrading, you may want to make sure everything is configured to your liking by looking through the app's options.

How to manage app subscriptions

To monitor your spending and prevent unforeseen fees, you must manage your app subscriptions on the Apple App Store.

The steps:

1. On the home screen of your iPhone, tap the App Store icon. This is symbolized by a blue icon with the white letter **"A."**

2. You'll need to sign in using your Apple ID and password if you haven't previously. Verify whether you are using the same Apple ID that you used to buy or subscribe to applications.

3. In the App Store, tap on your initials or profile image in the top right corner. You will then be directed to your account page.

4. To access all of your active app subscriptions, tap the **"Subscriptions"** section that appears on your account page.

5. This brings up a list of all the active subscriptions linked to your Apple ID, along with information about each one, including its name, price, and renewal date.

6. Tap on the subscription you want to cancel to get rid of it. One of the options you'll see is **"Cancel Subscription**." To complete the cancellation, follow the on-screen instructions. Make sure you read any further information provided about the cancellation, such as whether you may continue using the service until the conclusion of the current subscription cycle.

7. To move to a different subscription plan that the same app offers, touch **"Change Subscription**." Then, follow the instructions to choose a new plan and validate the change.

8. Additionally, you can re-subscribe in this area if you've already canceled your membership. To resubscribe, tap the app you want to use again and follow the on-screen instructions.

9. It's also possible to set up subscription alerts to prevent unforeseen expenses. Apple can notify you through email before a subscription renewal. To enable push notifications for a particular subscription, choose **"Subscriptions"** and then **"Notify Me"** next to it.

10. Regularly reviewing your app subscriptions is a smart idea, particularly if you download new applications often. By doing this, you may make sure you're not paying for services you don't need or use anymore.

How to leave reviews and ratings

You can rate and review apps on the Apple App Store in the following ways:

1. To begin, use Face ID or your password to unlock your iPhone.
2. On the home screen of your iPhone, tap the **"App Store"** icon. This will launch the App Store software.
3. Locate the app you want to review and rate using the search box at the bottom of the screen. Enter the name of the program or some associated keywords, and then hit the keyboard's **"Search"** button.

4. After locating the app you want to review, click or press its icon to see the product page.

5. To read details about the app, such as reviews, descriptions, and screenshots, scroll down the product page.

6. Touch the stars to rate the app under the "**Ratings & Reviews**" section, which is located beneath the app's icon and description. By clicking the "**Write a Review**" button, you can also write a review.

7. When you choose "**Write a Review**," a pop-up window with your review will show up. You have the option to type your review content, including a title, and provide a star rating. Provide an unbiased and instructive evaluation.

8. To publish your review, click **"Send"** after finishing it. You may be prompted to validate your review before it is posted.

9. Before your review is published, you may be asked to provide your Apple ID password or use Face ID to verify your identity.

10. Your rating and any further user reviews should now be shown on the app's product page, along with your review.

How to use privacy and permissions

1. **Accessing Privacy and Permissions**:
- Open the iPhone and go to the home screen.
- The **"App Store"** icon, usually a blue symbol with a white "A" on it, should be tapped.

2. **Review App Permissions**:
- The major functions of the App Store are app updates and downloads, but the Settings app is where you control permissions for applications. Navigate to your home screen and choose the **"Settings"** app by tapping on the gear symbol.

3. **Privacy Settings**:
- Tap **"Privacy"** after swiping down.

4. **App Permissions**:
- There are several sections under **"Privacy,"** including Location Services, Camera, Microphone, Contacts, and more. The permissions that applications can seek are represented by these categories.
- Press on the category (like Location Services) that you want to control.

5. **App List**:

- A list of applications that have asked to be allowed access to that specific category will appear. Accessible apps will be labeled **"ON,"** while inaccessible apps will be labeled **"OFF."**

6. **Manage Permissions**:
- To change an application's permission, just touch on its name.
- Depending on the permission category, you may then choose between alternatives like **"Allow While Using App," "Allow Once," or "Don't Allow."**

7. **App Store Specific Settings**:
- You can find similar options under the **"App Store"** section in your iPhone's settings if you want to modify permissions specific to the App Store, such as whether it may use your location to provide customized suggestions.

8. **App Updates and Privacy Information**:
- Apple added privacy labels to App Store applications, which tell you how your data is collected and used by the app. To help you make wise decisions, you can check these labels before installing or upgrading an app.

9. **App Store Restrictions**:
- Restrictions for the App Store can also be put up for more security and privacy. Usually, you can adjust this under the **"Screen Time"** area of your iPhone's settings.

How to access the app library in the Apple App Store

To use the App Library, go to:

1. Go to your home screen after unlocking your iPhone. The folders and app icons should be visible to you as normal.
2. On your home screen, swipe left to open the App Library. Your apps are automatically categorized into folders in the App Library, a special section, according to their use and kind.
3. You can discover a variety of folders in the App Library, including Recently Added and Suggestions. To see and launch the programs within these folders, just touch on them.

4. Use the search box at the top of the app Library screen to locate the program you're searching for if it's not in one of the folders. Just enter the name of the desired program, and it will show up in the list of results when you put it in.

5. Swipe down on the App Library page or hit the search box to reach the app categories. This will show you a list of categories to assist you in locating certain app categories.

6. To go back to your normal home screen with folders and app icons, just press or slide right from the App Library section.

Frequently Asked Questions

1. How do you access the Apple App Store on your iPhone 15 Series?
2. How do you search for an app and explore the app store?
3. How do you manage app subscriptions?
4. How do you manage your downloads?
5. How do you have privacy and permissions?
6. How do you use reviews and ratings?

CHAPTER SIXTEEN
FILES APP

Overview

The Files app houses all your contents including documents and its likes. With this app, you can easily organize, sort, and search for your files with ease.

How to access and navigate the Files App

Here's how to use your iPhone 15 Series' Files app and get around it:

1. **Using the Files App**:
- To reach the "**Search**" feature on your iPhone, slide right or downward on the home screen.
- Type "**Files**" into the upper search field, then press the "**Files**" app icon when it shows up in the search results.

2. **Navigating the Files App**:
- Explore and manage your files and folders using the user interface that appears when you launch the Files app.

Browse Locations

- Tabs like **"Search," "Recents," "Browse," and "Favorites"** are located at the bottom. You can examine your files in multiple places by tapping "**Browse**".

Viewing Files and Folders

- To open or see the contents of a folder or file, tap on it. Pinch motions may also be used to enlarge and reduce the size of thumbnails.

Creating Folders

- Press and hold the ellipsis (...) symbol, which is often found in the upper-right corner, to create a new folder, then choose "**New Folder**." Select the folder's location and give it a name.

Organizing Files

- Files and folders can be moved, copied, or deleted by choosing them and touching the corresponding action icon (which is often represented by an arrow-pointing folder, a copy icon, or a trash can).

Favorites

- You can easily favorite files or folders to easily retrieve them when needed. All you have to do is touch and hold a file or folder and choose "**Add to Favorites**."

Search

- Type keywords into the "**Search**" tab to locate files or folders easily.

3. **File Management**:

- The Files app allows you to handle files in the same way as you would on a computer. File and folder creation, renaming, transferring, copying, and deletion are all included in this.

How to browse your files

Here's how to use your iPhone's Files app to browse your files:

1. Locate and press the **Files app icon** on your iPhone's home screen to launch the application.
2. **Browse Locations**:
- **iCloud Drive**: When you launch the Files app by default, files saved in your iCloud account are accessible through iCloud Drive.

- **On My iPhone**: By choosing "**On My iPhone**," you can also see files that are locally saved on your device. For handling files that are not stored in iCloud, this option is helpful.
- **Other Locations**: You could notice other places, such as external storage devices if your iPhone supports them or third-party cloud storage services (like Google Drive and Dropbox), depending on the applications and services you use.

3. To open it, tap a place. Usually, there is a folder structure that arranges your files within each place. To open a folder and see its contents, tap on it.
4. A list of the files and folders within a folder or location appears when you touch on it. You may locate the desired file by swiping through the list.
5. Tap and hold on to a file or folder to execute an operation. A menu with choices to Copy, Move, Delete, Share, and more will appear as a result.

6. Use the search box at the top of the Files app to locate particular files if you have a lot of them. To get relevant results, just input the file name or keywords into the app.

7. By selecting the "**Sort**" option, you may arrange files according to size, date, or name. Use the three dots (ellipsis) symbol to create new folders and move files around. Then, choose "**New Folder**" or "**Move.**"

8. To examine a file's contents, tap on it. You can view, listen to, or read the file from inside the app, depending on the kind of file.

9. To share a file with someone, press and hold it, click "**Share**," and then choose the desired method (such as Mail, Messages, or AirDrop)

10. Choose to download files from iCloud Drive for offline use. Select "**Keep Offline**" from the three dots that appear next to a file to make sure you can view it without an internet connection.

How to manage files and folders

You can simply manage, browse, and access your documents and files using the Files app. It may be done as follows:

1. To locate and launch the app, swipe down from your home screen and input "**Files**" into the search box.

2. When it opens, the layout resembles that of a computer's file explorer or Finder. At the bottom of the screen, you'll see numerous options: Recents, Browse, Search, and Edit.

3. **Browsing File and Folder**:
    ● To see your files and folders, tap the "**Browse**" tab.
    ● If you have set up additional associated cloud services like Dropbox or Google Drive, you'll see a list of places like iCloud Drive, On My iPhone, and others.

4. **Creating Folders**:
    ● Press and hold the three dots (typically in the upper right corner) to bring up the menu, and then choose "**New Folder**."
    ● After giving your folder a name and selecting its location, click "**Done.**"

5. **Moving and Organizing Files**:
- To relocate a file, drag it to the intended folder after long-pressing on it to make it lift off the screen.
- Moreover, you can pick several files using the **"Edit"** option, and then choose **"Move"** to move them to a folder.

6. **Renaming Folders or Files**:
- To edit a file or folder, touch its name at the top after selecting it with your finger.
- To save the modified name, press the **"Done"** key on the keyboard after making your edits.

7. **Deleting Files or Folders**:
- Tap the file or folder that you want to remove.
- To remove the chosen item, tap the trash can symbol at the bottom.
- Exercise caution as it's not always possible to retrieve lost data.

8. **Sharing Files**:
- To share files, choose them and press the **share icon**, which is often an upward arrow.
- Select the sharing option you want to use, from Mail, Messages, AirDrop, or other installed applications.

9. **Searching for Files**:
- Apply the search function located at the top of the screen to locate files or folders by name with ease.

10. **Accessing Cloud Services**:
- You can view and manage files saved in cloud services—like iCloud, Dropbox, and Google Drive—if you've connected them. These services will show up in the Files app.

11. **Favorites and Tags**:
- For convenient access, you can tag and favorite files. After putting your finger on a file, choose "**Tag**" or "**Add to Favorites**."

How to access iCloud drive

Here's how to use your iPhone to access iCloud Drive:

1. If your iPhone isn't already unlocked, start by unlocking it.
2. Your iPhone's default app is the Files app. It resembles the symbol of a blue folder. Usually, you can use the search bar at the top of your home screen or swipe down to discover it on your home screen.
3. To access the Files app, tap its icon.
4. **Go to the iCloud Drive page:** A list of Locations should appear on the left side of the Files app once it is open. Click "**iCloud Drive**" to see the files and folders stored on your iCloud Drive.
5. Your iCloud Drive's contents are now visible to you. Just like in any file manager, you can browse through folders and files.
6. To see any file, just touch on it. You may also edit the file directly from the Files app using suitable applications like Pages for documents, Numbers for spreadsheets, or Photos for photos if the file type is compatible.
7. To upload files to iCloud Drive, hit the Files apps '**+**' icon in the upper left corner, then choose "**Upload**." After that, you may choose the file from your device to upload.

How to connect other cloud services in the Files app

The steps:

1. Check that the most recent version of the software update (iOS 17) is installed on your iPhone. Select **"Settings" > "General" > "Software Update"** to see if there are any updates available, then install them.
2. Download the app for the cloud service you want to link to the Files app, if you haven't already. For services such as Dropbox, OneDrive, and Google Drive, for instance, download the corresponding applications from the App Store.
3. Launch the just downloaded cloud service application and log in using your login details.
4. **Turn on the Files App Integration**:
   - To connect iCloud with the Files app, you must first ensure that you are logged in using your Apple ID under **"Settings" > [Your Name] > "iCloud."** Switch on iCloud Drive.
   - **Regarding Third-Party Services:** The Files app may be integrated with several cloud services, such as Dropbox and Google Drive. It may be necessary for you to activate this integration from the cloud service app's settings. Search for **"Files"** or **"Document Provider"**-related options.
5. Launch the iPhone's Files app.
6. If the **"Browse"** option isn't already chosen, press it at the bottom of the Files app. Next, choose **"Edit"** located in the upper-right corner, then **"Add"** to include a new place.
7. A list of cloud services that are accessible ought to appear. To connect, tap on the desired one.
8. Enter your login information for that particular cloud service if requested. For the Files app to access your files on the cloud service, you also need to provide permissions.
9. After connecting, the Files app should allow you to access, view, and manage the files that are stored on the cloud service.

How to search for files

To search for files in the Files app on an iPhone, follow these basic steps:

1. From the home screen of your iPhone, launch the **"Files"** app. usually; the symbol has the appearance of a blue folder.
2. To access the locations of your files, tap the **"Browse"** button at the bottom of the screen. You can see files that are saved on your smartphone, in third-party applications like Google Drive, or cloud services like iCloud Drive.
3. Locate the place where you want to do a file search. You can press **"iCloud Drive," "Recents,"** or any other folder where you have files saved.
4. There ought to be a search bar at the top of the screen. Pressing on it will initiate the search feature.

5. Type in the search phrases you want to use to locate your files using the on-screen keyboard. This might include any text that may be in the file, the file name, or keywords.
6. The Files app will begin providing search results that are relevant to your query as you enter. To access or see the file, just touch on any of these results.
7. If there are a lot of search results, you can narrow down your search by using more keywords or filters, if any are accessible.

8. After you locate the file you want, touch on it to open it or carry out further operations like transferring, copying, or erasing it.

How to view and share files in the Files App

Using the Files App to View Files:

1. Locate and open the **Files app** to launch it from your iPhone's home screen.
2. Your files can be saved in a list of locations and folders that you can view within the Files app. iCloud Drive, On My iPhone, and any other third-party cloud storage services you've linked, such as Dropbox or Google Drive, could be among them. To access your files, tap the relevant directory or folder.
3. A list of files will appear after you've navigated to a folder or location. To open and see a file, tap on it. Documents, photos, movies, and other file formats are supported by the Files app.

Using the Files App to Share Files

The iOS sharing function, which lets you, transmit files through a variety of applications and ways is usually used to share files via the Files app.

This is how a file can be shared:

1. Locate the file you want to share by opening the Files App.
2. To share a file, press and hold it. This will bring up a menu with many options.
3. From the menu, choose the "**Share**" option.
4. A share sheet with a list of applications and ways to distribute the file will show up. Messages, Mail, AirDrop, third-party applications, and more methods are available for sharing.
5. You will need to input the recipient's information or choose them from your contacts, depending on the sharing method you've selected.
6. To finish the sharing procedure, adhere to the on-screen instructions.

How to tag and sort files

Using the Files App on an iPhone, you can categorize and organize files in the following broad ways:

1. Find the "**Files**" app icon on the home screen of your iPhone. That seems to be a blue folder.
2. **Navigating to your Files App**:
- To access the "**Files**" app, just tap on it.
- Usually, other sections appear, such as **"Browse," "Recents," "On My iPhone,"** and **"iCloud Drive."** Select the folder where your files are kept.
3. Locate the folder or place where the files you want to categorize and sort are kept.
4. **Tagging Files**:
- Tap on the file or files that you want to tag. You can choose more than one file if necessary.
- After its chosen, press the toolbar's "**More**" option (shown by three dots) or the ellipsis (...) button.

5. **Adding Tags**:
- Scroll through the menu that displays and find an item labeled "**Tags**" or "**Add Tags.**"
- Press and hold it to add new tags or choose from ones that already exist. Using tags makes it easier to classify and arrange your files for quick access.

6. **Sorting Files**:
- You can often press the "**Sort**" or "**Arrange**" option, which is typically shown by an icon with arrows or lines, to sort files inside a folder.
- Decide on the sorting settings you want, such as size, date, or name. You can arrange files on your device in either ascending or descending order.

7. Generally, you can press the "**Browse**" tab and search for the "**Tags**" section to browse files with specified tags. You can also choose the desired tag there, and all files connected to that tag will be shown.

Frequently Asked Questions

1. How do you access and navigate the Files App?
2. How do you browse or manage files and folders?
3. How do you access iCloud drive?
4. How do you tag and sort files in the Files app?
5. How do you view and share in the Files app?

CHAPTER SEVENTEEN
APPLE MUSIC

Overview

In this chapter, you will learn about playing songs on any of your iPhone 15 Series via Apple Music. Additionally, you will also learn how to create playlists, subscribe to Apple Music, and so much more.

How to sign in to Apple Music

Here are the steps:

1. First, get your device unlocked. The home screen ought to be visible.
2. To locate the Apple Music app, either swipe through your home screens or uses the search feature. On a white background, there is an emblem featuring a musical note. To launch the app, tap on it.
3. Usually, the Apple Music app will ask you to create an account or log in. Look for the **"Library"** link at the bottom of the page if you aren't sent straight to the sign-in screen. Tap on it.

4. At this point, you must log in using your Apple ID; if you don't have one, choose the **"Create New Apple ID" or "Don't have an Apple ID or forgot it?"** options to create one. On the other hand, if you already have an Apple ID, choose "**Sign In**" and fill out the boxes using your password and Apple ID.

5. You could be required to provide further verification, such as Face ID or inputting a code that has been given to your trusted devices, according to your security settings. To finish this stage, adhere to the instructions shown on the screen.

6. If you're new to Apple Music, you'll be able to customize your music collection and choose your preferred genres. You can customize your Apple Music experience by following the instructions. If you're just logging into an already-existing Apple Music account, your preferences and library ought to be set up.

7. After successfully logging in, you are free to start using Apple Music. You can create your playlists, explore and listen to a large music, playlist, and album collection, and do much more.

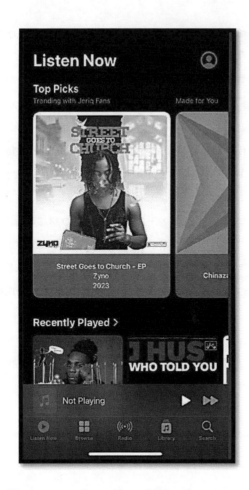

How to Subscribe to Apple Music on your iPhone 15 Series

These easy methods can be used to sign up for Apple Music on the iPhone 15 Series:

1. To begin, unlock your iPhone 15 Series. Use your password or Face ID to complete this step.
2. On your iPhone, find the Apple Music app. usually represented by a vibrant musical note symbol, you can find it on your home screen or, if you've arranged your applications that way, in the App Library.
3. Click the **"Sign In"** button and input your Apple ID and password if you haven't previously. On the off chance that you don't have one, you can hit **"Create New Apple ID."**

4. The Apple Music app has many tabs down the bottom, including **"Browse,"** **"Radio," "For You,"** and **"Library."**

5. You should notice a banner or a section promoting Apple Music under the "**For You**" menu. "**Try it free**" or a similar phrase could be shown. Click or tap this area or banner.

6. There are several ways to subscribe to Apple Music, including individual, family, and student subscriptions. After deciding which plan best meets your requirements, touch on it.

7. You may be asked to verify the method of payment. You will need to add a valid payment method to your Apple ID if you haven't already. To input your payment information, adhere to the on-screen instructions.

8. You will be able to check your subscription information after verifying your payment method. Verify that everything seems to be in order, and then approve the subscription. You may be prompted to utilize Face ID or enter your Apple ID password to verify.

9. Also, you will have access to the extensive catalog of music, playlists, and other content as soon as your membership is validated. You can immediately begin browsing and enjoying your favorite tunes.

10. By pressing the download symbol next to the material you want to keep, you can download songs and albums for offline listening.

How to Browse and Play Music

Use these instructions below to browse and play songs on Apple songs on your iPhone 15 Series:

1. Before getting started, confirm that your Apple Music membership is current. If not, you can use the Apple Music app to sign up for one.

2. To take advantage of the newest features and enhancements, make sure your iPhone is running the most recent version of iOS.

3. On your iPhone 15 Series, find the Apple Music app. It's the white-backed emblem with a musical note.

4. Enter your Apple ID and password to log in if you haven't already.

5. There are several areas on the Apple Music app's home screen where you may find music. Recommendations based on playlists, new releases, your listening history, and other factors are available.

6. To locate certain tracks, albums, or musicians, click the magnifying glass symbol located in the lower right corner to open the search bar. Enter the name of the desired song, album, or performer and hit **"Search."**

7. By selecting the **"Browse"** option at the bottom, you may listen to music. You can discover carefully chosen genres, playlists, and music choices depending on moods here.

8. Press the **"+"** button to start a new playlist, give it a name, and begin adding music. Alternatively, press the **"Library"** tab at the bottom and choose **"Playlists."**

9. Tap the song or album you want to listen to when you've found it. The play button (a triangle symbol) may then be tapped to begin listening. To access

more choices, such as adding the album to your playlist or library, you can also touch its cover.

10. To download music for offline playback, press the three dots (...) next to a song or album, then choose "**Download**." This feature is helpful for times when you don't have access to the internet. Apple Music provides a selection of radio stations and performances. By selecting the "**Radio**" option at the bottom, you can go to them.

11. Select "**Recently Played**" from the "**Library**" menu to see the music you've recently listened to.

12. Use the Control Center on the Lock Screen or swipe up from the bottom of the screen to expose it while you're listening to music.

13. As Apple Music gets to know your taste in music, it will provide tailored suggestions under the "**For You**" tab.

14. Apple Music is compatible with many devices. While a song is playing, press the **AirPlay symbol** and choose the relevant device to switch between devices for playback.

How to Create a Playlist

The steps:

1. Start by unlocking your iPhone 15 series and making sure you have an internet connection.

2. To access Apple Music, find the app on your iPhone's home screen. Apps usually have it on the bottom row and have a musical note icon for it.

3. You need to enter your Apple ID and password to access Apple Music if you haven't done so previously.

4. To access the Library, swipe left on the screen to see the "**Library**" tab. You can access your music collection by doing this.

5. **Proceed to create a new playlist:**
- "**Playlists**" will be at the top of the Library screen. Endeavor to tap on it.
- Press the "**+ New Playlist**" button now. Usually, it's located in the upper-right corner of the screen.

6. A window will appear asking you to identify your playlist. After giving your playlist a name that reflects its concept or goal, hit the **"Done"** key on the keyboard.

7. Return to your Library or use the search function to locate music to add to your recently made playlist.

8. Select the three dots (...) that appear next to the music title after you've identified one you wish to add.

9. From the list of options that display, choose **"Add to a Playlist."**

10. Select the newly created playlist from the list.

11. To add a song to the playlist, go back and repeat it for each song.

12. You can rearrange the music in your playlist by tapping and holding on to a song, then dragging it to the correct spot.

13. Songs can be deleted from your playlist by tapping the three dots (...) next to the title of the song, then choosing **"Remove from This Playlist."**

14. To save your playlist, touch **"Done"** in the upper-right corner of the screen once you've included all the songs you want.

15. Now that your new playlist is ready, go ahead and enjoy it. To play it, just touch the title in your library.

How to Share Apple Music with Family Members

Here's how to share Apple music with family members:

1. Verify that you have the Family Plan subscription for Apple Music. If not, you can sign up by selecting the Family Plan option on the Apple Music app.

2. Take a look at your iPhone 15 Series' **"Settings"** app.

3. To access your Apple ID at the top of the screen, scroll down and touch it.

4. Next, choose **"Family Sharing."**

5. To invite a family member, tap **"Add Family Member"** and input their Apple ID email address. An invitation to join your Family Sharing group will be sent to them.

6. An email invitation or an iOS device notice will be sent to the family member you have invited. To become a member of the Family Sharing group, they must accept the invitation.

7. After accepting the invitation, your family members need to use the "**Settings**" app on their iPhone 15 Series.
8. Tap on their Apple ID after swiping down.
9. Then choose "**Media & Purchases**."
10. Click on "**Subscriptions**."
11. Under **"Apple Music,"** the Family Plan ought to be shown. Click "**Join**" or "**Activate**" to begin sharing your Apple Music collection.
12. As of right now, every family member in your Family Sharing group is eligible for the Family Plan's access to Apple Music. Without paying extra, they may make playlists, listen to their favorite songs, and use all of Apple Music's features.
13. Go to **"Settings"** > **[Your Name]** > **"Family Sharing"** to control the group's members, payment options, and other configurations as the group organizer.
14. Recall that the Family Sharing coordinator is in charge of paying for the subscription, and each member of the family has to have their own Apple ID.

How to Listen to Music Shared with You

You can find new music to appreciate or hear your friends' favorite songs by listening to shared music on Apple Music.

Here's how to use your iPhone 15 Series to do it:

1. To start, unlock your iPhone and make sure you have a Wi-Fi or mobile data connection to the internet.
2. To access Apple Music, find the app on your iPhone's home screen. Usually, it takes the form of a vibrant musical note symbol. To launch the app, tap on it.
3. The "**Library**" tab is often located at the bottom of the Apple Music app after you've opened it. If not, click "**Library**" to open your music collection.
4. You can often find shared music by opening a message in the Apple Music app or by receiving a notice. You can usually locate songs shared by friends under the "**For You**" or "**Shared with You**" tabs, or by checking your Apple songs alerts.

5. Tap the shared music that you want to listen to when you've located it. This will direct you to the page for that song or album.

6. You have the option to add a song or album to your music library for offline listening by tapping the **"+ Add"** button, or you can hit the **"Play"** button to begin streaming the music right now.

7. After deciding on your favorite choice, you may begin to listen to the shared music. As necessary, change the playback and volume settings.

8. Using the sharing tools included in the Apple Music app, you can like, comment on, or even share the music that your friend shared with you with others if you like it.

How to Download Music for Offline Listening

To use Apple songs to download songs to your iPhone 15 Series for offline listening, follow these steps:

1. Make sure the Apple Music app is up to date by updating it. If not, get the most recent version from the App Store.

2. If you haven't done so already, sign up for Apple Music. A current membership is required to download songs for offline listening. Open the Apple Music app, choose the **"For You"** option, and then follow the on-screen instructions to begin a trial or subscribe.

3. On your iPhone 15 Series, open the **Apple Music app**.

4. To locate the music you want to download, use the search box or browse the different tabs. You can check music based on genres, playlists, albums, or artists.

5. Tap the song or album to bring up the information page once you've located the one you want to download.

6. A download icon will appear on the information page. It resembles a cloud with an arrow pointing down. The music or album will start downloading to your device when you tap this icon.

7. To keep track of your download progress, hit the **"Library"** tab at the bottom and choose **"Downloads."** From there, you'll get a list of all the songs and albums that are now downloading.

8. After the song has finished downloading, you can listen to it offline without using the internet. The music you downloaded can be found in the **"Downloads"** section of your library.

9. In the Apple Music settings, activate the **"Cellular Data"** option to save cellular data. When there is no Wi-Fi, you can use your cellular connection to stream music; however, new music cannot be downloaded using this method.
10. To organize your offline downloads and save room on your device, go to **"Settings" > "Music" > "Downloaded Music."** From here, you can delete any tracks or albums that you no longer need.

Note that music downloaded via Apple Music is subject to DRM (Digital Rights Management), thus to access and enjoy your downloaded content, you must have an active Apple Music membership. You will not be able to listen to the tracks you downloaded once your membership expires unless you want to renew it.

How to Change or Cancel Your Apple Music Subscription

To change or cancel your Apple Music membership on an iPhone 15 Series, adhere to the following instructions:

Changing Your Apple Music Membership

1. On your iPhone 15, find the Apple Music app and tap to open it. Make sure the Apple ID associated with your subscription is used when you log in.
2. To access your account, just tap the profile icon, which is often found in the upper-right or upper-left area of the app's UI. You can access your account settings by doing this.
3. To manage your Apple Music membership, scroll down and choose **"Subscriptions**."
4. Select Apple Music by locating and tapping on **"Apple Music"** under the **"Active"** subscriptions column.
5. This option allows you to go from one kind of plan to another, for example, from an individual to a family plan or the other way around. To make your choice, adhere to the on-screen directions.
6. If you make a subscription modification, Apple can ask you to confirm it. Examine the specifics and verify the modifications.

Canceling Your Apple Music Membership

The steps:

1. First of all, ensure you follow the first 3 steps above.
2. To cancel your membership, go to the **"Active"** subscriptions area and choose **"Apple Music**."
3. Click **"Cancel Subscription**." You may be asked to provide a reason for the cancellation.
4. Apple will request clarification of the cancellation. Examine the details and verify the cancellation. This subscription will continue to function until the end of the current payment cycle.

5. Following cancellation, you won't be billed for the subsequent monthly cycle and your Apple Music membership won't automatically renew. Apple Music will be available to you until the conclusion of the current subscription month.

Always keep in mind that the Family Organizer is the only one who can change your Apple Music subscription if you're a part of a Family Sharing plan.

How to Connect Apple Music to Other Devices

Use these procedures to connect your iPhone 15 Series to additional devices to stream Apple Music:

1. Make sure that iOS 17 is the most recent version installed on your iPhone 15 Series. Go to **"Settings"** > **"General"** > **"Software Update"** to see if there are any updates available, then install them.
2. Ensure that your iPhone is connected to a Wi-Fi network by connecting it to one. Using cellular data to stream music might use up a lot of data.
3. Turn on your iPhone and open the Apple Music app. It is located on your home screen and may also be found via an App Store search.
4. Use your Apple ID and password to access your Apple Music account if you haven't previously.
5. To locate the songs, albums, or playlists you want to listen to on different devices, browse your music collection or the Apple Music catalog.
6. To begin playing music on a different device, tap on it.
7. Use the Control Center to access AirPlay by swiping down from the top-right corner of your iPhone 15. A range of settings, including playback options, will be shown to you.
8. Press and hold the AirPlay symbol in the Control Center.
9. Select the destination device to get a list of devices that may be used for playback. Other Apple products like HomePods, Apple TVs, and speakers with AirPlay connections might fall under this category. Choose the device that you want to broadcast music to.

10. The song will begin to play on the selected device after you've made that choice. Playback controls (pause, skip, and volume adjustments) are available from your iPhone.
11. To cease the other device's music streaming, go back to the Control Center, hit the AirPlay icon once again, and choose "**iPhone**" or "**Disconnect**."
12. You can now use the selected device to listen to your Apple Music.

Note that for AirPlay to function properly, your iPhone and the target device need to be linked to the same Wi-Fi network. Make sure your target device is compatible with Apple Music and AirPlay as well.

How to Manage Your Subscription

Here is a step-by-step guide to assist you in changing your membership plan, updating your payment method, or canceling your subscription:

1. On your iPhone 15 Series, find the Apple Music app and tap to launch it. Verify that the Apple ID you are using to log in is the same as the one connected to your Apple Music subscription.
2. Press and hold your initials or profile image in the app's upper-left corner. You can access your account settings by doing this.
3. Locate and touch the "**Subscriptions**" area after swiping down. A list of your active subscriptions, which includes Apple Music, will be shown.
4. To see the information and administration options for the "**Apple Music**" subscription, tap on it.

5. **Subscription Settings:**

Here are the options here:

- **Change Plan**: Tap "**Change Plan**" and follow the instructions to choose a new Apple Music plan (switching, for example, from Individual to Family).
- **Payment Information**: To add or modify your credit card information, choose "**Payment Information**" and follow the on-screen instructions. This will update your payment method.

- **Cancel Subscription**: To end your Apple Music membership, choose this option and follow the instructions to make sure you've made the right choice. It should be noted that you may keep using Apple Music till the conclusion of the current subscription cycle.
6. The application will show you a confirmation page when any modifications are made. After making the modifications, check and validate them.
7. Depending on the modifications you made, you could be asked to use Face ID or passcode for verification or enter your Apple ID password.
8. You will get a confirmation notice when your changes are approved, and your Apple Music membership will be adjusted as a result.

Recall that the Family Organizer is the only person with the ability to modify the subscription if you are on a Family plan. To handle the subscription if you are not the organizer, get in touch with them.

How to Customize Apple Music Settings

On the iPhone 15 Series, adjusting your Apple Music preferences is a terrific way to improve your music-listening experience.

Try these steps to customize Apple Music to your taste, whether it's by changing the quality of your music, making personalized playlists, or fine-tuning your preferences:

1. On your iPhone 15 Series home screen, launch the Apple Music app.
2. Your profile image is represented by an icon in the app's lower right corner. To see your Apple Music profile, tap on it.
3. One of the gear wheel icons is located in the upper right corner of your profile page. To access your settings, just tap on it.
4. **Customize your Apple Music Settings:**
- **Sound Quality**: You can change the way your music sounds as it downloads or streams by going to the **"Music Quality"** area. Downloads, Wi-Fi streaming, and cellular streaming are all available to you. Select **"High Quality"** for optimal audio quality or **"Data Saver"** if you want to minimize data use.

- **Cellular Data**: You can change the amount of cellular data used by Apple Music for downloads and streaming by tapping on "**Cellular Data.**"

- **Downloaded Music**: Choose the location on your iPhone where you want to save your downloaded music in this area. The options are "**Downloads**" and "**iTunes Media.**"

- **Library**: It is possible to personalize the settings of your collection by turning on or off features such as **"Add Playlist Songs," "Add Playlist Albums," and "Add Music Videos."**

- **Playback**: Under "**Playback**," you can choose how songs are added to your queue by adjusting the "**Play Next Song**" option or by turning on "**Crossfade**" for a seamless transition between tracks.

- **Show in Library**: Select the kinds of information that show up in your library. It is up to you whether to display or hide items such as "**Cloud Music**" and "**Apple Music Mixes.**"

- **Automatic Downloads**: Turn on "**Automatic Downloads**" if you would want songs you add to your collection to be downloaded automatically.

5. To save your changes, be sure to press the "**Done**" button located in the upper-right corner after making the necessary modifications.

How to Listen to Audiobooks in Apple Books on iPhone 15 Pro

Using Apple Books to listen to audiobooks on the iPhone 15 Series can be done by following the steps below:

1. Verify that the most recent iOS version is installed on your iPhone 15 Series. To see whether there are any updates available, choose **"Settings" > "General" > "Software Update,"** download the update, and then install it.
2. On your iPhone, launch the "**Apple Books**" app.
3. Find titles you're interested in by browsing the "**Book Store**" or "**Audiobooks**" section if you haven't previously downloaded or bought audiobooks.

4. All you have to do is touch the book's cover and follow the instructions to buy or download it. Some audiobooks can be downloaded for free, while others need to be bought.

5. After obtaining audiobooks, choose the **"Library"** option located in the lower portion of the screen.

6. To access your audiobook collection, tap the **"Audiobooks"** option in your library.

7. Look through your collection of audiobooks to find the one you want to listen to.

8. To open the audiobook, tap its cover. The author's details, title, and cover art will be visible to you. The play button (a triangle within a circle) is located underneath that. To begin listening, tap it.

9. You have access to on-screen controls while you're listening to an audiobook.

10. To stop playing, use the stop button (two vertical bars).

11. To continue playing, tap the triangle-shaped play button once more. The slider is another tool for navigating the audiobook.

12. To adjust the pace at which you listen, just touch the playback speed symbol, which often resembles a speedometer, and choose the preferred speed.

13. To advance to the subsequent chapter or segment, use the forward button, which is often symbolized by a right arrow.

14. To return to the preceding chapter or segment, use the rewind button, which is often symbolized by a left-pointing arrow.

15. By pressing the bookmark or note icon, which is normally located in the playback controls, you can also add bookmarks and notes while you're listening.

16. It is possible to exit the Apple Books app while your audiobook is playing, and it will persist in the background.

17. Without unlocking your iPhone, you can access playback controls from the lock screen by swiping left or right.

18. For the best possible listening experience, ensure your Bluetooth speaker or headphones are connected to your iPhone.

How to Play an Audiobook

The methods below can be used to play an audiobook in Apple Books on the iPhone 15 Series:

1. If your iPhone hasn't been unlocked before, start by doing so. Proceed to enter your passcode or use Face ID to complete this step.
2. Find the **"Apple Books"** app on your iPhone to access Apple Books. Usually, it features a white symbol with many books on it. To launch the app, tap on it.
3. Open the Apple Books app and choose **"Library"** from the menu at the bottom of the screen. You can access your digital bookshelf by doing this.
4. Use the search box at the top of the page or browse through your library to discover the audiobook you want to listen to. It may be necessary for you to touch on **"Audiobooks"** to filter your collection just for audiobooks.
5. To start listening to an audiobook, touch the cover or title after you've located it.
6. These are located at the bottom of the screen. Play/pause, rewind, quick forward, and volume controls are a few of them. To begin listening to the audiobook, use the **play button** (a triangle symbol).
7. You can choose a different speed by tapping the playback speed button, which is often indicated by a '1x' or '1.0x' symbol.
8. Use the progress bar or the chapter symbol to get to the chosen chapter or section if you want to skip it.
9. You can also manage playback from the iPhone's lock screen or Control Center while the audiobook is playing. To use the playback controls in the Control Center, just slide down from the top-right corner of the screen.
10. Add notes to Apple Books or bookmark certain sections of the audiobook. Tapping on the bookmark or note symbol while listening will allow you to do this.
11. Tap the **AirPlay icon** in the Control Center or playback controls to make sure your audio output is configured appropriately if you wish to listen to the audiobook over headphones, AirPods, or external speakers.

12. Hit the pause button on the playback controls to halt or pause the playing. The app can be closed to stop your audiobook automatically.
13. When you're ready to continue listening, open **Apple Books**, navigate to your Library and touch the audiobook again. It should start up where you left off.

Frequently Asked Questions

1. How do you sign in and subscribe to Apple Music?
2. How do you browse and play music?
3. How do you create a playlist in Apple Music?
4. How do you download music for offline listening?
5. How do you listen to music shared with you in Apple Music?
6. How do you change or cancel your Apple Music subscription?
7. How do you connect Apple Music to other devices?

CHAPTER EIGHTEEN
APPLE PAY AND FAMILY SHARING

Overview

Chapter eighteen discusses Apple Pay and Family Sharing on your iPhone 15 Series. Apple Pay allows you to make purchases in stores and online and Family Sharing allows you to communicate with your family members.

Apple Pay

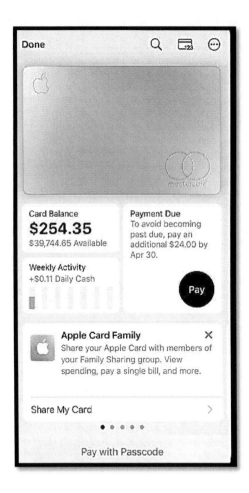

Numerous features included in devices make our regular tasks more convenient. Contactless payment, which eliminates the need to always carry your actual bank card with you, is one of its key advantages. The most prominent feature of the iPhone that was released to transform debit or credit cards from physical to virtual is Apple Pay. Payments can now be made in a couple of seconds using your iPhone. Only when you have correctly configured Apple Pay on your iPhone can any of these occur. The majority of consumers run into problems while using Apple Pay for contactless purchases at retail establishments.

Setting up Apple Pay

Even for those who are setting up Apple Pay for the first time, the process is rather simple.

Here are the steps:

1. Open the "**Wallet App**" on your iPhone 15 Series.

2. The "**Plus button**" symbol will then appear in the upper-right area of the screen. Simply tap it.

3. You can now choose from a variety of payment methods to add to Apple Pay, including applying for an Apple card or using a debit or credit card. Additionally, if supported in your area, you can choose to use the sophisticated capability known as transit.

4. Once you've chosen your preferred payment method, a box called **Add Cards** will appear. Here, you can add cards that were previously added to your prior iPhone by simply entering the CVC for authentication. Alternatively, add a whole new card and take a tour. Simply tap the option to "**Add a Different Card**."

5. After that, if the wallet app prompts you to do so, you can either input the credit/debit card's necessary information manually or hold it up to the camera. Your card will be immediately scanned.

6. You may now see your card in the Wallet app when Apple verifies all the details with your bank. If everything checks out, this process should take some time. Additionally, you will be notified through Apple Pay when your credit or debit card is ready to be used.

Once you have correctly configured Apple Pay by following the thorough instructions above, proceed with the following steps to use Apple Pay on your iPhone.

How to Use Apple Pay on iPhone 15 Series via Face ID?

The steps:

1. First of all, keep your phone close to the reader.

2. Next, regardless of how your iPhone is configured double-press the side button. When it launches, Apple Pay will be enabled, and your default card will be seen on the iPhone screen.
3. To confirm your face ID, now glance at your iPhone's screen at the happy face that appears.
4. The transaction will be completed in a matter of seconds once it validates you.

How To Choose Default Card for Apple Pay on iPhone 15 Series?

You must choose one of the cards you have added to your Wallet and Apple Pay as your default card for making purchases. When you use Apple Pay, the default card will be shown and you won't be prompted to choose from the other possible cards in your wallet.

Here are the steps:

1. Navigate to the "**Settings**" section on your iPhone.
2. After that, choose "**Wallet & Apple Pay**."
3. At this point, the "**Transaction Defaults**" section will be visible to you.
4. Select the default card from the list of possible cards under the transaction default section.

How To Enable & Use Apple Pay Express Transit on iPhone 15 Series?

Impressive is the new function that Apple Pay has added: Express Transit. Every transaction is now exempt from the need for further authentication. All you have to do to use fast transportation is set it up by adding the card and, once again, authenticating yourself. After that, at the time of transactions, no more verification will be needed. All you need to do is put your iPhone close to the NFC scanner. By doing this, you'll avoid authentication errors every time and complete transactions more quickly and easily. You will discover that this function saves more time. This function comes in handy in a lot of situations, such as metro stations, where you can use express transit to complete the necessary transactions in a matter of seconds if your metro card is out of balance and you need to quickly add the balance. To ensure that you never find yourself in a scenario where you need to do rapid transactions but are unable to use express transit, all you have to do is set up the express transit option on your iPhone.

Setting up Express Transit

1. Open the iPhone's **"Settings"** app.
2. Next, choose "**Wallet & Apple Pay**" by tapping on it.
3. At this point, the "**Transit Card**" option will be visible to you.
4. In addition, choose the "**Express Transit Card**" option found under the transit card section.
5. At last, choose the card and continue by following the directions shown on the screen.

You can now conduct transactions going forward without using Face ID or passcodes after your first card setup verification is finished.

How To Use Express Transit for Making Payments?

You can continue paying with express transit if you are in an area that accepts it, such as a metro station, retail center, or transportation network.

After completing the above-mentioned basic setup for express transit on your iPhone, do the following actions:

1. Hold the iPhone up to an express transit reader that is compatible.
2. Your transaction will be completed in a split second without requiring any verification, including passcodes or Face ID.

How to add a debit or credit card

The steps:

1. On your iPhone 15 Series, find and launch the **"Wallet"** app. usually, it has an image of a credit card with a blue and white symbol.

2. Locate the **"+"** (plus) symbol in the Wallet app's upper right corner. To start adding a new card, tap on it.
3. Choose "**Credit or Debit Card**" to get a list of available cards. Pick "Credit or Debit Card" to add a personal card.

4. **There are two ways you may add your card:**
- **Manual Entry:** If you choose this option, you will have to manually input the card number, expiry date, security code (CVV), and billing data.
- **Scan Card:** As an alternative, you can scan your card using the camera on your iPhone. Your iPhone will instantly recognize and enter the card information if

you place your card within the frame. Verify the information again to make sure they are accurate.

5. You could be prompted to go through and accept the terms and conditions from Apple Pay and your card issuer after entering your card information. After reading them, choose "**Agree**" or "**Accept**" to go on.

6. A procedure of verification will now be applied to your card. This might include getting a one-time verification number from your bank through text, email, or phone call. Kindly enter the code as directed.

7. You could be asked to configure extra security measures for Apple Pay, such as a PIN or Face ID verification, depending on your bank's policies.

8. The Wallet app will display your card after it has been successfully added. It may now be used for in-app purchases, web purchases, and contactless payments at participating businesses.

9. Choose which of the cards in your wallet to use as your primary payment method by tapping on the card and choosing "**Set as Default Card**." It will become the main card for Apple Pay transactions as a result.

How to find locations that support Apple Pay

Use the following methods to locate establishments that accept Apple Pay on the iPhone 15 Series:

1. Open the iPhone 15 and go to the home screen.

2. Locate and press the "**Maps**" app icon, which is often pre-installed, to launch it.

3. You must allow Location Services for the Maps app if you haven't previously. Check that "**Location Services**" is enabled by going to **"Settings" > "Privacy" > "Location Services"**

4. Type the name of the location or kind of business where you want to use Apple Pay into the search box at the top of the Maps app. You can look **for "coffee shops," "grocery stores,"** or a store's exact name.

5. Following the input of your search query, Maps will provide a list of findings on the interface. These are the locations that meet the parameters of your search.

6. Check for the Apple Pay logo in the search results, next to the listings. This emblem signifies that Apple Pay is accepted as a form of payment at this institution.
7. Tap on the listing of a particular establishment that accepts Apple Pay to get additional details about it.
8. You should find a section mentioning approved payment options in the location's comprehensive information. If Apple Pay is supported, it needs to be mentioned there.
9. You will receive turn-by-turn instructions to a location by tapping on the **"Directions"** button if you locate one that accepts Apple Pay and wishes to visit there.
10. Use Apple Pay at the checkout counter to purchase once you get to the store. All you have to do is place your iPhone 15 close to the contactless payment terminal and, when asked, confirm the transaction using Face ID or your password.

Do not forget that not every company may accept Apple Pay, so it's a good idea to make sure beforehand, particularly for bigger transactions. Furthermore, the accessibility of Apple Pay may differ depending on the nation and location, so be sure it's accepted where you live.

How to change your shipping and contact details

Follow the steps below to change your shipment and contact information in Apple Pay on the iPhone 15 Series:

1. On your home screen, find and press the **"Wallet"** app icon. You can control your Apple Pay settings using this app.
2. Open the Wallet app, then search for and press the **"Apple Pay"** icon to see the Apple Pay Settings. Usually, it takes the form of a vibrant card-shaped logo.
3. If you have more than one card linked to Apple Pay, choose the one for which you want to modify the contact and shipping information. To access the card's settings, tap on it.

4. This will display your card data, along with the shipping and contact details that are currently in effect.

5. Depending on your iOS version, the language for the **"Shipping Address" or "Shipping"** option may differ significantly. Tap on it to change your shipping address.

6. Tap the **"Contact"** or **"Contact Information"** option if you need to change your contact details.

7. At this point, you can update your contact details or shipping address as needed. Any necessary information, including your name, address, phone number, or email address, should be modified.

8. After making the necessary adjustments, locate the **"Save"** or **"Done"** button at the bottom of the screen. Press it to save your changes.

9. You could be asked by Apple to confirm the modifications. A verification code may be sent to the email address or phone number linked to your Apple ID to do this. To finish the verification procedure, adhere to the on-screen instructions.

10. A notice confirming your modifications will appear on your screen when they have been saved and validated.

How to pay in an application or on the internet

The steps:

1. Verify that your iPhone 15 Series device has Face ID enabled for authentication and that it supports Apple Pay.

2. You must configure Apple Pay on your smartphone if you haven't previously. To add credit or debit cards to Apple Pay, go to **Settings > Wallet & Apple Pay** and follow the instructions.

3. Open the app that you want to use to buy something or make a payment. Verify if the app accepts Apple Pay as a form of payment.

4. Look through the app to choose the product or service you want to purchase.

5. After deciding what you want to buy, either add it to your cart or use the app's unique checkout procedure.

6. After adding the item to your cart, go to the next screen.

7. Look for the payment options, and choose **Apple Pay** if prompted.

8. Use Face ID to verify the transaction. To use Face ID, just glance at your smartphone or press your finger on the fingerprint sensor. Enter the passcode on your smartphone if asked.

9. The credit or debit card you've connected to Apple Pay will be used by the app to execute the payment after authentication.

10. The app will provide you with a transaction confirmation as soon as the payment is authorized. Your smartphone may notify you that the payment was successful.

11. When not in use, make sure your iPhone is secured and protected. Although Apple Pay enhances transaction security, you should still take the necessary safety measures to safeguard your device and payment details.

How to set up and manage Family Sharing

When you enable up to six family members to share media—including music, movies, TV series, apps, books, and—most importantly—subscriptions—without requiring them to share an Apple ID, Apple's Family Sharing feature tries to save you money. This implies that you may share services like iCloud+, AppleOne, or the family plan for Apple Music with every member of your family at no additional cost if you sign up for them.

For children, it goes one step further: in addition to creating their own Apple ID, they can also remotely adjust Screen Time permissions, authorize purchases and downloads using Apple's Ask to Buy verification system, set up Apple Cash (at least in the US), and set up a cellular Apple Watch that doesn't require an iPhone to be paired. In essence, it's the best choice for families with lots of iOS users who download applications, play games, and subscribe to Apple Music—all for free.

Setting up Family Sharing

1. First of all, ascertain that every member of the family owns an Apple ID. Otherwise, they may go to **Settings > [your name] > Sign Out > Create Apple ID** to create one.

2. Navigate to your iPhone's Settings.

3. To access your Apple ID preferences, scroll down and hit [your name].
4. Then choose **"Set up Family Sharing."** See the directions shown on the screen.

5. Pick one individual to take on the role of Family Organizer. This individual will be in charge of overseeing the Family Sharing configurations.

6. **Invite Family Members:**
- Type your family members' email addresses in, or click **"Invite in Person"** if they are nearby and carrying their Apple devices.
- An invitation to join your family group will be sent to them.

7. Every member of the family has to look for the invitation in their messages app or email.

8. To join the family group, click the link and adhere to the on-screen instructions.

Managing Family Sharing

The Family Organizer may oversee many facets of Family Sharing when it is configured, including:

1. **Purchase Sharing:**
- App Store, iTunes, and Apple Books purchases may be shared across family members. Navigate to **Settings > [your name] > Family Sharing > Share My Purchases** to make this enabled.

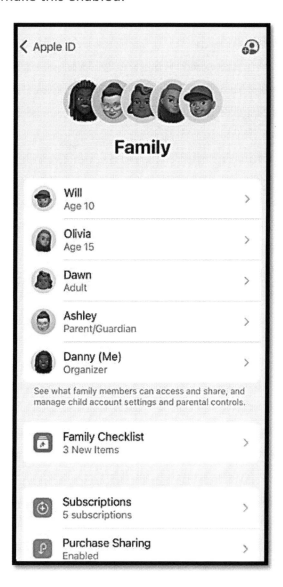

2. **Location Sharing**:
- When you select **"Share My Location"** on the Find My app, you can let family members know where you are.
3. Family members may share the Family Organizer's Apple Music Family Plan subscription.
4. Go to **Settings > [your name] > Family Sharing > Add Family Member >** and choose the subscription to share, such as Apple News+ or Apple Arcade.
5. Go to **Settings > Screen Time > Family** to set screen time limitations for your children or other family members.
6. **Ask to Purchase (Children):**
- If a kid is less than eighteen, Ask to Buy can be activated. This means that purchases of apps and media will need parental consent.
- Navigate to **Settings > Screen Time > Family > [Name of kid] > Request Purchase**.
7. iCloud allows family members to exchange calendars and images. This is configurable in the settings of the corresponding applications.
8. The Family Organizer has the option to allow the family to share an iCloud storage plan. This makes it possible for everyone to share and back up their data on iCloud.
9. Go to **Settings > [your name] > Family Sharing > [family member's name] > Remove** in the Family Organizer to remove family members if necessary.

How to start a family group

The methods below can be used to create a family group in Family Sharing on the iPhone 15 Series:

1. Take a look at your iPhone 15 Series' **"Settings"** app and open it.
2. To access your Apple ID at the top of the screen, scroll down and touch it
3. Then choose **"Family Sharing."**
4. To set up Family Sharing if you haven't previously, press **"Get Started"** and adhere to the on-screen instructions.
5. If Family Sharing is already configured, choose **"Add Family Member."**

6. Families may be invited to join your group by sending emails to their Apple IDs. You may email them an invitation link or invite them through iMessage.

7. You can tap "**Invite in Person**" if the person you want to invite is nearby, and they can accept the invitation on their smartphone by following the instructions. A notice will be sent to the invited family members' iPhones or other Apple devices.

8. To accept the invitation and become a member of the Family Sharing group, they can touch the notice.

9. After your family members join the group, use the family payment option to share purchases you make from the iTunes Store, App Store, and Apple Books.

10. Also, appoint a family organizer to oversee the approval of purchases made by family members who are younger than eighteen.

11. Share iCloud storage, Apple Music, Apple TV+, Apple Arcade, and other services with your family. Returning to options and selecting the Family Sharing section will allow you to adjust these options.

12. Furthermore, go to your Apple ID settings and choose **"Family sharing"** to manage your family group. You can then change the family organizer, update the sharing options, and add or delete family members.

13. You can now make use of Family Sharing on your iPhone 15 Series after setting up your family group and configuring sharing settings.

How to check if a member has accepted your invitation

You can choose to find out whether a member has accepted your invitation to Family Sharing by following these steps:

1. Locate and press the "**Settings**" app on your home screen to begin using it. This will launch the Settings app on your iPhone 15 Series.

2. Your name and profile image for your Apple ID should appear at the top of the Settings menu. Ensure you tap on it.

3. Hover your cursor over and search for "**Family Sharing.**" You should also tap on it to continue.

4. Under the "**Family Members**" area, a list of your relatives ought to appear. You will see on this list who has and has not accepted your invitation.

5. If you've extended an invitation to a person and they haven't accepted it yet, an **"Invited"** status will appear next to their name. If they accept your invitation, their name will be added to your family sharing group list.

6. When someone accepts your invitation, you can also get alerts on your iPhone. Usually, the notification center on your smartphone is where these alerts show up.

7. You may also speak with a family member directly to find out whether they have accepted the invitation. Text messages, phone conversations, or other messaging applications may be used for this.

How to join a family group

Here's how to use Family Sharing on your iPhone 15 Series to join a family group:

1. A family member must set up Family Sharing before you can join a group. The Family Organizer will be this individual. On their iPhone, they may do this by heading to Settings, pressing their name at the top, and choosing **Set Up Family Sharing.** Set it up by following the directions on the screen.

2. To become a member of the family group, you must receive an invitation from the family organizer. To do this, they need to go to Settings, touch their name at the top, choose Family Sharing, and then click **Add Family Member**. They will need to either create an Apple ID for you if you don't already have one, or input your Apple ID email address.

3. An invitation will be sent to you via email or as an iPhone notice. To accept the invitation, open the email or notice and click the link. You can also go to Settings, touch your name at the top, and then choose Invitations if you don't see the email or notice. After tapping the Family Organizer's invitation, choose **Accept**.

4. You can share access to music, apps, and other material that you have bought with other family members. Establishing a common payment mechanism is required. The Family Organizer has the option to set up Family Sharing with a separate payment method or to use their credit card for family spending. To configure the payment method, adhere to the on-screen instructions.

5. Choose what information you want to keep private and what you wish to share with your family. Select Family Sharing after going to Settings and tapping your name. You have the option to share your purchases, location, Apple Music, and more from this point on. Moreover, if necessary, you can invite other family members.

6. After you become a member of the family group, you can enjoy pooled resources and advantages. For instance, you can give your family members' access to Apple TV+, music, and applications that you have bought. Find my can also be used to find family members who have given you their location-sharing information.

How to enable Find My

To activate and use Find My on an iPhone, follow these basic instructions:

Enabling Find My

1. An iCloud account is required to use Find My. If you haven't already, go to **"Settings"** on your iPhone, hit your name in the upper right corner, then choose **"iCloud."** If required, log in or establish an Apple ID.

2. Scroll down to the **"Find My"** option under the iCloud settings, and turn it on. It can ask for your Apple ID password to be entered to verify.

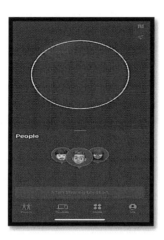

Using Find My

If your iPhone is lost or stolen, you can use Find My to find it after you've activated it.

Using Another Apple Device:

- Use the Find My app if you own another Apple device (iPhone, iPad, or Mac). Locate your missing iPhone by opening the Find My app, selecting the **"Devices"** option, and picking it from the list. It may be set to Lost Mode, have a sound play to aid in finding it, or see its position on a map.

Using a Web Browser:

- A computer or other device's web browser can also be used. Visit www.icloud.com to access iCloud, then log in using your Apple ID.
- Select **"Find iPhone."** This will display a map on which your Apple devices are located. To access its settings, choose your misplaced iPhone.

Using Lost Mode:

- You can use iCloud or the Locate My app to place your iPhone in Lost Mode if you can't locate it. This lets you trace the whereabouts of your smartphone, locks it, and shows a personalized message on the screen.
- If you think your iPhone may have been stolen, you can also remotely delete it to safeguard your data.

Report to Authorities:

- Notify your local police enforcement of the theft if your iPhone is taken. They may be able to help get it back.

Note that Find My depends on your missing iPhone having an active internet connection, and that GPS reception and signal strength may affect how accurate the position is. Make sure Find My is always turned on and that you know how to use it in case you have an emergency and need to find your iPhone.

Frequently Asked Questions

1. How do you add a debit or credit card to Apple Pay?
2. How do you choose your default card and reorganize your cards?
3. How do you find locations that support Apple Pay?
4. How do you change your shipping and contact details?
5. How do you set up and manage Family Sharing?
6. How do you invite members of the family to sharing?

CHAPTER NINETEEN
APPLE HEALTH AND CONNECTIVITY

Overview

Concerned about your health status and connectivity on your new iPhone 15 Series? Chapter nineteen talks about Apple Health, how to set it up, and use it to track your health. Additionally, you will learn how to connect Bluetooth devices, connect to a Wi-Fi network and so much more.

How to set up Apple Health

The steps:

1. Ensure that the most recent version of iOS 17 is installed on your iPhone before you start. By selecting **Settings > General > Software Update**, you can check for updates. Then, you can download and install any updates that are available by following the on-screen instructions.

2. Your iPhone comes with the Apple Health app pre-installed. To launch it, just look for the Health app icon on your home screen. Alternatively, you can use the integrated search function by sliding down on the home screen and entering "**Health**."

3. The Health app will ask you to establish or modify your health profile when you first use it. This includes providing personal data like your height, weight, sex, and age. Precise data is essential for monitoring fitness and health.

4. Apple Health lets you collect data about your fitness and health from many sources, such as the iPhone itself and other applications and gadgets. You can add or delete data sources from this screen by tapping on your profile image in the upper-right corner of the Health app and selecting **"Devices & Sources**."

5. The Health app offers the ability for you to establish a Medical ID. In an emergency, you may obtain this information via the lock screen. To configure your Medical ID, touch on your profile image and choose **"Medical ID**." Enter the required information, including medical conditions, emergency contacts, and allergies.

6. The Health app offers several categories for monitoring various facets of your health, including sleep, diet, exercise and more. Examine these categories and click on each one to add information or establish connections with related devices and applications.

7. The Health app allows you to establish customized exercise and health goals. For example, you may aim for a specific number of steps per day or a certain quantity of sleep every night. The software will monitor your development and provide analysis.

8. You can connect your health records to the Health app directly from certain healthcare facilities and providers. If you have access to it, you can see your test results, medical data, and more all in one location.

9. It's critical to go through your Health app privacy and data sharing choices. To guarantee that your data is safe, you can choose what information is shared with other applications and services.

10. To get the most out of Apple Health, measure your fitness and health progress using the app frequently. You'll get more insightful information the more data you enter.

How to use Apple Health to track health issues

Here are the steps to use Apple Health to track health issues:

1. Open the **"Health"** app on your iPhone to access Apple Health. You can use Spotlight Search to look for it if it's not on your home screen.

2. You will be asked to establish or update your health profile when you first use the app. Give truthful details about your height, weight, sex, and age. Many health measures will be computed using this data.

3. You can arrange and monitor several areas of your health with the aid of the Health app's wellbeing and health categories, which include **"Activity,"** **"Mindfulness," "Nutrition,"** and **"Vitals.**

4. Manually enter health data to monitor certain health conditions, or you can connect compatible health equipment (smart scales, fitness trackers, etc.) to sync data automatically. To enter data by hand:

➤ Press on the category (such as **"Vitals"** for blood pressure or heart rate) that you want to monitor.

➤ Select "**Add Data Point**" or a related menu item.

➤ Provide the pertinent data, such as your blood pressure and heart rate at the moment.

5. On the "**Summary**" page, choose your own fitness and health objectives. Tap **"Show All Health Data"** to see your monitored data and create objectives for physical activity, diet, and other areas.

6. Build a Medical ID profile with all the personal information you need in the "Medical ID" area of the Health app. Emergency personnel may still obtain this information even if your phone is locked. You can also activate Emergency SOS to promptly contact for assistance in an emergency.

7. Your health data over time is visually shown through the Health app. Through the app's several areas, you can see trends and patterns in your sleep, exercise, and other indicators.

8. A large number of fitness and health applications developed by third parties are compatible with Apple Health. These applications provide a more complete picture of your health by transferring and receiving data with the Health app.

How to manage workouts in Apple Health

Here are the steps:

1. Open the Health app on your iPhone 15 Series to have access to the Apple Health app. It's usually located on your home screen.

2. You will be asked to create your health profile if you haven't already. Enter your information, including height, weight, sex, and age. The app will use this data to monitor your progress and provide accurate fitness suggestions.

3. The Health app has many tabs located at the bottom. Hit and hold the **"Browse"** tab, like a heart.

4. To find the **"Activity"** section, go down the **"Browse"** tab. You can examine your fitness stats and manage your routines here.

5. View a variety of fitness measures, such as your daily steps, distance run or walk, flights climbed, and more, under the **"Activity"** area. Tap the **"Workouts"** option to examine your exercise history.

6. To manually add a workout, press the **"+"** symbol, which is often located in the upper right corner of the screen. After choosing the exercise you want to add (yoga, cycling, jogging, etc.), input the pertinent information (distance, time, and any further remarks you like to add).

7. To observe your development over time, you can go through your workout history. Your most recent workouts will be shown at the top.

8. Workouts can be edited or deleted by tapping on them to see their information. From there, choose the **"Edit"** or **"Delete"** option according to the changes you want to make.

9. Scroll down the **"Activity"** column to view trends in your workouts and activities. You'll discover statistics and graphs that shed light on your fitness path.

10. Choose the **"Goals"** option located in the **"Activity"** section if you'd like to establish particular fitness goals. This enables you to monitor your progress toward reaching your intended fitness benchmarks.

11. Data from other fitness applications and gadgets may be synchronized with Apple Health. The Health app's **"Sources"** page is where you link the devices or applications you use to log your exercises to do this.

12. Don't forget to check out the other areas of the Health app, including sleep, diet, and heart health, to keep an eye on your general health and well-being.

How to connect to a Bluetooth device

Using Bluetooth on your iPhone, follow these steps to establish a connection:

1. To access the Control Center, swipe down from the top-right corner of the screen.
2. To activate Bluetooth, tap the symbol. An alternative is to choose "**Bluetooth**" under "**Settings**" and turn it on.
3. Verify that pairing mode is enabled on the Bluetooth device you want to connect to. Typically, this entails pressing a certain button on the device, or a set of buttons, until it goes into a discoverable condition.
4. On your iPhone, go to **"Settings" > "Bluetooth."**

5. Tap the device you want to connect to from the list of accessible Bluetooth devices that appear under "**My Devices**."
6. You will be prompted on both your iPhone and the Bluetooth device to confirm a pairing request or enter a PIN, if necessary. To finish pairing, adhere to the on-screen directions.
7. The device will appear as "**Connected**" in your iPhone's Bluetooth settings when the connection is completed. The Bluetooth symbol is also shown in the status bar.
8. The Bluetooth device that is linked may now be used for its intended purpose. If it's a Bluetooth headset, for instance, you can use it for music playback and calls.

9. To unpair a Bluetooth device, choose **"Settings" > "Bluetooth,"** touch the name of the device, and select **"Disconnect**." This will unpair the device while preserving the pairing details for later use.

10. The device will be completely removed from your iPhone's Bluetooth list if you choose to **"Forget This Device**" rather than **"Disconnect**."

How to pair and unpair a Bluetooth accessory

Follow these instructions to pair and unpair Bluetooth accessories, whether you want to connect wireless headphones, a keyboard, a speaker, or any other compatible device

Pairing a Bluetooth Accessory

1. Ensure your Bluetooth gear is in pairing mode to ready it for use. To learn how to do this specifically, see the user manual that comes with the attachment. Typically, an LED light will flicker or a pairing indication will show up if you press and hold a certain button or set of buttons.

2. Also, ensure that your iPhone is switched on after unlocking it.

3. To access the Control Center, swipe down from the top-right corner of the screen. After that, to turn it on, hit the **Bluetooth** icon. Another option is to choose **"Settings" > "Bluetooth"** and turn on the switch by toggling it.

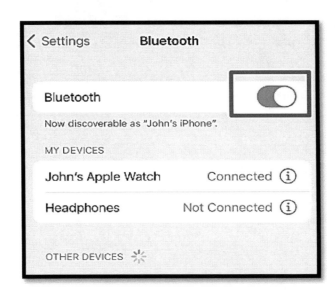

4. At this point, your iPhone will look for Bluetooth devices that are nearby. Your desired pairing attachment ought to be listed among the compatible devices under **"Other Devices" or "Discoverable Devices."**

5. To pair the accessory, tap the name of the connected device from the list. When instructed on-screen, follow those steps to finish pairing. This might include verifying a passkey or entering a PIN on your accessory, however, other devices could connect on their own without any input needed.

6. If the accessory supports it, you'll hear a confirmation sound after a successful pairing. It will also appear as **"Connected"** in your iPhone's Bluetooth settings.

Unpairing a Bluetooth Accessory

To separate or unpair a Bluetooth device from your iPhone, follow these steps:

1. Endeavor to check your device is turned on and unlocked.

2. Select **"Settings" > "Bluetooth."**

3. The "My Devices" section has a list of every paired device.

4. Locate the Bluetooth item you want to unpair and hit the (i) symbol next to its name to begin the process.

5. To unpair the attachment from your iPhone, touch **"Forget This Device"** on the ensuing screen.

6. Verify your selection when asked. Your iPhone will now be unpaired and the accessories unplugged.

How to connect to a Wi-Fi network

Here are the steps to connect:

1. If it hasn't been unlocked before, start by doing so. Your home screen will appear.

2. Navigate to the **"Settings"** app on your home screen to access the settings. It's often located on the home screen of your applications and is symbolized by a gearwheel icon.

3. Scroll down to the **"Settings"** menu and choose **"Wi-Fi."** The option should appear in the second part of the menu.

4. Ensure that the Wi-Fi toggle located at the top of the screen is in the "**on**" position. If enabled, it ought to be green.

5. When you turn on your iPhone, it will look for Wi-Fi networks that are accessible. Under **"Choose a Network..."** you'll see a list of networks. The names (SSID) and signal strength of the nearby networks will be shown.

6. To connect to a Wi-Fi network, choose it by tapping on it. You'll be asked to enter the password if the network is protected. After entering the proper Wi-Fi password, click "**Join.**"

7. The chosen Wi-Fi network will be attempted to be connected to by your iPhone. It should connect in a few seconds if the network is accessible and the password is valid.

8. When you are connected to Wi-Fi, a checkmark will show up next to the network you have chosen, and the Wi-Fi symbol will show up in the upper-left corner of your iPhone's screen.

9. Open a web browser or any other program that needs an internet connection, and make sure you're connected to the internet.

How to set up a personal hotspot

Here are the steps:

1. Ensure that your device is unlocked and that the home screen is shown.
2. To access the Control Center, slide down from the top-right corner of the screen. Press the Wi-Fi symbol to momentarily disable it.
3. Click the "**Settings**" app from your home screen to open Settings Now. This seems to be a gearwheel.
4. To find "**Personal Hotspot**" in the Settings menu, scroll down and tap on it.
5. There is an option at the top of the Personal Hotspot settings. Turn it on to make your hotspot functional.
6. After turning on your hotspot, you can customize it to your preferences. By selecting "**Wi-Fi Password**" and inputting a password of your choosing, you can secure your Wi-Fi network. To link additional devices to your hotspot, you will need to enter this password.
7. Other devices can now connect to your active and configured personal hotspot. Navigate to the Wi-Fi settings of the device you want to connect to, then search for your iPhone's network name (SSID) among the accessible networks. If you established a password in the previous step, tap on it and enter it.
8. Your iPhone's cellular data will be used to provide the other device with internet access once it is linked to your hotspot. To find out how many devices are connected, you may see the status of your hotspot on the screen of your iPhone.
9. To save battery life and data consumption, turn off your personal hotspot after you're done using it. Just return to the iPhone's Personal Hotspot settings and flip the switch off.

How to connect to a visible and hidden network

To connect an iPhone to both visible and hidden Wi-Fi networks, follow these steps:

Connecting to a visible Wi-Fi Network

1. Open your device and go to the home screen.
2. Launch the **Settings** app.
3. After swiping down, choose **"Wi-Fi."**
4. Verify that the Wi-Fi is enabled (it ought to be green).
5. Tap on the name of the network you want to connect to from the list of available Wi-Fi networks that should show up under "**Choose a Network**."
6. You will be requested to enter the network password if the network is password-protected. After entering the password, click "**Join**."
7. Await the iPhone's Wi-Fi network connection. The network name will have a checkmark next to it, and the Wi-Fi symbol will show up in the status bar at the top of the screen after you're connected.

Connecting to a Hidden (Non-Broadcast) Wireless Network

1. To access your iPhone's Wi-Fi settings, choose the first four steps mentioned above.
2. Since the secret network doesn't broadcast its name, hit "**Other**" at the bottom of the list of accessible networks.
3. The hidden Wi-Fi network's precise name (SSID) must be entered when requested. Put it inaccurately.
4. Next, input the secret network password and choose the network security type (WPA2, WEP, etc.).
5. Using "**Join**" will allow you to join the undiscovered Wi-Fi network.
6. Await the network connection on your iPhone. The network name will have a checkmark next to it, and the status bar will display the Wi-Fi icon once it is connected.

Frequently Asked Questions

1. How do you set up Apple Health?

2. How do you use Apple Health to track health issues?
3. How do you manage workouts in Apple Health?
4. How do you connect to a Wi-Fi network?
5. How do you set up a personal hotspot?
6. How do you connect to a visible and hidden network?

CHAPTER TWENTY
BASIC FUNCTIONALITIES

Overview

Here comes the last chapter. Chapter twenty discusses the basic functionalities found in the new iPhone 15 Series including using the do not disturb mode, the various tips and tricks, how to turn on dark mode, how to pin apps to the screen, and a whole lot more.

Tips and Tricks

Over time, your iPhone comes with different features and functions that a lot of people aren't aware of. However, in this section, you will get to see the different tips and tricks that will make the use of your iPhone 15 Series (iPhone 15, iPhone 15 Plus, iPhone 15 Pro, and iPhone 15 Pro Max) worthwhile.

1. **Turn off the always-on display (15 Pro only)**

The always-on display function of the iPhone 15 Pro accentuates the clock and reduces the background. By default, it is enabled, but you could discover that it consumes your battery or isn't all that helpful. Thus, you have the option to disable it. Now that you have opened Settings, choose **Display and Brightness**, and turn off the **"Always On"** option. You can configure it to turn off at night as part of sleep mode if you don't want it off all the time and want it on during the day. Select **Sleep** under **Settings > Focus**. Under the **'Schedule'** menu, you can arrange for a sleep focus to turn on at a certain time every night. Your always-on display will turn off at night once it's activated.

2. **Enable the haptic keyboard**

Apple included haptic feedback to their default keyboard with iOS 17. This implies that you will experience faint vibrations or taps underneath the display while you write. Simply choose **'Keyboard feedback'** under **Settings > Sound** and **Haptics** to activate it. Adjust the **'Haptic'** setting.

3. Battery percentage indicator

You can enable a new battery percentage indicator to see the real percentage shown in your status bar battery symbol. Navigate to **Settings > Battery** and turn on the **'battery percentage'** option to enable it.

4. Change your notification style

In iOS 17, the quantity, or **"count,"** of notifications now appears by default at the bottom of your lock screen to inform you of the amount of unread messages. However, you can change this to show a stack of notification windows or a list of real alerts. Simply go to **Settings > Notifications** and choose one of the two other choices under **'Display As'** at the top of the screen.

5. Hide a personal message behind Face ID

You can now secure a particular note in Notes with Face ID verification. It's no longer sufficient to just lock it with the password on your phone. Navigate to **Settings > Notes**, choose the **'Password'** option, and then press it to activate this function. After choosing **"Use Device Passcode,"** enable **"Use Face ID"** on the next screen. Not only is it no longer necessary to enter a password to open notes. Lock a particular note by long pressing on it inside the app, and then selecting **"lock note"** from the pop-up menu that shows up. It will verify that you are attempting to access it using Face ID the next time you try to open it.

6. Edit or unsend iMessages

Occasionally, when you communicate, you'll probably both instantly regret it and want to take it back or make a humiliating mistake. Maybe even both. Fortunately, iOS 17 offers a fix for such issues. iMessages can now be edited or unsent at this time. To do this, open **Messages**, enter your message as usual and then long-press it to send it. **'Edit'** and **'Undo send'** are available options in the drop-down menu. Select the one you want to use at that moment. However, be aware that even if the recipient doesn't have iOS 17, they will still be able to read the message and it won't display as unsent.

7. **Delete Duplicate Images**

With the aid of Apple's most recent Photos app, you can quickly and simply remove duplicate images from your iPhone and iCloud storage. Just click on "**Albums**" after opening Photos. Once you reach the list towards the bottom of the page that says "**Duplicates**," scroll down. You can now opt to manually choose each picture you want to remove by clicking the delete trash can symbol at the bottom, or you can click "**merge**" next to each match.

8. **Drag foreground subjects away from backgrounds into new documents**

The ability to take subjects out of their picture backgrounds and share them as cutouts in any app is one of the amazing new capabilities of iOS 17. You can simply drag and drop it into another document or onto a picture that you may be working on in Photoshop, Pages, or a comparable program if you know the appropriate approach. To remove the subject from the background, just touch and hold it as usual. Then, hold onto it with the same finger and use your other hand to swipe the app out of the one you want to put it into and open it.

If Pages is the program of choice, for example, open it, create a new document, or open an existing one, and then just drop the picture. If there's another method you'd want to share them, just press and hold the subject, wait for the white line to form around it, and then tap **'share'** to choose the location, or **'copy'** to open the app manually and paste it in.

9. **Manually enable macro mode on or off**

Another helpful feature is the manual macro mode switch since the auto-switching between 1x and macro on certain phone generations has been a little startling. Reopen **Settings > Camera**, then simply flip the "**Macro Control**" option on and off.

When you launch the camera app and point your camera in the direction of an item, the macro logo should show up in yellow on the screen. It's turned on by default, but you can turn it off simply by tapping the logo when it shows up.

10. Customize Spatial Audio

Using the front-facing Face ID sensors, iOS 16 offers an intriguing feature that allows you to customize the Spatial Audio in your AirPods. AirPods 3 and AirPods Pro (first and second generation) are compatible with it. Simply open the case for your AirPods, check to see whether they're connected, and then launch the Settings app to begin using it. Locate "**Personalized Spatial Audio**" on the screen that appears when tapping on the AirPods in the list. Then choose "**Personalize Spatial Audio**" from the menu that appears on the next screen. It will now walk you through a process where it measures your face and ears using the front-facing depth sensors. Based on that information, it creates a customized Spatial Audio profile that you can use with your AirPods attached.

11. Check your current Wi-Fi network's password

Seeing the network password that you're connected to is one function that maybe ought to have been around for a long time. iOS 17 allows you to. Go to **Settings**, choose **'Wi-Fi'**, and then tap the information symbol next to the network you are currently connected to. 'Password' will appear on the next screen. When you tap it, Face ID will be used to verify that it is you and display the passkey.

12. Add stops to your Apple Maps route

You can add stops along the route to your final destination in Apple Maps on iOS 17. Simply continue with navigation as normal, entering your intended destination into Maps, and then tapping the drive or vehicle symbol. You will now see a list under **'Directions'** where you can choose **'add stop'** before beginning the turn-by-turn navigation. Enter the places you want to see, and then rearrange the stops. Tap **'Go'** to begin the navigation process, which will include your stops along the route.

13. Quick Note

You can, of course, start composing a note in the Notes app very fast thanks to an iOS feature called Quick Note. Simply choose **Control Center** and locate the control that has a + sign and resembles a note page. Start a new note in the Notes app right now by tapping it.

14. **Back tap to screenshot**

You can take a snapshot or swipe down the alerts by tapping the back of your iPhone twice or three times using a neat technique. Furthermore, it is a feature of the accessibility settings. Locate **'Touch'** by opening **Settings > Accessibility**. On the next screen, **'Back Tap'** will be located at the bottom. Choose **'Double Tap'** and select **"Screenshot"** or any other function you can choose from the list. Now, the phone will snap a screenshot when you press the back twice.

15. **Type to Siri**

Typing Siri commands is another accessibility feature for those who may have trouble speaking or hearing. However, you must first allow it. Navigate back to **Settings > Accessibility** and locate **'Siri'** towards the bottom. Turn on 'Make to Siri' from the next page, and you can now make requests and see the replies on the screen when you activate Siri by pressing and holding the side key.

16. **One-handed mode (also known as reachability)**

With iOS 17, there's a feature that makes it simpler to reach the top of the screen with one hand—or, more precisely, your thumb. Reachability is a feature that allows you to more easily access the upper half of the screen by swiping down from the bottom of the screen when it's enabled. Simply go to **Settings > Accessibility > Touch**, then turn on **"Reachability."**

17. **Quick-dial Siri Shortcut**

You can add a quick dial shortcut icon to your home screen so you can instantly call a priority contact without having to go through your contacts list. Get your iPhone's Shortcuts app open, hit the '+' in the corner, and choose **'Add Action'** to do this. If there isn't already a recommended contact where it says "**call**," tap "**+,**" and then "**contact**" on the screen that appears. Select the person you want to quickly call. Select **'Add to Home Screen'** from the menu by tapping the share icon, which is the little square with an upward pointing arrow. You can customize the icon and name of the contact on the next page. After making these changes, you can press "**Add**" and then "**Done**" to add the contact to your Home page and easily call your most essential contact(s).

Using Do Not Disturb

Use these easy steps to enable the iPhone 15 Series' "Do Not Disturb" feature:

1. To begin, swipe down from your iPhone's top right corner to bring up the Control Center. You can quickly access many options, including "**Do Not Disturb**," from here.
2. Turn on Do Not Disturb by locating the crescent moon symbol in the Control Center. The "**Do Not Disturb**" toggle is located here. To activate Do Not Disturb mode, tap on it. The crescent moon symbol will glow purple while it's active, signaling that notifications are muted.
3. Tap and hold the crescent moon symbol to change the Do Not Disturb settings. The Do Not Disturb settings page will open as a result. You can adjust settings such as:

- **Turn On Automatically:** You have the option to program Do Not Disturb to activate and deactivate at certain intervals, such as when you're sleeping.
- **Allow Calls From**: When using Do Not Disturb, you have the option to accept calls from anybody, your favorites, certain contact groups, or none at all.
- **Repeated Calls:** If this option is enabled, in case of an emergency, a second call from the same individual will be sent through in three minutes.
- **Silence**: Select whether you want alerts to come through on your phone even while it is locked, or if you want it to remain absolutely quiet.

4. If you've configured Bedtime in the Clock app, you can choose to have Do Not Disturb turned on during your bedtime. This will automatically turn off alerts when it's time for you to go to bed.

5. Go back to the Control Center and press the crescent moon symbol once again to turn off Do Not Disturb. This will stop the function from working and return your phone to its regular notification system.

6. As an alternative, you can use the Settings app to access the Do Not Disturb settings. Select **"Settings" > "Do Not Disturb"** to see and modify the available settings.

How to use focus mode

To use Focus Mode on your device, follow the steps below:

1. To access the Control Center, swipe down from the top-right corner of the screen.

2. To activate Focus Mode, find an icon in the Control Center that looks like a crescent moon. This is the symbol for Focus Mode. To activate Focus Mode, tap on it.

3. You can select from a variety of Focus Modes, including **"Personal," "Work," "Sleep,"** and custom modes that you can build, by touching the Focus Mode icon. Choose the mode that works best for the task at hand or the circumstances.

4. Limit the alerts and calls from certain contacts in each Focus Mode. This is useful for avoiding distractions and maintaining relationships with significant people and applications. After selecting the Focus Mode you want, hit **"Customize."** From there, you can choose which contacts and applications can send alerts when the mode is active.

5. Focus Mode can also be set to switch on and off automatically at certain intervals. Go to **Settings > Focus > Scheduled** and enter your desired timetable for each Focus Mode to do this.

6. A status indicator that shows you which Focus Mode is active at the top of the screen appears when Focus Mode is engaged.

7. Notifications received while in Focus Mode will be compiled into a summary for easy access. You can swipe down from the top of the screen to see these alerts.

8. This can be done by simply returning to the Control Center and tapping the Focus Mode symbol once again.

How to multitask

The different methods:

Using the App Switcher

- Swipe up from the bottom border of the screen and stop in the center.

Switching Between Applications

- An open app list can be found in the app switcher. To navigate between them, swipe left or right, then press the app you want to go to.

Using Slide Over

- Use the Slide over function on newer iPhones with bigger displays. To access the dock while using an app, slide up slightly from the bottom.
- To launch an application in a floating window, drag it from the dock and drop it on the screen's left or right border. By moving the handlebar at the top, you can change the floating app's size and location.
- To navigate between Slide Over applications, slide horizontally from the screen's right edge to see the Slide over app switcher.

Use Split View

- Open an app, and then slide up from the bottom to reveal the dock to use it.
- In the app switcher, drag an application from the dock and place it in the space between two programs. You will be able to use two applications simultaneously as a result.

Close Apps in the App Switcher

- Swipe applications up or off the screen to the top to close them in the app switcher. While it may not directly save battery life, this may help you keep track of the open applications.

Use Picture-in-Picture (PiP) mode

- YouTube and other video applications support PiP mode. When using one of these applications to view a video, you may swipe up to return to the home screen and the video will resize and become a smaller window that you can move about.

How to pin apps to the screen

Here's how to pin apps to the screen:

1. If your iPhone is locked, use Face ID or your password to unlock it.
2. Search the App Library or your home screen for the app you want to pin.
3. Press and hold your finger on the app icon to do a long press. Holding it will cause an options menu to appear.
4. Go to the "**Edit Home Screen**" or a similar option from the menu that displays.
5. Switch to "**Jiggle mode**" to watch your app icons jitter and a little "x" or negative (-) symbol appears in the upper left corner of each icon.
6. Locate the app you want to pin, then drag & drop it to the desired spot on the home screen. It may be positioned next to other applications or moved to a different page.
7. Exit "**Jiggle mode**" by tapping the Done or Finish button, which is often located in the upper or lower right corner of the screen, once you've positioned the app in the correct spot.
8. Test the pinned app by swiping up from the bottom to get out of editing mode and confirm that the app is pinned. At this point, the app ought to remain pinned to the home screen.

How to turn on dark mode

To activate dark mode on an iPhone, follow these steps:

1. Launch the "**Settings**" app.
2. Scroll down and touch on "**Display & Brightness.**"

3. You have two appearance options in the **"Display & Brightness"** settings: **"Light" and "Dark."** Tap on **"Dark"** to activate dark mode.

4. Instantaneously, your iPhone will enter dark mode; the UI will now have lighter text and objects against a dark background.

5. Additionally, you can program dark mode to turn on and off automatically according to the time of day. To configure your iPhone to switch between settings automatically, choose **"Light until Sunset" or "Dark until Sunrise"** under **"Settings" > "Display & Brightness" > "Automatic."**

How to reduce and increase font size

To increase font size:

1. Tap the **Settings** app, which has the appearance of a gear symbol, to launch it from your home screen.

2. Scroll down and choose **"Accessibility."**

3. Locate and press **"Display & Text Size"** from the Accessibility menu.

4. The **"Text Size"** option in this case has a slider. To enlarge the typeface, slide it to the right. There's a preview of the text that appears as you slide.

5. You can also activate **"Bold Text"** just below the Text Size slider if you'd like the text to be even more readable. As a result, the writing will be thicker and simpler to read.

6. Click **"Apply"** in the top right corner of the screen when you're happy with the font size.

7. The modifications will need to be confirmed by you. Enable the new font size by tapping **"Continue"**.

The majority of applications on your iPhone and the interface should now have bigger, easier-to-read text.

Reduce Font Size

1. To access the accessibility options, follow the previously specified procedures once again.

2. Select **"Display & Text Size"** once again by tapping on it.

3. To decrease the text size, move the Text Size slider to the left this time. You can get an indication of how the writing will become smaller as you move.
4. Click "**Apply**" in the top right corner of the screen after adjusting the font size to your preferred level.
5. To ensure that the changes are accurate, click "**Continue**."

Recall that the system and built-in applications are mostly impacted when you change the text size in the accessibility settings. You may need to make individual adjustments to font size under the app's settings for some third-party applications.

How to use crash detection

To activate and use crash detection on an iPhone, follow these basic instructions:

1. Ensure that the operating system on your iPhone is current. Safety and emergency services-related enhancements and new features are often included in software upgrades.
2. Crash detection is often linked to the Emergency SOS function. Follow the steps below to enable it:
- Launch the iPhone's Settings app.
- After swiping down, choose "**Emergency SOS**."
- Verify that "**Auto Call**" is on. This function will automatically make five fast presses of the power button to summon emergency assistance.

3. If your iPhone senses an impending accident or other emergency, you may designate emergency contacts to receive notifications. To carry out this:
- Launch the iPhone Health app.
- At the upper right corner of your profile photo, tap on it.
- After swiping down, choose "**Medical ID**."
- Tap "**Edit**" in the upper right corner. e. To add emergency contacts, press "**Add Emergency Contact**."
4. Accelerometers, gyroscopes, and other sensors in iPhones are capable of detecting sudden acceleration or atypical motions that might indicate a collision. Your iPhone may immediately activate the Emergency SOS function if it senses such movements.

5. Manually initiate Emergency SOS by quickly tapping the power button five times if you think you've been in an accident or other emergency circumstance and your iPhone hasn't recognized it automatically. This will alert your specified emergency contacts and start a call to emergency services.

6. If an emergency SOS is activated, your iPhone will make a call to emergency services and provide your medical ID number so that first responders may see it. Observe whatever directions the emergency services operator provides on the screen.

How to use the water-resistant feature

Here are the steps:

1. Make sure you are aware of the water resistance rating of your iPhone before subjecting it to any water. Different iPhone models—such as IP67 or IP68—have differing degrees of water resistance. The phone's rating lets you know how deep and how long it can stay immersed in water.

2. Verify that all ports, including the SIM card tray and charging port, are firmly shut and sealed. Open ports allow water to enter readily, therefore when near water, keep them shut.

3. If you want to submerge your iPhone or use it in harsh environments, think about investing in a high-quality waterproof cover for additional protection.

4. Although your iPhone could be water-resistant, prolonged submersion is not recommended for it. Do not immerse it in water, and if it does get wet, take it out right away.

5. The water resistance of the device may be compromised by high-pressure water, such as that from a shower or jet spray. Avoid placing your iPhone near sources of high-pressure water.

6. Take your wet iPhone out of the water and give it a little shake to get rid of extra moisture. For drying, use a lint-free, clean cloth. A totally dry surface is required before charging or reusing it.

7. Before attaching your iPhone to a charger, make sure it is completely dry. A charging port that has water in it might break.

8. The SIM card tray of iPhones has a water damage indication. It could change color if it comes into contact with water, suggesting possible water damage. If you need to contact warranty support, keep this in mind.

9. Wear and tear over time may cause your iPhone's water resistance to deteriorate. Periodically checking the seals to make sure they are clean and clear of dirt is a good idea.

Troubleshooting Issues

Your iPhone 15 Series is due to experience one issue or the other as time goes on.

Here are some of the problems and potential solutions you can try out:

How to fix iPhone 15 Black Screen Issue

Several iPhone 1T models have had black screen problems, commonly referred to as the "black screen of death," after installing recent versions of iOS 17. Users say that when they swipe, tap, or make movements, the device stops responding. **Try these steps if the screen on your iPhone 15 Series turns dark and it stops working.**

- Increase the volume.
- Decrease the volume.
- Press and hold the side button for one minute.

These instructions, which are direct from the Apple Store's technical support team, should restore your iPhone to its original condition.

How to fix iPhone 15 Series Battery Life Problems

If your battery life goes down faster than expected, it may be because of one issue or the other. If the issues are severe, a hardware problem may be the cause. Should that be the case, you should either bring your iPhone 15 to an Apple Store or get in touch with Apple customer care. These solutions have been effective for us over the years, and they may be able to resolve your battery problems in a matter of minutes without requiring you to speak with customer support.

The solutions include the following

Restart your device

Before doing anything else, we always advise resetting your iPhone 15 if the battery is depleting quickly. After waiting a minute, turn on your iPhone 15, iPhone 15 Plus, iPhone 15 Pro, or iPhone 15 Pro Max again. If it continues to drain rapidly, go to the further procedures listed below.

Update your Device

For the iPhone 15 series, Apple will frequently issue new iOS 17 software upgrades. While milestone upgrades (x.x) normally provide a combination of enhancements and fixes, point updates (x.x.x) are mainly focused on correcting problems. Even while the business may not mention battery life improvements in the change log for an iOS 17 update, new software always can aid with problems with battery depletion.

Lower the screen's brightness

Your phone's battery will be depleted if you use the brightest display setting all the time. For your iPhone 15, we strongly advise turning on Auto-Brightness to assist in saving battery depletion.

This is how you do it:

- Open the **Settings** application.
- Touch on **Accessibility**.
- Text Size & Tap Display.
- Confirm that Auto-Brightness is turned on.

Disable the Always-On Display

Although Always-On Display is a helpful feature, it may cause your iPhone 15's battery to discharge faster. The function is turned on by default, but you can test disabling it if you don't need it to check whether your phone runs on a longer battery life.

Here's how to carry it out:

- Select **Settings**.
- Touch the **Display and Brightness** button.
- The Always-On display can be turned on or off by swiping down to find it.

Turn off 5G

The iPhone 15 series, like the iPhone 13 series, is capable of a 5G connection, which has the potential to deplete your battery significantly more quickly than LTE. Navigate to the settings on your iPhone 15 Series if you don't need to use 5G or don't need to use it constantly. You'll want to commit a few 5G settings to your memory bank. You should open the Settings app; choose **Cellular**, then **Cellular Data Options**, and finally **Voice & Data** to locate them.

You should see three options if you're at the correct place:

- 5.G On
- 5G Auto
- LTE

If you turn on 5G on your iPhone 15, it will use it anytime it is available, even if it means depleting the battery. The 5G Auto feature only makes use of 5G when it won't adversely affect the battery life of your phone. The majority of users should choose 5G Auto, which is the default setting.

Examine Your Apps

Apps may sometimes negatively affect how long your phone lasts on a charge, so if you see unusual drains, you should look into them.

The iPhone 15 series makes it very simple to check the performance of an app. Here's how to carry it out:

- Open the **Settings application**.
- Choose **Battery**.
- Navigate to the Battery Usage tool.

This app for monitoring battery usage allows you to see which applications are using up your iPhone 15's power and when. Frequently used applications will consume more battery life than hardly ever used ones. You should look into an app further if you see that it's using a lot of power and you don't often use it. Try removing the app from your smartphone to check if things work properly if that's the case. We advise getting the most recent update from the developer if the program is crucial to your daily activities. If it doesn't work, you may have to revert to an earlier iOS 16 version, if that's an option.

Deactivate Keyboard Haptics

Regretfully, Apple claims that using keyboard haptics may shorten your iPhone's battery life. You should disable keyboard haptics if you don't require them.

- Open the **Settings** app.
- Select **Sounds and Haptics**.
- Tap **Keyboard Feedback**.
- Turn off haptic feedback.

Reset All Settings

You might also attempt to reset every setting on your device. Be aware that doing this can lead your device to forget known Wi-Fi networks, so be sure to have your details saved someplace before proceeding.

- Open the **Settings** app.
- Touch **General**.
- Tap Reset or Transfer on your iPhone.
- Tap **Reset**.

- Tap **Reset All Settings**.
- If you have a passcode enabled, enter it here.

You will need to reconnect your iPhone 15 to Bluetooth devices and Wi-Fi networks when the operation is finished.

Opt for Low Power Mode

By disabling services that can deplete your battery, Low Power Mode prolongs the life of your battery. Low Power Mode is switchable on and off at any time. In addition, your iPhone will notify you to switch it on when its battery drops below 20%. Add Low Power Mode to your Control Center if you haven't already. Swiping in from the upper right corner of the screen brings up the Control Center menu.

Here's how to carry it out:

- Open the Settings menu.
- Tap Control Center.
- Touch on Customize Controls.
- On the Low Power Mode screen, tap the green + symbol.

You will see a battery symbol in the Control Center the next time you use your device. To switch your device's Low Power Mode on or off, tap it.

Low Power Mode can also be enabled via your settings. Here's how to carry it out:

- Open the Settings app.
- Tap **Battery**.
- Select the **Low Power Mode**.
- Turn it On.

How to fix lost 5G on iPhone 15 Series

5G connection is supported by the iPhone 15, iPhone 15 Plus, iPhone 15 Pro, and iPhone 15 Pro Max. You must, however, be using a plan that supports 5G. It's not a glitch if you open the **Settings app** on your phone, go to the Cellular area, and see that there are no 5G options. It most likely indicates that your carrier does not provide a 5G-enabled package for you. If so, the only networks you'll notice are "**LTE**" and "**4G**." You will need to upgrade or modify your plan to use the 5G network offered by your carrier. Make sure 5G service is accessible in the locations you often visit before you make this decision.

See the following maps for further details:

- AT&T 5G Layout
- T-Mobile 5G Map
- Verizon 5G Map

You may find that your iPhone 15 model on AT&T is connected to 5Ge even though it isn't linked to a Wi-Fi network. This network is not AT&T's 5G. The carrier's LTE-A service has been rebranded as 5Ge, or 5G Evolution.

How to fix iPhone 15 Bluetooth Problems

You should force your iPhone 15 to forget the problematic Bluetooth connection if it starts to have trouble connecting to one or more of your devices.

Here's how to carry it out:

- Open the **Settings** app
- Turn on Bluetooth.
- Using the "i" in the circle, choose the link.
- Click on "**Forget this Device**."
- Try reestablishing contact with the Bluetooth device.

Try resetting the Network Settings on your iPhone if it doesn't work:

- Open the **Settings app**.
- Touch General.
- Tap Reset or Transfer on your iPhone.

- Tap **Reset**.
- Select **Reset Network Settings**.

It will take a few seconds to finish this procedure. Also, it will make your iPhone forget which Wi-Fi networks it is connected to, so be sure to have your password(s) ready. Resetting your iPhone 15's settings to their original factory settings is another option you might attempt. This ought to be the very last option.

Here's how to carry it out:

- Navigate to **Settings**.
- Select **General**.
- Select Reset iPhone or Reset Transfer.
- Choose **Reset**.
- Select **Reset All Settings**.
- If you have a passcode enabled, enter it here.

If none of those solutions resolve the issue, get in touch with Apple customer support. Get in touch with the manufacturer of the product if Apple isn't the one who manufactures it.

How to fix iPhone 15 Wi-Fi Problems

Here are a few possible solutions that have previously worked for us if you're experiencing slower-than-usual Wi-Fi speeds and/or lost Wi-Fi connections. Look into the Wi-Fi connection that's giving you trouble before tampering with your phone's settings. Try rebooting your router if you're connected to your home network through Wi-Fi. Go into the Settings app on your iPhone 15 if you are unable to access the router it is linked to or if you are certain that the problem is not related to your ISP or router. You should forget about the problematic Wi-Fi network in this place.

Here's how to carry it out:

- Tap **Wi-Fi** under Settings.
- To choose your connection, just press the circle's "i."

- From the top of the screen, choose Forget this Network. (Note: You'll want to have your Wi-Fi password ready since doing this will make your iPhone forget it.)

Try resetting your network settings if this doesn't work:

- Open the **Settings** application.
- Choose **General**.
- Tap Reset or Transfer on your iPhone.
- Tap **Reset**.
- Hit the Reset Network Settings button.

How to fix iPhone 15 Charging Problems

You should attempt hard resetting your iPhone 15 if you have problems with wireless charging. This may be accomplished by holding down the side button until the phone turns off, then pressing and releasing the volume up and down buttons. After restarting the device, check to see whether charging functions properly. Before charging your phone, take out any credit cards or security passes that you may have stored in your iPhone case. You might also try taking off your case and using that method to charge your iPhone 15.

How to fix iPhone 15 Cellular Data Problems

Here are a few things you may try if your iPhone 15 suddenly shows a **"No Service"** indicator and you are unable to connect to your cellular network. First, confirm that your location is not experiencing an outage. Look for reports on social media, or use the platform to connect with your service provider. If the issue is not associated with a network outage, you could try restarting your iPhone to see if it resolves the problem. Try using Airplane Mode for 30 seconds before shutting it off if that doesn't work. Also, if the issue persists, you may want to consider entirely turning off Cellular Data.

Here's what you have to do to do that:

- Open the **Settings** app.

- Select **Cellular**.
- Turn off cellular data.
- Turn it back on after a minute of deactivation.

How to fix iPhone 15 Sound Problems

Loud and clear audio should be projected by your iPhone 15's speakers. However, before contacting Apple customer support, try these simple fixes if your sound begins to crackle or sound muffled. Try rebooting your iPhone first. If the phone's sound is still absent or distorted, check to see if anything is obstructing the speaker grille or the Lightning port on the bottom of the device. Restart your phone if you notice a sudden decline in call quality. Additionally, you should make sure that nothing is obstructing the device's reception, such as dirt or your screen protector if you have one. If you're using a case, you may also try taking it off to see if it helps. Try rebooting your iPhone if the microphone abruptly stops functioning or begins to cut out on its own.

If the device's microphone is still broken, you may attempt to restore it from a backup. If restoring is unsuccessful, you should contact Apple since there may be a hardware issue at hand.

How to fix iPhone 15 Activation Problems

Here are a few things you may do if you're having trouble activating your new iPhone 15 during setup. Make sure Apple's systems are operational first. When iOS Device Activation is shown in green, Apple services ought to be operating as intended. Moreover, confirm that you are on iOS 17, the most recent version. The iOS 17 update for the iPhone 15 resolves a problem with migration and activation during setup.

If it still doesn't function, try these fixes:

- Ensure that your device provider has an active plan for you.
- Turn your phone back on.
- Look for updates to your carrier's settings. Enter **Settings**, then **General**, then **About**. You'll be prompted to either OK or **Update** if there is an update available.

Get in touch with Apple or your service provider if none of those solutions work.

How to Solve Face ID Issues on the iPhone 15

Here are some things you may try if you're experiencing problems with Face ID. First, confirm that the most recent version of iOS 17 is installed on your iPhone 15. If you're experiencing problems with the most recent version, check your Face ID settings.

- Select **Settings**.
- Navigate to Face ID and Passcode. Be aware that to get in, you'll need to enter your passcode if you have one.

Once you're in there, confirm that Face ID is configured on your phone and that the functions you want to use Face ID for are active at the moment. Verify that you are actively staring at the screen if you are experiencing trouble unlocking your phone with your face. You may need to set up an alternative look in Face ID if you often change your appearance.

Here's how to do that:

- Select Settings.
- Select **Face ID and Passcode**.
- Tap the option to **set up an Alternate Appearance**.

Additionally, you should check to see if anything (dust, grime, etc.) is obstructing the FaceTime camera on your phone. The front of the phone houses the FaceTime camera. Once you have your Face ID set on your phone, make sure you are scanning your face in a well-lit area. It may also be necessary to level the iPhone or move it closer to your face.

How to Solve Overheating Issues with the iPhone 15

Here are several fixes for an iPhone 15 that is overheating. If you're using a case, start by removing it to see if it helps. A further thing you should attempt is turning the phone off and back on. Also, attempting to use the phone in Airplane Mode is another option.

Frequently Asked Questions

1. How do you use focus more on your iPhone 15 Series?
2. How do you use crash detection?
3. How do you turn on dark mode?
4. How do you pin apps to the screen?
5. How do you use the water-resistant feature?

CONCLUSION

The iPhone 15 series which includes the iPhone 15, iPhone 15 Plus, iPhone 15 Pro, and iPhone 15 Pro Max provides a plethora of new features and updates that, depending on your needs and the phone you're replacing, can make the purchase worthwhile. It's cheaper and simpler than ever to update to the iPhone 15 generation for every particular new feature, no matter how little. It's difficult to argue against upgrading to the iPhone 15 series if you can trade in your old phone and get the new one for free or at a large discount. Apple and carriers provide good trade-in incentives based on the age and condition of your current iPhone.

The cameras on the iPhone 15 and iPhone 15 Plus are a significant improvement, particularly with the added capability to use the 48MP sensor as a 12MP 2x optical zoom lens, even before we've had a chance to work with the models personally. This preserves excellent picture quality while adding significant adaptability. Before making any snap decisions, it's important to examine the 5x **"tetraprism"** zoom lens on the iPhone 15 Pro Max more closely, but if you've ever wanted to capture sharper images of distant scenes, it's worth contemplating an upgrade. The iPhone 15 generation's USB-C port is a wonderful feature, allowing you to charge your phone using the same cable as your Mac, iPad, and other USB-C compatible devices (assuming they have USB-C versions as well). However, we wouldn't say it's a feature that has to be updated right away since iPhone owners already have Lightning cords.

INDEX

(

(Optional) Unblock a contact, 77

1

120Hz ProMotion, 8
12MP 2x optical zoom lens, 338
12MP ultrawide, 4

2

24MP super-high-resolution, 1

4

48 MP primary, 1
48 MP primary camera, 1
48MP camera's capability, 1
48MP sensor, 7, 338

7

72-hour passcode grace period, 14
72-hour timeframe, 14

A

A Quick Word on eSIM, 28
A16 Bionic, 3, 4, 10
AAA memberships, 13
ability to produce 3D spatial video, 2
Access Additional Camera, 133
Access Archived Notes, 178
access Siri Settings, 83
Access the Bookmarks Menu, 118
Access the Dual SIM, 30
access the passcode settings, 61
access the Shortcuts application, 14
Access Voicemail, 101
Accessibility, 37, 38, 87, 95, 320, 325, 329

accessing applications, 11
Accessing Bookmarks, 119
accessing the dropdown menu, 14
activate Private Browsing, 110
Activate Silence Unknown Callers, 95
activate Siri through voice, 80
activating a Focus mode, 11
activating your new iPhone 15, 336
activating your new iPhone 15 during setup, 336
activation of a compatible iPhone, 13
Adaptive Audio, 18
Adaptive Audio and Personalized Volume, 18
Add a Bookmark, 118
add a bookmark in Safari, 118
Add a contact in the block, 77
Add Bookmark, 118, 119
Add Cellular Plan, 30
Add contacts to favorites, 102
Add Contacts to the Call, 71
Add People, 169, 177
Add Tabs to the Tab Group, 114
Add to Bookmarks or Favorites, 192
added capability, 19, 338
Adding Events, 162
Adding Other Accounts and Setting, 28
Adding Other Accounts and Setting Preferences, 28
Additional controls, 72
additional useful one for iOS Mail, 37
Adjust Brightness, 135
Adjust Calendar Preferences, 163
Adjust Camera Settings, 132, 134
Adjust Color, 135
Adjust Safari Settings, 106
Adjust the High Dynamic Range, 135
adjust your Caller ID preferences, 66
Advanced Search Techniques, 111
aesthetic appeal, 9
AirDrop, 21, 22, 151, 152, 177, 199, 258, 259, 263
AirTags can be shared with more people, 20
Alert Emergency Contacts, 98
Allow Siri When Locked, 80
altered audio file., 76
amazing quality, 1
amazing quality and manageable file, 1

amount of rings, 95

an Action button, 1

an iCloud backup, 27

angular edges, 8

Animoji, 67

Answer voicemail, 101

Answering a Call, 94

anticipation among technology enthusiasts, 8

Apple account information, 25

Apple and carriers, 338

Apple devices, 42, 109, 169, 170, 177, 215, 247, 296, 299, 302

Apple ID., 24, 28, 39, 40, 42, 68, 85, 170, 202, 228, 232, 234, 267, 269, 273, 295, 301, 302

Apple logo, 26, 34, 35, 39

Apple Maps, 36, 198, 319

Apple News app, 208, 209, 214

Apple products, 27, 37, 277

Apple stores, 6

Apple unveiled the latest version, 6

Apple's built-in translation tools, 106

Apple's largest updates, 1

Apple's privacy and design regulations, 83

Apple's systems, 336

Apple's video and voice calling app, 63

appropriate usage of language, 22

app's content search, 208

Archive a Note, 178

Assassin's Creed Mirage, 10

assign unique ringtones, 17

AT&T and Verizon, 6

Attach the message to an email, 177

authorized retailers, 6

Auto Call, 97, 326

Auto-Answer Calls, 95

Autocorrect, 15

Autocorrect gets an improvement, 15

Await the iCloud data restoration on your iPhone, 32

B

Background App Refresh, 28

Backup your Old Device, 31

Base storage, 3, 4, 5

Basic Camera, 152

Basic Camera settings, 152

basic instructions, 44, 60, 117, 193, 227, 301, 326

basic instructions for configuring an iPhone's Focus function, 44

basic queries to detailed inquiries, 87

Battery life, 3, 4, 5

Battery Percentage, 28

Be Cautious with your Number, 96

Begin the Group Call, 72

big files, 22

Black Titanium, 4, 5

Block All Cookies, 111

block or report a contact, 99

Block Specific Numbers, 95

Blocked Contacts, 76, 77, 98, 99, 100

Blocking Calls, 98

Blocking on Third-Party Applications, 99

blur images or videos, 22

Bookmark the Page, 119

bookmarks bar or a folder, 118

Bookmarks Folder, 121

bookmark's name, 118, 119, 120, 121

brightness adjustments, 133

bringing new features, 63

bringing new features and bug fixes, 63

broad overview, 76, 145, 232

built-in web browser on iOS devices, 107

business launched 6TB, 1

C

Calendar app, 154, 155, 159, 161, 162, 163

Camera App, 130, 152

Capture a Photo, 132

capture a video of an interesting event, 14

capture sharper images, 339

Capture the Video or Photo, 149

cellular connection, 28, 275

Cellular Data., 280, 336

cellular network, 22, 335

cellular signal, 13

change Siri's replies, 84

change the event's information, 162

Change the Folder, 120

Change the Name, 120

Change the Notifications, 210

Change the URL, 120

Change Voicemail Greeting, 101

charging connector, 1

Charging port, 3, 4, 5

Check for Updates, 63
Check whether the contact has been blocked, 77
Check with your Carrier, 96
Check-In feature, 16
Choose a Result, 184
choosing **Share Link**, 70
circular button, 167
clever software, 1
Close the Discussion, 81
cloud storage services, 76, 257, 263
color settings, 136
Colors, 4, 5, 9
communication hurdles, 87
comparable outcome, 2
compatible services, 133
comprehensive overview, 5
comprehensive overview of the iPhone 15, 5
comprehensive overview of the iPhone 15 and iPhone
    15 Pro series, 5
CONCLUSION, 338
Configure a Voicemail Welcome, 101
CONFIGURING THE NEW IPHONE 15 SERIES, 25
Confirm the block, 77
confirm the SIM card, 29
Connect your outdated iPhone to a network., 31
Consecutive Siri Requests, 19
Consistently update iOS, 96
constraints in production capacity, 8
contact cards, 16
Contact Posters, 16, 22
Contact Posters feature, 16
contemplating an upgrade, 339
Content Blockers, 111
content sharing, 21
Control Center, 44, 46, 48, 50, 75, 76, 95, 99, 128,
    158, 166, 271, 277, 278, 282, 309, 310, 313, 320,
    321, 322, 323, 332
Control with Ring Switch, 85
convenient solution, 20
Conversation Awareness, 18
Conversational Awareness with AirPods, 18
cost-effective, 9
cost-per-use model, 13
CPU, 3, 4, 5, 10
crash detection, 326, 338
Create a grocery list in Reminders, 17
create a new note, 166, 176, 179
Create a New Note, 167

Create a Tab Group, 114
crescent moon, 44, 50, 95, 99, 321, 322
current Apple ID or create a new one, 44
current iPhone, 9, 338
current map on Google Maps, 36
current map on Google Maps for iOS, 36
current safety capabilities, 13
customizable Siri's replies, 83
Customize Siri, 81
Customize your News Preferences, 204

D

Daily View, 157
data and apps, 27
Daylight, 135
Death Stranding, 10
Declining a Call, 94
Delete a Note, 178
Delete password verification messages, 17
Delete password verification messages automatically,
    17
delete Siri and Dictation History, 89
Delete Voicemail, 101
Deleting Events, 163
derive various advantages, 16
designate emergency contacts, 326
developing future environments, 2
device's microphone, 336
device's settings, 85, 177, 214, 244
dialogue. Siri, 81
dimensional format, 7
Disable Passcode, 61
Display & Brightness, 58, 109, 206, 325
Display Size, 3, 4, 5
displaying the current time, 13
Do Not Disturb, 46, 48, 49, 50, 95, 99, 321, 322
Double Tapping with Two Fingers, 190
double-tap, 36, 190
Double-Tap, 190
Download and Install, 23, 63
Downloading the iPhone Calendar App, 154
Drag and Drop, 116
Drag the Slider, 97
DuckDuckGo, 111
During the Call, 94
Dynamic Island feature, 12

E

edit photos, 136
Edit the Bookmark, 120
Edit Time and Date, 148
Editing Events, 163
Editing Photos, 136
Editing Videos, 137
Emergency Contacts, 50, 98
Emergency SOS, 13, 21, 93, 97, 98, 307, 326, 327
Enable Emergency, 97
enable Filter Unknown Senders, 96
enable the battery percentage view., 28
Enabling elements, 188
Enabling iCloud and External Calendar Sync, 163
encountering unsolicited explicit images or videos, 22
End the Call, 72, 74
engaging gaming experience, 2
enhanced level of customization, 17
Enter your Apple ID and password to log in., 32
Entertainment, 87
executing a Shortcut, 11
Exit Tab Groups, 115
Explore Details, 184
explore neighboring areas, 198
Explore Other Tabs, 204
explore the environment, 184
Exposure Control, 152
extensive personalization options, 16

F

FaceTime, 22, 28, 63, 64, 65, 66, 67, 68, 69, 70, 71, 72, 73, 74, 75, 76, 77, 91, 98, 99, 338
FACETIME, 63
FaceTime camera, 338
FaceTime interface, 72
feature Apple's first 3nm mobile processor, 1
feature thinner, 9
Features, 5, 105, 133, 188
features Apple's latest, 7
features Apple's latest 5x zoom lens boasting, 7
featuring the cutting-edge technology, 8
ferries, 188, 193
few mobile service providers, 96
filmmaking and photography, 133
Filters, 67, 135, 152, 199

Find my iPhone, 42
find new information, 208
finish setting, 46
First of all, launch **Settings**., 65
First, Back Up Your Old Phone, 25
Firstly, launch the **Contacts** app., 66
flagship smartphone, 6
fluid visuals, 8
Fluorescent, 135
focal length telephoto, 2
FOCUS AND SECURITY, 44
Focus settings, 48, 50
Follow-Up Questions, 81
Font Color, 170
Formatting and Options, 168
four versions in the series, 1
Frequently Asked Questions, 24, 43, 62, 77, 89, 103, 124, 153, 164, 179, 199, 214, 226, 235, 253, 265, 283, 303, 315, 338
Front camera, 4, 5
front-facing, 133, 319
front-facing (selfie) camera, 133
Full-Screen Preview, 108
function of the Action button, 11

G

generate tailored prompts, 15
generation's USB-C port, 339
get eSIM activation, 29
Get the **Phone app** open., 96
GETTING STARTED, 3
Give your Command, 80
granting access to different functions, 53

H

Handling Dual SIM Configurations, 30
hardware issue, 336
hardware-accelerated ray, 2, 10
hardware-accelerated ray tracing, 2, 10
HDR, 134, 135, 152
heavy 8.47-ounce iPhone 14 Pro Max., 9
high refresh-rate display, 8
highly anticipated iOS 17 update, 15
Home automation, 86
Home Screen, 14, 34, 165, 234, 321, 324

How, 22, 24, 25, 28, 31, 33, 34, 38, 41, 43
How do you add contacts to favorites?, 103
How do you add media to your note?, 179
How do you answer or decline calls?, 103
How do you apply filters?, 153
How do you avoid unwanted phone calls?, 103
How do you block unwanted callers, 77
How do you change between the rear and front cameras?, 153
How do you change Siri's voice?, 89
How do you change the name Siri calls you?, 89
How do you create a personal focus?, 62
How do you delete an event?, 164
How do you disable and delete a focus?, 62
How do you download and install the new iOS 17?, 24
How do you edit images?, 153
How do you edit Siri's response?, 89
How do you enter into live mode?, 153
How do you make an emergency call?, 103
How do you manage blocked contacts?, 103
How do you manage calendars?, 164
How do you organize and search notes?, 179
How do you pin apps to the screen?, 338
How do you set up a Focus?, 62
How do you set up a passcode?, 62
How do you set up Apple ID?, 43
How do you set up physical and eSIM?, 43
How do you share photos and videos?, 153
How do you sort notes?, 179
How do you take panorama, portrait, and record slo-mo videos?, 153
How do you turn on dark mode?, 338
How do you use crash detection?, 338
How do you use Siri to create events?, 164
How do you use Siri?, 89
How do you use tab groups?, 124
How do you use the calendar app?, 164
How do you use the water-resistant feature?, 338
How do you view calendars?, 164
How do you view notes in folders and attachments?, 179
How do you view saved tabs?, 124
How do you view websites in Safari?, 124
How do you wake up and unlock your new device?, 43
How to access and use iCloud, 41
How to access the maps app, 180
How to access the News app, 200

How to Access the Notes app, 165
How to add a bookmark, 118
How to add contacts to favorites, 102
How to add media to your note, 170
How to add someone to a call, 74
How to adjust and straighten the perspective, 140
How to allow calls from emergency contacts when you silence notifications, 49
How to answer or decline calls, 94
How to apply filters, 142
How to avoid unwanted phone calls, 95
How to begin navigation, 188
How to block people from reaching you on different call apps, 98
How to block unwanted callers, 76
How to bookmark a map, 192
How to bookmark a page, 118, 124
How to bring back Safari to the home screen, 113
How to carry out a safe and advanced search, 110
How to change between dark and light theme, 109
How to change between the rear and front camera, 133
How to change how tab groups are arranged, 116
How to change language in Safari, 112
How to change Siri's voice, 83
How to change the Camera aspect ratio, 127
How to change the name of tab groups, 115
How to change the name Siri calls you, 85
How to change the way Siri responds, 84
How to change when your phone locks automatically, 58
How to choose a transportation mode, 186
How to clear browser search history, 122, 124
How to copy and paste edits to images, 147
How to create a new guide, 197
How to create a new note, 166
How to create a Personal Focus, 46
How to create a smart folder, 176
How to Create an Event, 159
How to customize map settings, 193
How to customize your newsfeed, 209
How to deactivate a Focus, 50
How to delete a bookmark, 121
How to delete a Focus, 50
How to delete a tab group, 116
How to Delete an Event, 161
How to delete or archive notes, 178

How to disable image mirroring for the front camera, 134

How to download and install iOS 17, 22

How to edit a bookmark, 120

How to Edit an Event, 161

How to edit photos and videos, 136

How to edit Siri's response, 81

How to edit time, location, and date, 148

How to end navigation, 191

How to enter into Live Mode, 128

How to erase data after ten failed passcode entries, 59

How to explore nearby areas, 198

How to fix iPhone 15 Activation, 336

How to fix iPhone 15 Activation Problems, 336

How to fix iPhone 15 Sound Problems, 336

How to follow channels and publications on the news app, 208

How to get directions, 184

How to get your current location, 181

How to launch the camera app, 125

How to make an emergency call, 92

How to make calls via the Contacts list, Keypad, and Favorites, 90

How to make corrections in case Siri doesn't get what you say, 87

How to manage blocked contacts, 99

How to mark my location, 196

How to navigate the news app, 203

How to open a bookmark, 119

How to organize and search notes, 173

How to power on and off your device, 34, 43

How to preview website links, 107

How to read articles on the news app, 204

How to record a slo-mo video, 148

How to record a time-lapse video, 145

How to report an issue, 194

How to revert an edited video or image, 146

How to rotate the map, 190

How to rotate, flip, and crop images, 138

How to search for a location, 182

How to Search for an Event, 162

How to see the overview of your route, 192

How to set a Focus to activate, 48

How to set a Focus to activate automatically, 48

How to set the flashlight to be on always, 128

How to set up a Focus, 44

How to set up Apple ID, 38

How to set up Apple News, 202

How to set up physical and eSIM, 28

How to share and collaborate on your note, 177

How to share and save on the news app, 206

How to share photos and videos, 149

How to Solve Face ID Issues on the iPhone 15, 337

How to Solve Overheating Issues with the iPhone 15, 338

How to sort notes, 172

How to take panorama images, 144

How to take pictures and videos, 130

How to take portrait images, 143

How to take steady shots with your Camera timer, 129

How to transfer data from old device, 31

How to translate a webpage or image, 106

How to turn off the passcode, 60

How to type and format your note, 169

How to undo and redo edits, 139

How to use a reading list, 108

How to use enable Siri, 78

How to use Siri, 80, 220

How to Use Siri to Create Events, 164

How to use tab groups, 114

How to use the search bar on the news app, 211

How to use the voicemail function, 100

How to view all missed calls, 102

How to view all the tabs in a tab group, 117

How to view attachments in notes, 173

How to view notes in folders, 175

How to view notifications on the news app, 210

How to view saved tabs, 113

How to view search history, 122

How to view search results, 183

How to view websites, 104

How to view websites in Safari, 104

How to wake and unlock your device, 33

How to zoom in and out on the map, 189

I

iCloud Backup, 25, 27, 31, 32, 42

iCloud Drive, 42, 149, 256, 258, 260, 261, 262, 263, 264

iCloud notes, 178

iCloud storage tiers, 1

iCloud synchronization, 163

iCloud-stored documents, 42

iMessage, 28, 36, 38, 149, 150, 177, 221, 299

iMessage thread, 36

immediate visual feedback, 2

impact on Siri's replies, 85

improved energy economy, 2

in-camera functions, 1

Incandescent, 135

Incoming Call Notification, 94

incorporating emoji pictures, 17

Information retrieval, 87

innovative addition, 12, 14

innovative feature, 7, 13, 16, 22

installation of iOS 17, 17

Integration with applications, 86

introduce an iPhone 15 "**Ultra**" model, 6

introduce spatial video recording functionality, 7

INTRODUCTION, 1

iOS 17 operating system, 17

iPhone 12, 5

iPhone 13, 5, 6, 330

iPhone 14 Pro and Pro Max models, 13

iPhone 14 Pro series, 10

iPhone 14 series, 5, 8, 13

IPhone 15, 3, 4, 5

iPhone 15 generation, 6, 8, 338, 339

iPhone 15 Plus, 1, 3, 6, 7, 8, 10, 12, 63, 68, 100, 316, 329, 333, 338

iPhone 15 Pro, 1, 3, 5, 6, 7, 9, 10, 11, 12, 63, 68, 100, 316, 329, 333, 338, 339

iPhone 15 Pro Max, 1, 3, 6, 7, 9, 10, 11, 12, 63, 68, 100, 316, 329, 333, 338, 339

iPhone 15 series, 5

iPhone Calendar App Views, 155

iPhone Calendar App Views and Icons, 155

iPhone Maps app, 183, 186, 189

iPhone Mini model, 6

iPhone Mini model in the iPhone 14 generation, 6

iPhone owners, 339

iPhone X back in 2017., 12

iPhone XS, 28

iPhone's Camera app and launch, 140

iPhone's home screen, 51, 57, 74, 107, 112, 154, 162, 189, 191, 192, 193, 206, 256, 263, 271, 273

iPhone's Notes app, 176

Island on non-pro versions, 1

iTunes or Finder Backup, 32

J

journaling application, 15

Journaling is a beneficial practice, 15

K

Keep Up with a Publication or Channel, 208

L

Language Translation, 87

larger amount of storage, 7

Launch a new reminder., 17

launch a new tab, 110

Launch Finder or iTunes., 32

launch **Safari**, 113, 121

Launch **Safari** from your home screen., 122

Launch **Safari**., 110

Launch **Settings**., 64

Launch the **"Settings"** app., 59, 66, 109, 325

Launch the aforementioned app, 99

Launch the iPhone, 53, 97, 98, 110, 261, 326

Launch the iPhone Health app., 326

Launch the iPhone's Settings app., 97, 98, 326

Launch the iTunes Finder., 32

Launch the **Photos app**, 151

Launch your iPhone's **"Settings"** app., 63

launching the application, 17

launching the Notes app, 169

level the iPhone, 338

lightbulb image, 135

lighter device, 9

Lightning cords, 339

List View, 156

Listen and Respond, 80

Listen to Voicemail, 101

Live Activities, 13

Locate the **Maps app icon**, 181, 189, 192, 193

Locate the person you want to block., 99

locating local sites of interest, 87

Location Services, 28, 194, 196, 198, 221, 223, 251, 292

Loud and clear audio, 336

Lower the screen's brightness, 329

M

Mail app by Apple more, 37
main procedures, 48
main upgrade, 1
majority of users, 2, 330
Making Calls from Contacts, 90
Making Calls from Favorites, 92
Making Calls from the Keypad, 91
Manage Caller ID, 66
Manage Cookies and Website Data, 110
Manage Group Tabs, 114
manageable file sizes, 1
Managing Events, 162
Managing the Group Call, 72
MAPS APP, 180
Medical ID, 98, 306, 307, 326
Memoji, 67
Messages, 16, 17, 22, 37, 38, 67, 73, 96, 99, 175, 182, 183, 197, 198, 199, 206, 207, 221, 225, 258, 259, 263, 317
Messages app, 16, 67, 73, 221
Messages application, 16, 17, 96
messaging applications, 76, 300
Microsoft Word, 15
minimize ambient noise, 18
Missed Calls, 102
missing iPhone, 42, 302
Modify the camera's location, 130
modifying the color and font, 17
monitoring personal belongings, 20
Monthly View, 158
Move Data from Android, 25, 27
multifaceted virtual assistant, 81
Multilingual Support, 86

N

NameDrop, 21
Natural Conversation, 87
Navigate to a Website, 104
Navigate to Face ID and Passcode, 337
Navigate within a Website, 105
Navigation, 87, 187, 191
navigational directions, 191
necessary customizations, 46
new 24MP super-high-resolution setting, 1

New Contact Posters, 16
New Journal app, 15
New Messages improvements, 16
New Messages improvements and features, 16
newest A17 Pro processor, 10
NEWS APP, 200
Night Mode, 153
No more 'Hey, Siri', 19
notable distinctions, 12
notes accessible and well-organized., 173
NOTES APP, 165
Notifications & Focus, 49
now program, 46
numerous accounts, 178

O

On your iPhone, launch the **Phone app.**, 100
one-of-a-kind passcode for optimal protection, 58
Open Camera app modes, 14
Open Camera app modes with new shortcut actions, 14
Open **Settings**, 28, 76
Open Several Tabs, 106
Open the **"Files"** app, 42
Open the Notes app, 166, 176
Open the **Settings** app., 331, 332, 334, 336
Open the **Settings** application., 99, 329, 331, 335
Operating System, 3, 4, 5
optical quality zoom, 7
Organize your Notes, 169
Organizing notes, 172
Organizing notes on the iPhone Notes app, 172
overall listening experience, 18
Overview, 3, 25, 44, 63, 78, 90, 104, 113, 125, 154, 165, 180, 193, 200, 215, 227, 237, 254, 266, 284, 304, 316

P

Panorama, 131, 144, 152
Panorama Mode, 131
particular account, 178
particular folder, 168, 175
particular new feature, 338
particular website, 104, 215
party calling applications, 17

Passcode, 53, 54, 55, 57, 59, 60, 61, 98, 317, 337

pencil icon, 167, 172

peppermint mocha, 27

periscope-style 10x zoom lens, 7

periscopic camera, 2

Personalization, 86

Personalize your Feed, 210

phone in Airplane Mode, 338

Photo Mode, 131, 152

photographers, 2

physical or eSIM, 25

pin apps, 316, 324, 338

Pinch Gesture, 189, 190

Pinch to zoom on videos, 35

Place your physical SIM card, 29

Portrait Mode, 131, 152

Portrait Orientation Lock, 158

possesses an AirTag device, 20

powerful A17 Pro processor, 10

Powering off, 34

preferred webpage, 104

preserves excellent picture quality, 339

Press the top-level list view., 158

prevent blurriness, 130, 144

Prevent Cross-Site Tracking, 111

prevent significant inconvenience, 14

preview website, 107, 124

previous iPhone during setup, 28

previous Lightning charging technology, 11

Price, 3, 4, 6

Privacy & Security, 110, 111

Pro models offer, 9

Pro Res mode, 2

procedure of configuring Apple News, 202

processing software, 15

produce images, 1

provider of automotive assistance services, 13

providing Siri instructions, 88

Q

quality 24MP photographs, 7

Quick Start, 25, 26, 27

quicker peak performance, 2

quicker transfers, 2

Quicker zooming in on Apple Maps, 36

R

Raise to Wake, 33

range of significant upgrades, 5

reaching contentment, 119

Reader symbol, 111

real-time on-location editing., 2

Rear cameras, 4, 5

Rearrange Tab Groups, 116

recent version of iOS, 23, 68, 81, 269, 304, 337

recently released AirPods Pro 2, 11

Recents Tab, 102

recipient's device, 22

Record a Video, 132

record immersive mixed-reality, 1

record immersive mixed-reality scenes, 1

record incredible visuals, 2

recorded moments, 149

red record button, 137, 146, 149, 150

Refresh rate, 3, 4, 5

Regarding Publications, 209

registration of AirTags, 20

regular intervals, 146, 153

reliable cellular data network, 88

reliable cellular data network or Wi-Fi, 88

remove a Focus from an iPhone, 50

Remove a tab group, 116

Remove/Delete Tabs from a Tab Group, 115

Removing the Lightning connector, 1

Report an Issue, 195, 196

Report as Spam, 96

Report Spam Calls, 96

Reset network settings, 68

Reset Siri, 89

Resident Evil 4, 10

Resident Evil Village, 10

resolution and balancing light, 1

Restart your iPhone, 89

Restore Backup, 32

Restore the Data, 32

resulting images, 7

Retrain Siri, 88

roads, 188

Rotate an Image, 138

Rotate the Map, 190

S

Samsung Galaxy S23 Ultra, 7
satellite-based Roadside Assistance, 13
Save an article, 207
Save Voicemail, 101
saving battery depletion, 329
scanned documents, 170
screen protector, 336
search engine query, 118
Search Engines, 111
Search for Camera., 14
Search for Events, 163
Search for Location, 183
Search for your Destination, 186, 188
Search Nearby, 183
Search Using Safari, 105
second-generation AirPods Pro, 18
Security and Privacy, 81
security risks associated with disabling the passcode., 61
Select **Cellular.**, 336
Select **Contacts** or **Recents.**, 96
Select the Camera Mode, 131
Select the person to block, 77
selecting Settings, 25, 28, 304
selection of titanium frames, 10
Send Apple Feedback, 88
sending messages, 81
sending unsolicited explicit photographs, 22
Sensitive content warnings, 22
Series Action Button, 11
Series Camera app, 135, 144, 149
Series' Camera app, 130, 148
Series Cameras, 7
Series Design, 8
Series Displays, 7
Series Dynamic Island, 12
Series Maps app, 194, 196
Series Release Date, 6
Series Roadside Assistance via Satellite, 12
Series using the Contacts list, 90
Set Passcode, 57
set up an **Alternate Appearance**, 337
Set up Call Forwarding, 96
Set Up Manually, 27
Set Up Voice Recognition, 79
Setting Reminders, 163

Setting up the Physical SIM Card, 29
Setting up Voicemail, 100
Setting up Your New iPhone, 26
Settings app, 28, 48, 49, 57, 59, 85, 86, 97, 98, 100, 112, 141, 217, 221, 251, 299, 314, 319, 322, 325, 326, 330, 331, 332, 333, 334, 336
Settings app's **"End Focus Mode" button**, 48
several fixes for an iPhone 15, 338
Shake to undo, 36
Sharing an article, 206
sharing and saving, 1
sharing capabilities, 21
Sharing Events, 163
Sharing is easier with AirDrop and NameDrop, 21
Sharing Pictures and Videos, 150
showcase various features, 13
Sign In to Your Apple ID, 63
significant improvement, 338
Siri & Dictation History, 89
SIRI ON YOUR IPHONE 15 SERIES, 78
Slide to Place an Emergency Call, 97
snap decisions, 339
social media, 133, 144, 145, 149, 151, 225, 335
social media applications, 133
Software Update, 23, 63, 114, 261, 277, 280, 304
Speak Naturally and Clearly, 80
Speak Screen, 38
Speak slowly and clearly, 87
special characters, 57
specific benchmarks, 10
specific Camera mode, 14
specific message by swiping, 16
specifications, 3, 24, 218, 219
Specifications and Features, 3
standard 3x zoom lens, 7
StandBy mode, 13
StandBy Mode, 13
stock market data, 87
stunning photos and recording, 125
stunning visuals, 8
Super Retina XDR OLED display, 8
support eSIM, 29
Swipe and Hold, 108
swipe down from the top-right corner of the screen., 48, 309, 310, 322
Swipe down to hide the keyboard in iMessage, 36
Swipe down to listen to the text, 38
Swipe down to save email drafts, 37

Swipe left or right to remove digits in the calculator, 38

Swipe left to view details in the Message, 38

Swipe right to go back, 38

Swipe Up from the Bottom, 191

Sync the appointments, 42

T

Tap and drag to select images, 37

Tap and drag to switch scrubbing speed, 37

Tap and hold to archive messages, 37

Tap and hold to change keyboards, 36

Tap and hold to open closed tabs in Safari, 36

tap the square symbol, 110

telephoto camera, 2

Telephoto option, 1

terrific technique, 129

tetraprism, 7, 339

the **"Add Action"** option., 14

The **"New Tab Group"** button, 114

the 7.27-ounce iPhone 14 Pro, 9

the A17 Pro, 1, 10

The ability to use offline Maps, 21

the age and condition, 338

the backup provider, 32

The calendar app, 154

the calendar icon located, 158

the Camera app, 14, 107, 125, 126, 127, 128, 129, 130, 131, 133, 134, 135, 136, 137, 138, 140, 142, 143, 144, 145, 146, 148, 150, 152, 153

the customizable Action button., 11

The fundamental instructions, 189

the iOS 17 version, 21

the iOS version, 75, 113

The iPhone 15 generation's USB-C, 339

The iPhone 15 models, 8

The iPhone 15 Pro, 7, 12

the iPhone 15 Pro is 6.6 ounces, 9

the iPhone 15 Pro Max, 6, 7, 9

the iPhone 15 Pro models, 7, 10

the iPhone 15 series, 1, 338

The iPhone Pro's Action Button, 2

the iPhone's settings., 80

the latest versions of the iPhone, 11

The Lightning port, 11

The Maps app gets a boost, 20

The new Apple OS is iOS 17., 63

the new device, 25, 27

the News app, 200, 201, 202, 203, 204, 206, 207, 208, 209, 211, 213, 214

the physical volume buttons, 150

the process of creating Shortcut actions, 14

The recently introduced 5x zoom lens, 7

the **Safari app icon**, 117, 119

The second-generation AirPods Pro features, 18

The shutter button, 150

The toolbar's icons, 168

the United States, 20, 159

the upper-right corner, 14, 17, 44, 67, 71, 99, 102, 119, 128, 133, 137, 139, 147, 148, 159, 161, 162, 191, 194, 204, 255, 261, 272, 280, 306

Third-Party applications, 82

thumbnail icon, 150

thumbnail photos, 17

thumbnail preview, 138, 144

Time-Lapse, 133, 145, 153

Time-Lapse mode, 153

Timer options, 152

tons of additions to the new iOS 17, 13

touching the grid symbol, 105

Transfer Directly from iPhone, 27

Translate, 11, 106, 107

translate a webpage, 106, 124

Translating a Web Page, 106

Translating an Image, 107

trouble finding Safari, 113

Troubleshooting, 68, 328

Truecaller or RoboKiller, 96

trustworthy third-party app from the App Store, 96

Turn it back on after a minute of deactivation., 336

Turn off cellular data., 336

turn on dark mode, 316, 325, 338

Turn on the Gridlines, 141

Turn Passcode Off, 61

Turn your phone back on., 337

Turning on, 29, 34

Turning on the eSIM, 29

typical sharing techniques, 177

U

Underline, 169

Unfollow Channels or Topics, 210

unidentified AirTag, 20

unlocking your phone, 135, 337

unlocking your smartphone and granting access, 53

unsolicited calls, 76, 95, 96, 97, 99

upgrading to iOS 17, 17

upper-right corner of the screen, 44, 128, 133, 137, 147, 148, 162, 272

upward-pointing arrow, 107, 118, 119, 149, 150, 151, 176, 198

usage of the USB 3.1 Gen 2 standard., 12

USB 3 rates, 2

USB 3 speeds, 12

USB Type-C, 1

USB-C, 1, 2, 3, 4, 5, 11, 12, 339

USB-C compatible devices, 339

USB-C versions, 339

Use a USB cord to connect your outdated iPhone to your PC., 32

Use Commands Wisely, 88

use of wireless Earbuds, 18

Use Private Browsing, 110

Use Reader Mode, 111

Use Siri for Multiple Tasks, 81

use StandBy mode, 13

Use the Edit Button, 116

Use the Front-Facing Camera, 133

Use the Maps app, 192, 193

Use Third-Party Apps, 96

use USB-C to transfer, 2

using iCloud Keychain, 42

using iTunes or Finder, 22

using multiple call apps, 98

Using Siri, 166

Using Spotlight Search, 166

USING THE CALENDAR APP, 154

USING THE CAMERA APP, 125

Using the Maps app, 181, 182

Using the Notes app on an iPhone, 166

Using the Notes app on an iPhone from the 15 Series, 166

USING THE PHONE APP, 90

USING THE SAFARI APP, 104

utilizing a cropping technique, 7

V

variety of Portrait Lighting effects, 143

variety of subjects, 87

Verify Language and Region Settings, 88

Verify Website Certificates, 111

Verify Your Connection, 87

Video and Portrait, 14

Video Mode, 131, 152

View and Edit Photos and Videos, 132

View and Manage Calendars, 162

View on Map, 184

View Recent Calls, 102

View your Captured Media, 150

Viewing Several Calendars, 163

Viewing the Calendar, 162

Vision Pro, 1, 2, 7

Visual Voicemail, 101

Voice Commands, 86

Voice Feedback, 85

Voice Memos, 11

Voice search, 111

voicemail feature, 100

voicemail greeting, 101, 102

Volume buttons, 97

volume control and playback control., 87

volume on your AirPods or iPhone, 18

Volume Up/Down Buttons, 95

W

Wake Siri Up, 80

Waking up, 33

Warn About Harmful Websites, 110

water-resistant, 327, 338

water-resistant feature, 327, 338

Weekly View, 157

What are the new features of iOS 17?, 24

What Siri can do for you?, 86

What's new in iOS 17?, 13

White Balance, 135

White Titanium, 4, 5

wide range of activities, 81

widgets, 13, 223

Wi-Fi. Siri's functionality, 88

wonderful feature, 339

Write Your First Note, 168

Y

Yearly View, 159

Your Wi-Fi information, 25

Made in the USA
Las Vegas, NV
29 February 2024

86477280R00199